THE CIVILIANS

AN ANTHOLOGY OF SIX PLAYS

EDITED BY
STEVEN COSSON

Playscripts, Inc.

Published by Playscripts, Inc.
450 Seventh Avenue, Suite 809
New York, New York, 10123
www.playscripts.com

Cover design by Sara E. Stemen
Text design and layout by Jason Pizzarello

First Edition: April 2009
10 9 8 7 6 5 4 3 2 1

ISBN-13: 978-0-9819099-0-5

Library of Congress Cataloging-in-Publication Data

The civilians : an anthology of six plays / edited by Steven Cosson.
   p. cm.
 ISBN 978-0-9819099-0-5 (pbk.)
 1. American drama. I. Cosson, Steven.
 PS625.C56 2009
 812'.608--dc22
                            2008053806

Contents

Foreword

I sometimes think The Civilians are the only necessary ensemble in New York.

That's an exaggeration, to be sure, but not by much. Steve Cosson has *led the company* over the last decade with a team of collaborators, most notably composer Michael Friedman. They have grown into a group that creates theater that is not only consistently thrilling, but that reflects the world we live in with a passion and depth unmatched by any of their peers. Steve has worked with a team of collaborators to build the company, but the central artistic partnership has been with composer Michael Friedman. I go to each new Civilians project filled with curiosity and excitement, because I know they make will open up the world in which I live in fresh and brilliant ways.

Their work is growing, too: the beautiful baubles of *Nobody's Lunch* and *Gone Missing* have been expanding to create the extraordinary vista of *This Beautiful City* and *Paris Commune* and the still-in-progress *Atlantic Yards*. Steve's work as a writer has been getting deeper and sharper and more confident, Michael's music continues to astonish with his range and complexity, and their combined dramatic imagination and ambition continues to expand at a breathtaking rate. They've been very good, so far; where their work promises to take them is breathtaking.

But it's not just Michael and Steve: The Civilians, large and informal as it is, is a real company of playwrights, directors, actors and designers. I can't single out any of the artists who work with them, much as I'd love to, because I'd be leaving out so many who are so amazing. The company attracts actors who, different as they are, seem similar in their ability to radiate a sympathetic intelligence onstage. The depth of their involvement in the creation of the work is evident in their proud, full-blooded ownership of the complex material they embody. It's a brave, beautiful and luminous group that take the stage whenever The Civilians perform.

The ethos of their work combines the best of the British Joint Stock tradition of collective creation with the rawness and immediacy that is so characteristically American. Their work is both of the New York downtown scene, with all the sophistication and hipness that implies, and of a much older American tradition of telling the stories of the people. They are in the world, and of it. Their theater embodies what is best in the form: connection to community and the highest artfulness, playfulness and seriousness side-by-side. They make the American theater a nobler profession; if they didn't exist, we'd be struggling to invent them.

But they do exist, and this book is a record of their first phase. It's terrific work, and they are only getting started.

—*Oskar Eustis*
Artistic Director
The Public Theater

Introduction

First, the name: when I founded The Civilians in 2001 I wanted a name that would suggest an outwards-looking theater company, one that would go beyond the familiar to investigate the world. I knew that vaudevillians described the people outside of show biz as "civilians." Apparently models use the term in a similar way as do many other insiders describe those on the outside. And outside is where my interest lay. I had grown weary of a theater that seemed to be a place where you went to get reassured, a place to get a message we already all believed in. I wanted a theater of discovery, a theater where I'd get surprised, feel the limitations of my ways of knowing, and hopefully leave with a sense that the world is a bigger and more complex place than what I had previously believed. I wanted to meet the people I didn't already know, those outside of my own experience, the others: the civilians.

But the idea behind The Civilians is more than a name. The company exists to make a different kind of theater possible. We would create original shows, and each project would begin with some sort of creative investigation into real life. For *Gone Missing* that meant interviewing New Yorkers and asking them about lost and found stuff. For a historical show like *Paris Commune,* Michael Friedman and I sought out first person accounts and transcripts in an effort to see this revolution through the varied perspectives of its players. Each of these investigations is then a leaping off point for a creative process. There is no set method. Some of the shows draw more on the contributions of a group, using verbatim interviews as the main source of text. Other projects such as Anne Washburn's *The Ladies* or Neal Bell's *Shadow of Himself* are playwright-driven. And hopefully future works will continue to evolve with new variations. But whatever the method or aesthetic, this combination of research, investigation and creativity serves to compel the artists involved to shed old ideas, recalibrate perceptions and hopefully discover the new forms and new stories that will keep theater a dynamic part of contemporary life.

—*Steven Cosson*
Artistic Director
The Civilians

Acknowledgments

The Civilians warmly acknowledges the theaters and individuals who have supported The Civilians work on these plays through their collaboration and friendship. The following is a partial representation of the many people who have helped to make it all possible:

Doug Aibel, Giles Anderson, Elizabeth Angell, Toni Amicarella, Beth Blickers, Renée Blinkwolt, Bill Bragin, Roger Burlingame, David Carpenter, Linda Chapman, Jessica Chayes, Alexandra Conley, Jason M. Cooper, Ellie Covan, Anne Dennin, Kurt Deutsch, David Dower, Julie Dubiner, Peter Dubois, Anne Dunning, Ari Edelson, Oskar Eustis, Angela Fiordellisi, Shirley Fishman, Peter Hess Friedland, Marion Friedman, Boo Froebel, Jennifer Garvey-Blackwell, Jenny Gersten, Fred Gilde, Kyle Gorden, Leslie Graham, Mandy Hackett, Adrien-Alice Hansel, Jessica Harris, Julia Hart, Patrick Herold, Christopher Hibma, Philip Himberg, Christopher J. Hogan, Allison Horsley, Morgan Jenness, Melanie Joseph, Chris Kam, Abigail Katz, Laurie Kauffman, Daniel P. Kim, Jeanhee Kim, Kelley Kirkpatrick, Elysabeth Kleinhans, Sarah MacArthur, Kristin Marting, Marc Masterson, Des McAnuff, Bonnie Metzgar, Scott Morfee, Ethan Morris, Jennifer Morris, Seiji Newman, Jim Nicola, Harold Norris, Tricia Paik, Janice Paran, Shoshana Kovac Parets, Thomas Pearson, Tali Pelman, Ted Pettus, Michael Ritchie, Jana Ross, Rebecca Rugg, Mark Russell, AnnaCatherine Rutledge, Stephen Siderow, Sara Stemen, Sarah Stern, Michael Stickle, Aaron Stone, Mark Subias, Olivier Sultan, Molly Tack, Peter Tear, Lou Viola, Ann Wagar, Donya Washington, Abby Weintraub, Erica Whyman, Tom Wirtshafter, George C. Wolfe

59E59, Actors Theatre of Louisville, American Repertory Theatre, The Assembly Rooms, Barrow Street Theatre, Center Theatre Group, Chashama, The Cherry Lane Theater, Dixon Place, Elevator Repair Service, The Foundry Theatre, Galapagos Art Space, Gate Theatre, Ghostlight Records, H-Art Management, Here Art Space, La Jolla Playhouse, New York Theatre Workshop, The Orchard Project, PS 122, The Public Theatre and Joe's Pub, SCAMP, SITI Company, Soho Rep, Soho Theatre, The Sundance Institute, Under the Radar, Universes, Vineyard Theatre, Z Space Studio

A special thank you to all of the individuals and institutions whose contributions to The Civilians have made these works possible.

CANARD, CANARD, GOOSE?

created by the company

written by Steven Cosson

from interviews, improvisations, writings,
and other contributions by the company:
Damian Baldet, Ayşan Çelik, Maria Dizzia, Aimée
Guillot, Anne Kauffman, Christina Kirk, Caitlin Miller,
Jennifer Morris, Charlie Schroeder,
Brian Sgambati, and Colleen Werthmann

additional text by Anne Washburn

music and lyrics by Michael Friedman

Playscripts, Inc.
website: www.playscripts.com
email: info@playscripts.com
phone: 1-866-NEW-PLAY (639-7529)

INTRODUCTION

Looking back on the creation of The Civilians' first show *Canard, Canard, Goose?* I am trying to distill exactly why immediately post-9/11 we chose to do a show about alleged geese abuse. There was no good reason. There were only circumstances, lots of bad reasons, and a deadline. As it is chronicled in the play—with great dramatic license—the making of the play was essentially a group of people stumbling ahead, using curiosity as our only guide, fueled by desperation.

The "making of" story begins when Bonnie Metzgar gave us a date to perform (November 13th, 2001) at Joe's Pub, the Public Theater's house nightclub. We planned out an idea for a project and set a first rehearsal, which turned out to be a few days after September 11th. With the smell of the smoldering Towers still everywhere in the city, our planned idea then seemed stupid and meaningless so we dropped it. Everything at that time was rollercoaster emotions, bizarre pronouncements from the cultural front and ominous signs from our political leaders. And perhaps because of all this confusion we decided to pursue a story with clear good guys (geese) and bad guys (Disney). Or we chose it because it offered escape from the city. Or we said yes because for whatever reason at that time this story was the right kind of stupid. The idea itself knew it was stupid, so there was no way to go but forward.

It turns out this was an ideal beginning for a theater company. Everyone was thrown into doing something new. Michael Friedman, for one, ended up writing songs for a musical for the first time. I learned many things, but perhaps most importantly I learned that The Civilians' process requires a leap into the unknown. Just as a solitary writer needs to create with some balance between the subconscious and the rational; a collaborative approach equally needs some push to suspend the usual ways of thinking and get to the interesting stuff. I learned that somehow the play is out there already in the world; that the way to find it lay in creating circumstances in which something unexpected might happen and then trying to find the points of connection. *Canard* certainly has its rough edges, but it's the way—like Anna Paquin—we learned to fly.

—*Steven Cosson*

CAST OF CHARACTERS

TWO FRENCH GIRLS, purposeful. Mysterious. French?

BILL LISHMAN, Canadian, Inventor, Pilot, Geese trainer. Mid fifties. Grey-bearded. Pilot goggles. Exuberant and full of the wonders of the world.

MARGIE MOORE, summer worker at the Long Lake Motel. Forties. Weary.

MOTEL OWNER, owns the Long Lake Motel. Sixties. Slow. Meek.

DINER GUY, wiseacre.

BARTENDER WOMAN, from NJ. Sensible, warm, animated, casual. No frills no bullshit.

SHIRLEY, works at the bank. Fifties. Short grey hair. Butch & straightforward.

SALLY, works at the bank. Thirties. Heavy. Friendly.

MOTEL OWNER'S WIFE, middle-aged. Originally from Texas. Long Lake Motel.

ADIRONDACK HOTEL OWNER, owns the Adirondack Hotel. Short, composed, plain looking but has something of an acquired refinement that comes with being in hospitality. From Buffalo.

WILDLIFE REHAB WOMAN, middle-aged. Clean, homey tailored look.

CHARMAINE, twenties. Long Lake native. Hotel cleaner and occasional goose sitter. Really could care less about it all.

WISE SOUNDING GUY, forties. He's a pilot and he's always got something he's thinking but not saying.

WOMAN WHO WORKS WITH THE GUY WHO RENTS PLANES, works at the Marina. Late 30s. Sensibly feminine.

GUY WHO RENTS PLANES, pilot at the Marina. Late 30s. Windblown, haggard, handsome. Leans on things.

CUSTOMER AT THE OTHER BAR, forties. Up from NJ. Horse-owner. A good drinker. Tough on the outside. Mushy on the inside.

BARTENDER MAN, bartender. Tall, thin, bald, languidly effeminate. Gold chain.

BOB, former cop. Sturdy. Regular guy.

GOOSE HATING OLD GUY, park and rec guy. Carhartt.

BRUCE MACKINNON, Canadian, Avian Control Expert.

RANDALL WATT, Air Force Chicken Tester.

ANNA PAQUIN, movie star. First at 19, then at 14.

TERRY KINNEY, actor.

4

Actors
DAMIAN
BRIAN
CHARLIE
COLLEEN
AYŞAN
JENNY
AIMÉE

ACKNOWLEDGMENTS

The premiere of *Canard, Canard, Goose?* was produced by The Civilians (Steven Cosson, Artistic Director) at HERE Arts Center, New York City, opening on January 25, 2002. It was directed by Steven Cosson with the following cast:

Damian Baldet
Ayşan Çelik
Aimée Guillot
Jennifer Morris
Charlie Schroeder
Brian Sgambati
Colleen Werthmann

And the following production staff:

Set Designer .... Louisa Thompson
Costume Designer .... Sarah Beers
Lighting Designer .... Gwen Grossman
Sound Designer .... Samuel C. Tresler
Stage Manager .... Terence Dale
Choreographer .... Jessica Wallenfels
Associate Director .... Anne Kauffman
Music Director .... Kris Kukul
Movement .... KJ Sanchez

Jennifer R. Morris, Damian Baldet, Colleen Werthmann, Ayşan Çelik,
Brian Sgambati, and Aimée Guillot
in *Canard, Canard, Goose?*

HERE Arts Center, New York City, 2002
Photo by Leslie Lyons

CANARD, CANARD, GOOSE?

Scene One

An empty stage. Sounds of morning. Someplace cold and misty at the edge of a lake. The TWO FRENCH GIRLS *enter, wearing yellow raincoats and berets. They pause, honk horns, look over their shoulders and wait expectantly. Sound of goslings approach. The* TWO FRENCH GIRLS *move on. Sounds of wind and a small snowmobile motor. Canadian inventor* BILL LISHMAN *is revealed; he's flying in his ultralight airplane. He wears old-fashioned pilot goggles.*

AN ACTOR'S VOICE. In the air. Somewhere. In Canada. Bill Lishman.

BILL LISHMAN. I started flying as a hobby, you know. You dream about it as a kid just flying through the air and it was a dream of mine so I started building ultralights in my backyard. I got about a hundred acres here in Ontario, so there was plenty of room to experiment with construction.

I love to fly in the fall watchin' the leaves change, looking down at my house at the foot of the river. One day I—just by sheer coincidence—got caught up in a gaggle of ducks. Now usually when you're flyin' around, the speed of the ultralight will intimidate or scare off a bunch of birds, but I just happened to be flying at their speed about twelve, fifteen feet away from them, so we just kept pace with each other. I was behind a couple of them and one of them kept turning around to see if I was still there. It was the most amazing experience. It's what led me to start my experiments with migrating geese. I wrote a book about it, *Father Goose.* And then the Hollywood people called and turned my story into a movie. *Fly Away Home.* Now take geese. Say they've lost their leader or mother, there's no one to point them in the right direction.

(Crudely made geese puppets appear. They fly around erratically like crudely made geese puppets who've lost their way.)

Well I figured if I could adjust the speed of the ultralight, it's about a 50 horsepower, but if I could just tweak it a little here and there-if I could find the right speed then these birds would follow me. We could fly together.

(Sound of a motor adjusting and then a flock of geese flying nearby. The geese puppets fly alongside BILL LISHMAN.*)*

But I tell ya, there's nothing better than flying up there in a river of geese. It's really special, like being a kid again.

(Sounds of honking builds. Wonderful honking.)

Scene Two

A member of the company, COLLEEN, *addresses the audience.*

COLLEEN. Everything that you're about to see is fact. Everything is exactly as it occurred, as we managed to remember it. Some of the fact has been edited. Names have been changed and within the company identities have been rearranged. There may have been a certain amount of reimagining.

That said, I state to you, the audience, unequivocally, that the things we are talking about are either completely real or altered slightly from real events. If you doubt the truth of this statement I have just made, I say to you that you are entitled to that doubt in as much as any human being has a right to be skeptical about received information, yet I will insist that despite this entitlement, if you persist in your doubt of the reality of people, events, or facts in this show you are erroneous in that persistence.

AIMÉE. Meeting of The Civilians. September 23rd, 2001.

(A scene, members of a theater company looking frazzled, numb and altogether distracted. It's Aimée's turn to report on the progress of their latest project.)

AIMÉE. Pass. Ayşan?

AYŞAN. Nada.

AIMÉE. Jen?

JENNY. Are you kidding? I can barely leave my fucking apartment.

COLLEEN. I have a quasi interview.

CHARLIE. I don't want to do a show about anything.

BRIAN. Quasi?

COLLEEN. Well, she talked to me, and I got notes.

*(*DAMIAN *examines a green Cheeto-like snack, a Seaweed Puff.)*

DAMIAN. The *amount* of seaweed in this puff will determine my willingness to eat it.

COLLEEN. It's a Seaweed Puff.

DAMIAN. If seaweed is a garnishing element, I can eat it. Otherwise I'm afraid I have to withdraw.

COLLEEN. What, you're a misogynist?

DAMIAN. I'm a—? No. Do you *mean* misogynist?

BRIAN. *(Helpfully:)* Because a girl bought it.

COLLEEN. Xenophobe. Sorry. A—something phobe, uh—fuck. What's the Latin for—

CHARLIE. Non-terrerius.

COLLEEN. Uh…but okay tell me this. Do you genuinely not like it? Or is it more that it *scares* you.

JENNY. Damian, say something moving about your childhood.

DAMIAN. "I was very young. I was on a beach."

COLLEEN. But did you know, for example, that seaweed actually *leaches* radioactivity from your body?

BRIAN. Get out.

      (COLLEEN *feeds* AYŞAN *a seaweed puff.*)

COLLEEN. Body of Christ.

AYŞAN. Amen.

COLLEEN. All I'm saying is that if you can't stand it, you can't stand it, but if it's just an amusing little aversion for you, you might want to rethink your stance. Also it has all these, I'm certain it has all these weird especially healthful minerals. And why not, you know? Why not be sophisticated?

AIMÉE. No, seriously. In case of nuclear attack?

COLLEEN. Uh…yes. If you're pretty far away when it happens it might be helpful.

DAMIAN. In that case. I'll give the puff a whirl.

      (BRIAN *is eating something else.*)

BRIAN. This isn't real cheese is it?

JENNY. It's tofu cheese.

CHARLIE. Since when are we a vegetarian collective?

COLLEEN. It actually leaches radioactivity from your body. That I know. I don't know about nuclear attack or dirty nukes or distance from the epicenter or any of that.

BRIAN. This cheese is really realistic.

JENNY. It's tofu pepper-jack.

BRIAN. It isn't bad.

JENNY. *(Looking at* CHARLIE:*) Someone* brought cookies last time.

AYŞAN. You thought it was real cheese?

BRIAN. Yeah. I did.

CHARLIE. Cookies are vegetarian.

AYŞAN. You are *crazy.* This tastes *nothing* like real cheese.

CHARLIE. Next time I'm bringing a hunk of meat. Just to make sure.

JENNY. *(Meaning the seaweed puffs:)* I like 'em.

COLLEEN. *Thank* you.

      (*Pause.*)

AYŞAN. Wow. That was like normal conversation, almost three minutes.

DAMIAN. Which included irony. Not dead after all. "Pfew."

JENNY. But was that irony or was it just sarcasm?

CHARLIE. That's—

BRIAN. That's what irony means now. Basically.

(*Pause.*)

CHARLIE. Can we do this already?

COLLEEN. Sorry. I thought everyone was enjoying the "normal conversation." Okay. So this is the 8th. And I'm up at Long Lake, which is this town upstate, this little town, on a lake. Anyway. Margie Moore at the Motel was telling me and Juergin that movie *Fly Away Home* was filmed up there, and that they trained all these geese to fly behind a light aircraft, an ultralight propeller aircraft, and basically they imprinted the little geese so that they'd think that Anna Paquin is their mother, or their goose leader, or the aircraft is their mother and after they've done this, and these geese are totally dependent on…Anna Paquin, or the plane, or both, I forget which, once they're done filming the movie they split. And they leave the geese behind. So these geese, their 'mother' is gone, their social system is fucked, and they have no leader and no concept of how to migrate. So they're all stranded there over the winter and they all die. Margie is telling us this and I'm outraged. I'm like, this is inexcusable! So I went back to my room and I wrote it down. Juergin is like 'Colleen, come on we're on vacation' and I'm all 'Disney isn't getting away with this one.' I said to Juergin 'That is the saddest fucking thing I have ever heard.'

(*The company seems to agree.*)

Okay, so here she is. This is Margie. Um, let me just look at my notes again.

(COLLEEN *prepares for a moment and then plays* MARGIE MOORE.)

MARGIE. You know, they shot that movie *Fly Away Home* here in Long Lake you know that movie where the little girl shows the geese the way home—with the planes? Yeah, well, you know, it was terrible, you know, those movie people came in here, raised those geese to follow planes, by imprinting them, you know, not on their mother, and then when they were done filmin' they up and deserted those geese. Yeah. And, since the geese didn't have anyone to show them the way down south they got stuck over there behind the Long Lake Diner. Yeah Hollywood up and left 'em. Just left 'em behind.

(*The company is moved by the story.*)

JENNY. Colleen, how many people can you fit in your station wagon?

(*Footlights. The company performs:*)

THE CIVILIANS THEME SONG

OOOH. OOOH. OOOH.
WE'RE THE CIVILIANS AND WE'RE GONNA GETCHA.
WE'RE HERE BY THE MILLIONS, DO WE ROCK? YOU
    BETCHA.
THE CIVILIANS ARE COMING.

THE CIVILIANS ARE COMING.
OOOH.

(Spoken over the Oooh's:)

We think pretty hard about stuff.
We decide on a thing.
We investigate stuff like timeless issues, and current events.
We interview strangers.
We don't use any recording devices.
We do little and mostly inconclusive research.
People bring snacks.
And then…
We make a show of it!

WE'RE THE CIVILIANS AND WE'RE GONNA GETCHA.
WE'RE HERE BY THE MILLIONS, DO WE ROCK? YOU
  BETCHA.
THE CIVILIANS ARE COMING.
THE CIVILIANS ARE COMING.
CIVILIANS. (x7)

Scene 3: Fly Away Home

CHARLIE. *(Movie trailer voice:)* Fly Away Home

AYŞAN. *(Movie trailer voice:)* To attempt the incredible, you have to achieve the impossible.

(The company tells/performs/confuses the plotline of "Fly Away Home.")

JENNY. Okay, well there's this whole—

AIMÉE. Jeff Bridges—

JENNY. Daniels.

AIMÉE. Jeff Daniels crashes the plane and he's like: "You must go on, you must go on."

DAMIAN. *(Playing Jeff Daniels:)* You must go on, you must go on.

BRIAN. And there's this scene in the shower

DAMIAN. And there's this ranger

BRIAN. She has soap in her eyes

DAMIAN. He's all: "I must clip their wings."

BRIAN. She's surrounded by all these fledgling geese.

DAMIAN. *(Playing the Park Ranger:)* I'm going to clip their wiiiiings!

BRIAN. She's naked and crying.

JENNY. And an important time element.

BRIAN. The geese are just confused.

(Pause. That didn't really work at all. Take two.)

CHARLIE. *(Movie trailer voice:) Fly Away Home*

AYŞAN. *(Movie trailer voice:)* To achieve the incredible, you have to attempt the impossible.

JENNY. Okay. There's this thirteen-year-old girl who is Anna Paquin and she's in a crash with her mom.

COLLEEN. This truck hits them.

DAMIAN. She wakes up and Jeff Bridges is her father—

JENNY. Jeff Daniels.

DAMIAN. Jeff Daniels.

(Set up of a hospital scene.)

CHARLIE. This is in the hospital. And I'm a pillow.

AYŞAN. He's very hairy, and he's all like "Your mom is dead, and now you're going to live with me."

COLLEEN. She's in Canada, in the middle of Canada, and her father is a freaky inventor pilot, and she has no friends, and she's all shitty and unhappy. She's raising geese eggs in a drawer full of her dead mom's scarves and a heat lamp and of course the eggs hatch and then there's a lot of endless —and this is all based on Bill Lishman and his work with ultralight aircraft— but the point is: these geese have no concept of how to migrate and they think Anna Paquin is their mother and so Anna Paquin has to migrate.

DAMIAN. She's the only one who can do it.

COLLEEN. Igor, the lame goose is bundled on the plane with her and he's wearing a little muslin jacket.

AYŞAN. Jeff Daniels crashes the plane at some point and he's all, "You must go on, you must go on."

BRIAN. "You must go on. You must go on."

JENNY. Uncle David played by Terry Kinney is in a truck down below helpin' out.

COLLEEN. She's flying, and the geese are following her, and she's flying into the airspace around New York and the military is going to shoot them down but decides instead that they love them.

DAMIAN. They're champions. The newscasters say: That's illegal! But that's inspiring!

AYŞAN. People are lined up cheering.

COLLEEN. They arrive in North Carolina just before the bulldozers (there are all these bulldozers) and the day is saved and Anna Paquin and Jeff Bridges are a family.

Scene Four

AYŞAN. On the ground. Somewhere. In New York.

(All The Civilians in one station with CHARLIE *in the way back. Sound: station wagon downshifting.* JENNY *wakes up.)*

JENNY. Where are we?

DAMIAN. Albany.

JENNY. This is Albany? This is not how I imagined Albany.

CHARLIE. You guys this is the capital of New York. Isn't it?

JENNY. It's like this creepy moon city, like a city on the moon.

CHARLIE. Or a city in Europe.

COLLEEN. My dad told me "You'd better be careful. A lot of people liked that movie. It was a very popular movie."

AYŞAN. What makes this such an indictment, this is such an indictment because Disney—people say they treat their *employees* like animals, but this is how they treat their *animals.*

BRIAN. Do you think the geese starve? Or is it one of those things where their little webbed feet aren't designed for the ice and they just get stuck there.

AYŞAN. I mean, what do you think it would take to get Disney to face the truth? Not just as a business, but as people, like before whoever their god is, before the faces of their children. I mean, these people are not *biologically* incapable of contrition.

CHARLIE. How far?

DAMIAN. 165 Miles

    (Pause.)

I had a great goose down parka in 5th and 6th grade—

BRIAN. Yeah, yeah. Parkas. I remember and they were great and everyone had them but then there was this sudden point after which only geeks wore them. I remember it was this distinct moment where I looked around and I suddenly realized that everyone else had abandoned the parka ship. I was like: "Heeey?"

JENNY. How do they get goose down off the goose? Is it a gathering thing?

COLLEEN. They kill them.

DAMIAN. They do not. They shear them. Like a sheep.

COLLEEN. And then they knit them little sweaters to wear until their feathers grow back.

AYŞAN. They kill them.

DAMIAN. My grandfather back in France said like one hundred years ago that to fatten up the geese, they'd stick a funnel in their little beaks, and pour the seed in and then they'd go like this *(Neck stroking jerk off gesture).* And I think that speaks volumes to the degree to which man will manipulate geese as a live product, which argues for the shearing theory.

(Intro to Poor Little Goose begins:)

BRIAN. I loved those parkas

AIMÉE. They were warm.

JENNY. They were great, they were poofy.

POOR LITTLE GOOSE

POOR LITTLE GOOSE
ALWAYS HONKING ALONE IN THE SNOW
NEVER KNOWING WHICH WAY YOU SHOULD GO
OR WHICH GAGGLE TO FOLLOW.

POOR LITTLE GOOSE
THEY JUST USED YOU AND LEFT YOU BEHIND
WITH NO MAMA AND NO HOPE TO FIND
ANY LOVE THAT'S NOT HOLLOW.

FLY AWAY HOME LITTLE GOOSE
YOU DON'T NEED ANNA PAQUIN TO SHOW YOU THE
    WAY
IF YOU FOLLOW YOUR HEART YOU CAN MAKE IT
    THERE
AND YOU WONT BE A POOR LITTLE GOOSE ANYMORE.

WE'RE ALL LITTLE GEESE
JUST LOOKING FOR LOVE
SO LOOK TO THE SKY
AND FLY AWAY FLY.

Scene 5

The company arrives in Long Lake. They are interviewing the locals.

CHARLIE. I know this sounds kinda weird but—

JENNY. We're looking for Margie Moore she works here.

COLLEEN. We're here from New York City.

AYŞAN. The geese…what happened to the geese?

AIMÉE. *Fly Away Home?* It's a movie.

(People of Long Lake, New York:)

MOTEL OWNER. Oh, Margie's back in Rochester…but I remember the planes—they flew right over there. And the birds would all follow. Yeah, I heard they left the geese here and they didn't fly south.

GUY AT THE DINER. The geese? They left them and we shot 'em. Just kidding.

MOTEL OWNER. They got stuck here for the winter.

BARTENDER WOMAN. Oh yeah, I know what you're talking about, the Disney movie. I didn't meet them. But I saw the planes with the geese following after. *(She squirts a soda gun into a glass.)*

GUY AT THE DINER. An airplane flew round the lake out here and the geese followed them. Not our geese mind you, but French geese. These geese only spoke French.

MOTEL OWNER. I don't know how they made it through the winter. I'm not sure they all did.

GUY AT THE DINER. No those geese behind the diner are local geese. When the movie crew was here, those geese, our geese, might have mixed with the French geese—I don't know what happened after—but when they made the movie all the geese hung out together.

CHARLIE. Did you see *Fly Away Home?*

BARTENDER. No I didn't watch it 'cause I saw the trailer and I cried. *(Soda gun.)* You want another beer?

CHARLIE. *(To* BARTENDER:*)* Uh. Yeah. Please.

> *(A desk bell.)*

ADIRONDACK HOTEL OWNER. The movie crew didn't stay at this hotel. I should know, I'm the owner. I mean, we served them food. We tended to their personal…stomachs. And we did their laundry. We're a catering service and a hotel, that's what we do. We feed people.

GOOSE HATING OLD GUY. Are you pro geese or anti geese because that will determine the length of this interview?

HOTEL OWNER. You know who you could talk to, there's Charmaine, she works here. She took care of the geese.

GOOSE HATING OLD GUY. The only good goose is one that's lying on its back with its feet in the air all brown and crispy.

CHARMAINE. I just goose sat. From six until dark.

MOTEL OWNER. I'm sorry I can't help. You could come back and talk to my wife. You know they go just about now. You might even see them flying in formation above your heads.

BARTENDER WOMAN. Yeah. I saw that trailer—the little girl who flies the airplane down South. Yeah. I cry at all those movies. Pocahontas. Frosty the Snowman. Yaah—when he melts. Now don't get me wrong, real life I do pretty good at. I can handle real life just fine. It's the movies I don't like.

MOTEL OWNER'S WIFE. What? No, that's not a goose. That's just a duck with one foot. Margie was real fond of him when she worked here. He can't go too far, you know. I mean, all he can do is hop around.

> *(At the Long Lake Bank:* BOB, BANK TELLER WOMAN, OLDER WOMAN AT THE BANK.*)*

BOB. I just want to let you guys know that I talked to Vincent over at the film studio and they don't know anything about you guys. I asked them—right after I talked to you, I gave them a call and they hadn't heard anything about you. So if it seemed like I didn't want to talk to you that's why. I mean, we really liked those guys.

(At the bank. Slashes indicate overlapping dialogue.)

BANK TELLER WOMAN. We were here for the filming. They were right over there on the lake. I saw them with all those sheep flying behind the plane. Geese. I always think of them as sheep—like a herd.

OLDER WOMAN AT THE BANK. Little Bob—my son Bob—and my husband Bob took 'em through the woods

BOB. They came up here for the foliage. They wanted to get shots of the geese flying over the fall foliage

BANK TELLER WOMAN. Everyone was really excited to help you know—

OLDER WOMAN AT THE BANK. Yep, she and I worked for them, servin' them food. And I would tend bar so when the guys would come in after shooting, they'd sit down and tell me all their stories / Stories about trudging through the mud.

BANK TELLER WOMAN. They'd go trudging through the mud. Sal, tell 'em about the mama goose!

OLDER WOMAN AT THE BANK. Oh, yeah, the mama goose—

BANK TELLER WOMAN. They would follow her around, you know, 'cuz they grew up with her and they thought she was / their mama

OLDER WOMAN AT THE BANK. their mama.

(The TWO FRENCH GIRLS *appear.)*

BOB. There were these girls who were always with them—and they spoke French. They were from French. France.

*(*JENNY *pulls* CHARLIE *aside.)*

JENNY. What's with all the French shit?

CHARLIE. These people are just confused, they mean French Canadian. Bill Lishman is Canadian, maybe he brought helpers from, you know, the French part.

JENNY. Ah. Quebecois.

(The TWO FRENCH GIRLS *exit.)*

WISE SOUNDING MAN. They wanted a clear cut in the background for the geese to land in and I wondered 'why do they want a clear cut?' but we took them around but they didn't have the kind of clear cutting they wanted. You're in the theater. You know what directors are like. They want a specific thing even if it doesn't…exist.

(At the bar, non-stop 9/11 coverage on the TV.)

BARTENDER WOMAN. Aw jeez, you guys are up here from New York. You came up here to get a break and look at me here, you must be sick of seeing this shit on the news—do you want me to change it to the MTV?

(She changes channels, we hear Mary J. Blige instead.)

WISE SOUNDING MAN. At one point they were looking for a documentable frost. They wanted to locate a reliable barometer. And I said, there isn't a reliable way of predicting weather conditions out here—you can put a bowl of water outside and see if it freezes.

GUY WHO RENTS AIRPLANES. They did try to get a bald eagle before. They wanted to film a bald eagle flying in the desert. But the US government wouldn't give them bald eagle eggs. So they found this guy, he had a seventeen-year-old bald eagle and they rented it. And then, *something…* happened with the plane and that bird went straight into the prop. I remember that because they had to pay out $42,000 in insurance.

OLDER WOMAN. *(Accusatorily:)* Why are you so interested in this movie?

*(*BARTENDER *gives beers to* CHARLIE *and* COLLEEN.*)*

BRIAN. *(To* COLLEEN:*)* Hey did you get the email I sent you with the *Fly Away Home* url?

COLLEEN. Yuh. I loved the online interview with Anna Paquin. "Die Hard with a Vengeance."

BRIAN. Yeah. Yeah. But did you click on the link to Bill Lishman?

COLLEEN. Who?

BRIAN. The Canadian Inventor Pilot Guy. The guy Charlie plays.

COLLEEN. No. They just got spy software at work. I can only surf so long.

BRIAN. He's flying South right now with a flock of whooping cranes. So they won't go extinct.

COLLEEN. Cool.

BRIAN. Yeah. But does it not seem peculiar that this Bill Lishman guy would let Disney perpetrate such evildoings?

COLLEEN. Why?

BRIAN. He's so obviously crunchy.

COLLEEN. Yyyy-eh. Well maybe they didn't tell him. Maybe he doesn't exist. He could be like a logo.

BRIAN. A logo?

COLLEEN. You know, like a humanizing corporate face. Like Betty Crocker.

BRIAN. Or Aunt Jemima.

COLLEEN. Yeah.

(They exit.)

CHARMAINE. They need someone to take care of the geese, to feed them. People know that I like animals so I guess they found out my name.

WOMAN WHO WORKS WITH THE GUY WHO RENTS PLANES. The two French girls, they called them the mama goose because they raised those geese and the geese followed them like they were their own mamas, right. They started on a boat, first—no, first it was just a horn and the girls always wore these yellow raincoats and honk their horns, and then they put the girls on a boat—and they'd wear their raincoats and honk the horn and the geese would swim after. And after they trained them like that then anyone could just wear the raincoats, like the pilots, and then the geese would just follow the planes.

CHARMAINE. They put chips in the geese to track them. Electronics. In their chests. So they could just pass something, a tracer, over them like *blip blip* to record them. So if one goose was tired or something they would pass the thing, the tracer over their chest and it would say, like, "#47." So they would record "#47 was lazy today."

WOMAN WHO WORKS WITH THE GUY WHO RENTS PLANES. But there would also be like a dominant male goose, and sometimes, because one would be like too weak, or too small. They'd lose one. Yeah, he'd just take one out. You know, the survival of the fittest.

CHARMAINE. They didn't really have a personality. They did their primming and grooming. It was boring.

WOMAN WHO WORKS WITH THE GUY WHO RENTS PLANES. I went up with them once, in the ultralight airplane. I think I was the only one who did. I guess no one else thought they could ask, but I did, and they took me up once. It was the most wonderful experience of my entire life.

CHARMAINE. They ate. And they shit. A LOT.

CHARLIE. That's super. Really. But do you know what they did with the geese when they were done filming?

CHARMAINE. I dunno. I think they went to Arizona.

BARTENDER WOMAN. I know what you're thinking. Zero population growth. Lower Siberia. But it doesn't get boring up here.

WILDLIFE REHAB WOMAN. You have to understand, we work very, very hard here. The people of Long Lake have ten weeks to make our living. We are up to our eyeballs in work.

(A different bar run by BARTENDER MAN *is set up.)*

BARTENDER MAN. Is he still talking about horses?

BARTENDER WOMAN. I'm a lifer. Been here twelve years. I moved up from New Jersey—I gave up drugs for alcohol. No, seriously. But you do have to drink a lot up here.

WILDLIFE REHAB WOMAN. I'll use myself as an example.

CUSTOMER AT THE OTHER BAR. Can I have another one? Still thirsty.

WILDLIFE REHAB WOMAN. Yesterday it was 28 degrees in the morning, that's an early frost. And at 28 degrees, pipes freeze.

BARTENDER MAN. Don't listen to him

WILDLIFE REHAB WOMAN. I have fourteen cottages with fireplaces and I had to close them down. I can't afford to burn wood for two days straight in order to rent them out. And it's like that for everybody.

ADIRONDACK HOTEL OWNER. It gets real slow here in the winter. It's scary.

WILDLIFE REHAB WOMAN. No one comes here then. No one. There's a couple weeks with the leaf peepers but they don't stay overnight.

BARTENDER WOMAN. What's that Stephen King book?

AIMÉE. *The Stand?*

BARTENDER WOMAN. *The Stand,* yeah that's it, *The Stand.* Where the whole country gets some killer virus and everyone dies.

CUSTOMER AT THE OTHER BAR. You got some of America's Most Wanted living out there, hidden in the mountains. The Adirondack State Park is twice the size of the Grand Canyon. You knew this was all a State Park, didn't ya?

CHARLIE. Oh. Sure.

BARTENDER WOMAN. I was home sick with the flu and Dougie brings me that book to read. *The Stand.* I was like…hello? What is this? Are you trying to give me a message or something? Am I dying here?

CUSTOMER AT THE OTHER BAR. They just build a fort. Make a fire. No one's ever gonna catch them.

(AIMÉE *and* CHARLIE *talk aside.*)

AIMÉE. Hey is your cell phone working?

CHARLIE. Fuck no. And I love it. I have no idea what's going on back home.

AIMÉE. Mine neither. Goddamn Sprint. Goddamn Sprint and goddamn Disney. I can't get these people to say anything about the lost geese. They must have gotten hush money or something.

CHARLIE. I'm not even checking my messages. It's amazing. I've been over at the Blarney Stone drinking with these guys—they want to take me hunting. But we won't shoot geese. One of them won't shoot geese. I think I could shoot a goose. They take these snowmobiles and go way out in the mountains—

AIMÉE. Are you out of your mind? You have to check your messages.

(The Adirondack Hotel. Desk bell dings.)

ADIRONDACK HOTEL OWNER. I remember they did another movie here a while back, there was a film crew here filming a documentary about Cold River, you know because of the hermits.

DAMIAN. You mean people hermits?

ADIRONDACK HOTEL OWNER. Oh yes, we've got several famous hermits.

DAMIAN. How did they get famous?

ADIRONDACK HOTEL OWNER. Oh you know. Folklore. This painting here. This is Noah Rondo, he's a famous hermit from up here—this is back at the turn of the century, a lot of people up here just lived off the land and kept to themselves. This is actually a funny story about Noah Rondo: he used to come in here, and paddle his boat across that lake, like twice a year to, I don't know, do his shopping, and he'd come in and have his dinner with the old codgers. And there used to be an old hotel over here and the Mrs. *(Laughs.)* he used to go knocking on the back door to see the Mrs. And the Mrs. wouldn't let him in but she'd crack the door open and give him a… pie…or cake…or something. And he'd do this every year, and then one year he's there and he's eating his pie and he looks up at her and says "Well, you're getting awfully rough and old!"

> *(Pause.)*

DAMIAN. Wow.

ADIRONDACK HOTEL OWNER. People come in here and they know who he is, they say, "Oh, look, you've got Noah Rondo there." In a small town like this one, everyone knows each other. You know what they say, they'll stab you in the back, but if you're ever in need, they'll be the first to help you out. We try to help each other out here. It can get really hard in the winter. It gets real slow here. Real slow. It's scary. Nobody comes up here then. Maybe a snowmobiler.

> *(Pause.)*

They drive trucks across the lake.

> *(She looks out across the lake as the afternoon light dims.)*

LONELY

THEY DRIVE TRUCKS
ACROSS THE LAKE
SO SLOWLY.

OVER THE ICE
ACROSS THE LAKE
SO SLOWLY
SO SLOWLY

IF I COULD FLY AWAY
IF I COULD FLY AWAY
AND LEAVE THIS COLD BEHIND.

LONELY.
I'M SO LONELY.
LONELY.
I'M SO LONELY.

SNOW FALLS DOWN
ACROSS THE LAKE
SO SLOWLY

OVER THE ICE
ACROSS THE LAKE
SO SLOWLY
SO SLOWLY

IF I COULD FLY AWAY
IF I COULD FLY AWAY
AND LEAVE THIS COLD BEHIND

LONELY.
I'M SO LONELY.

ADIRONDACK HOTEL OWNER. When it happened. I was asleep. My daughter called me and said, "Mom, we're being attacked." And I thought, "What? Attacked? Here?" *(Gestures out the window to a picturesque view of the Lake.)* No, I shouldn't joke. I just couldn't have imagined.

We were just devastated. Just. Devastated.

People came here to the hotel. A lot of people live alone up here in the mountains. I think they just wanted to be around other people. So we put the TV on here in this room. And it's been on ever since.

(Back to the bar.)

BARTENDER MAN. Are you still talking about horses?

CUSTOMER AT THE OTHER BAR. Can I have another one? Still thirsty. Sure, sometimes they get hurt. You see, when a horse falls and breaks her leg, I'm the first one over that gate. I'm the first one to throw myself on top of that horse. You have to throw yourself on her to stop her from getting up. See, because she's scared and she'll try get up and run and then she'll get tangled up in her harness and hurt herself more. So I'm the first one over to throw myself on that horse. The cops come after me for that. Tried to arrest me but I don't care because I love horses, so I'm the first one over.

GOOSE HATING OLD GUY. There is only one way to get rid of a goose. There is only one way to get rid of a goose.

CUSTOMER AT THE OTHER BAR. Yeah, we both hunt. I'll shoot most anything Well, I'll shoot bears—black bears. They're mean mother-fuckers. I don't give a fuck. And deer, I'll shoot deer. But I won't shoot geese.

BARTENDER MAN. I shoot geese.

GOOSE HATING OLD GUY. A couple of years back I asked the board if I could have permission to kill some geese but they said no, I couldn't do it out of season and then a couple of weeks later one of the member's son's trucks got shat all over by the geese and he just looked at me and said "kill 'em."

CUSTOMER AT THE OTHER BAR. See, geese mate for life. So, if you kill that male goose that female will never mate again. Never mate again. She'll be left alone.

GOOSE HATING OLD GUY. Each one of them can shit up to five pounds a day

CUSTOMER AT THE OTHER BAR. I just got divorced. That's really why I came up here. To get my head together after my divorce. I only meant to stay here three months and so far it's been…

BARTENDER MAN. Six

CUSTOMER AT THE OTHER BAR. Six

GOOSE HATING OLD GUY. Geese are a pain in the ass. One time my wife was hitting golf balls on the ball park and they wouldn't let her retrieve her ball. They'll attack you, but I'm not afraid, I'll kill 'em. They bite you and twist. Just bite and twist. Like they'll grab your finger or the back of your thigh, right here, and just twist. That hurts. But like I said I'll kill em. Grab their heads and twist, and twist and twist until their head snaps off. That's how I used to kill chickens on my farm.

CUSTOMER AT THE OTHER BAR. So, no I won't shoot geese, I can't do that.

WILDLIFE REHAB WOMAN. Those are photos of all the animals I've rehabilitated. I'm wildlife rehabilitation and those are some of the animals I've saved. Raccoons can be the most rewarding. Baby raccoons hug you and kiss you. They're like a mix between a kitten and a puppy. See that fawn there, her mother was hit by a car. I cared for her from when she was just a baby until she was a little over a year old. Then I took her to the woods to let her go. And she would run a little out into the woods and then run back to me. Then she would run a little farther and then run back to me, and then finally she ran a little farther out and just kept going. She was so beautiful. So happy to be out running. I saw her again last Christmas. I was out in the area where I released her and there she was. She came right up to me but she was different. She was so confident—an adult not a child. She came right up to me. I was standing there with tears running down my face looking in my pockets for a piece of apple. And I gave it to her and she ate it, looked at me and then ran off.

GOOSE HATING OLD GUY. The Canadian Government has a real problem on their hands. There are so many geese and so few hunters—down here we only get two weeks, and when the geese are up in Canada—the thing about Canada is: There's. Nobody. There.

WILDLIFE REHAB WOMAN. What do I feel about hunting? Well it's funny you know because I sell the hunting licenses for Long Lake. Everyone knows what I do, you know, it's a small town so people are always making jokes about it. But the people who hunt don't want the animals to suffer. They want a clean shot.

BARTENDER MAN. Sure, I feel bad sometimes when I shoot the geese. Like if I clip them with a bullet and then they're flapping around in the water and suffering. I don't like that. Yeah, I feel bad when that happens. You go through your day and you want a release and if that happens it's upsetting.

WILDLIFE REHAB WOMAN. It's usually the people who aren't from around here, they will do things like shoot the deer in the hip and then track it through the woods, you know torture it. That's just awful. The hunters up here they don't do that.

BARTENDER MAN. I get my two geese per season and that's it. Geese don't taste very good. They taste like grease.

CUSTOMER AT THE OTHER BAR. Yeah, they're greasy sons of bitches.

BARTENDER MAN. If I miss—if I can't get a clean shot, sometimes I won't shoot again. I take pictures instead. I send them to my sister in Florida and say, "Hey, that's what I saw on the lake today."

CUSTOMER AT THE OTHER BAR. It's beautiful. The way they fly in formation. Have you ever seen it? There's a leader and they all talk to each other. Yeah, there is something going on. There is something going on.

AIMÉE. Wonderful, but *Fly Away Home?*

WILDLIFE REHAB WOMAN. Yes. It was very beautiful but I didn't see it.

BRIAN. Hey, really, it's so nice of you to invite us over for dinner, and, uh, I'm really looking forward to the snowmobile race, and thanks for all the beers, and the scotch, and that other warm drink thing you made that I can't remember. And, I never would have known how much a goose can shit if you hadn't shared that with me, and I totally, totally appreciate the over-population issue, and if we didn't have to get back to the city, I mean New York City—I mean, maybe we'll come back and help out during goose season and shoot a couple, but really…really we just need to know what happened after they made *Fly Away Home* here. Did you ever see Bill Lishman, he's like a hairy Canadian bird guy, or maybe Anna Paquin, or Jeff Daniels slash Jeff Bridges? Did you see any alienated geese? I'm sorry, I mean, disoriented geese? There must have been, somewhere, a strange accumulation of goose bodies? As in goose corpses. Is Disney behind some sort of covert op here? I mean, we just need to know what happened.

ADIRONDACK HOTEL OWNER. I didn't even know there was a movie called *Fly Away Home.*

WOMAN WHO WORKS WITH THE GUY WHO RENTS PLANES. What? No. Who gave you your information?

BARTENDER WOMAN. No, the geese didn't stay here. They took them with them. I think they're in Arizona.

ADIRONDACK HOTEL OWNER. Have you talked to Tina over at the Blarney Stone? She worked for them.

BARTENDER WOMAN. Tina was going to go with them 'cause they liked her look. I says Tina go with 'em, go, you know, but she's got deep roots here.

WISE SOUNDING MAN. *Fly Away Home?*

BARTENDER WOMAN. Me, if I had a chance I'd go with them, do something different, do something new. If I had a chance to do something like that, feet don't fail me now, I'd go with the geese. Yeah, I'd go with the geese.

MOTEL OWNER'S WIFE. Uh uh. *(Meaning no.)*

DINER GUY. No, I never saw that movie they filmed here. I did see the other one though. The one with the girl who flies the little airplane south.

MOTEL OWNER'S WIFE. I don't know what my husband told you but Margie won't be able to help you. She doesn't know anything about it. She wasn't even here. Everything she heard she heard from me, and everything I heard I heard from the townspeople and it's just hearsay.

WISE SOUNDING MAN. *Fly Away Home?* No that was filmed in Minnesota.

WOMAN WHO WORKS WITH THE GUY WHO RENTS PLANES. No. No no no. The movie they were filming here was a French documentary. I think the geese must be—

GUY WHO RENTS AIRPLANES. These geese are still with those girls somewhere. I imagine in France. Cause they're not really wild birds. They've never lived in the wild. The girls who took care of them, the Mama Geese, they have to stay with them until they die. They're required by law. Until they die. I mean, I don't know how long a Canada Goose lives but it doesn't seem like something I'd like to do.

ADIRONDACK HOTEL OWNER. No. They were very, very good to those geese. Very good.

(Shit. Civilians take off their costume pieces.)

DAMIAN. Hey, remember this— "I mean, what do you think it would take to get Disney to face the truth." The truth, the truth, the truth…

AYŞAN. So?

DAMIAN. *Fly Away Home* was not a Disney movie.

AIMÉE. Well, it wasn't even filmed in Long Lake.

CHARLIE. Yeah. I kinda wondered about that thing at the end of the movie.

COLLEEN. What thing?

CHARLIE. That thing that said "*Fly Away Home* was filmed on location in Ontario."

JENNY. You watched *Fly Away Home?*

CHARLIE. Didn't all of you?

(General mutterings of 'no.')

BRIAN. I can not fucking believe that *Fly Away Home* was not filmed in Long Lake.

DAMIAN. Yeah that's two days spent in Long Lake. Two days of my life I'll never get back.

COLLEEN. I.O.U. two days of relevant, meaningful existence. Sincerely, your friend and colleague, Colleen E. Werthmann.

(Silence. JENNY looks out at the audience.)

JENNY. So what about…them?

COLLEEN. Oh. Fuck.

(All of the company looks out at the audience. Awkward shuffling of feet. Slowly, they sing, building confidence.)

THE CIVILIANS THEME SONG

OOOH. OOOH. OOOH.
WE'RE THE CIVILIANS AND WE'RE GONNA GETCHA.
     WE'RE HERE BY THE MILLIONS, DO WE ROCK?
          YOU BETCHA.
THE CIVILIANS ARE COMING.
THE CIVILIANS ARE COMING.

WE THINK PRETTY HARD ABOUT STUFF
WE DECIDE ON A THING
     WE INVESTIGATE STUFF LIKE TIMELESS ISSUES,
          AND CURRENT EVENTS
WE INTERVIEW STRANGERS
WE DON'T USE ANY RECORDING DEVICES
WE DO LITTLE AND MOSTLY INCONCLUSIVE RE-
SEARCH

PEOPLE BRING SNACKS
AND THEN...
NO MATTER WHAT HAPPENS
WE MAKE A SHOW OF IT!
(Blackout.)

THE FRENCH GOOSE SONG

CHARLIE. Ladies and gentlemen, we have a very special little treat for you tonight—no, no I'm sorry we can not give you a sad story about little lost frozen popsicle geese. There is no sad story about little sad chilly little imprinted-on-Anna-Paquin geese, no. Tonight we give to you ladies and gentlemen the real geese of Long Lake. They are from French. France. And do not be tricked, ladies and gentlemen, although these geese star in a "documentary," they are not amateurs. No. They are professional performers. And these geese live now in a comfortable tedious retirement with two French girls who wait ever so patiently for them to die. So, please help me welcome these very very talented geese to our stage, they are very very happy to be here, as they have nothing else to do.

GEESE.
          I'M LULU, I'M FIFI, I'M FEATHER, COLLETTE!
          I'M PEPE, I'M BRAD.

COLLEEN.
          I'VE HAD ALL KINDS OF LUCK.
          I'VE WADDLED THROUGH THE MUCK.
          I'VE PLAYED THE WILD DUCK IN KRAKOW.
          THROUGH ALL THE WORLD I'VE TOURED
          BUT IT JUST LEAVES ME BORED

GEESE.
          SO TELL ME WHAT AM I FIT FOR NOW?

JENNY.
          THEY SAY THE FIT SURVIVE
          BUT WATCH THE SHIT THAT I'VE
          PLAYED IN SOME LOUSY DIVE IN BILBAO.
          AND CHEKHOV'S SEAGULL TOO,
          I EVEN PLAYED THE ZOO,

GEESE.
          BUT TELL ME WHAT AM I FIT FOR NOW?

AYŞAN.
          AWAY FROM PARIS I'M FILLED WITH GOOSE ENNUI
          WHERE IS THE JOI DE VIVRE IN THESE WINGS?

BRIAN & DAMIAN.
          AND IN LA CAGE AUX FOLLES

LIFE WAS OH SO DULL
OUI, MON CHERI I KNOW WHY THE CAGED BIRD SING!

AIMÉE.
I FLEW THROUGH ASIA TWICE
AS MOTHER GOOSE ON ICE
PECKED AT FOIE GRAS AND RICE WITH CHAIRMAN
MAO

COLLEEN.
FOR HITCHCOCK ON HIS SET
I KILLED SUZANNE PLESHETTE!

GEESE.
BUT TELL ME WHAT AM I FIT FOR—

CHARLIE. Next year, Björk will be wearing one of them

GEESE.
WHAT AM I FIT FOR—

CHARLIE. Next year, The Civilians will do an exposé on *That Darn Cat*

GEESE.
WHAT AM I FIT FOR—

CHARLIE. *(To the company:)* I can't believe none of you even watched the movie. I mean, what—we try to do actually do something, like make a show that actually has some *content,* you know like DO something like ABOUT something—I mean, I know we're just a bunch of theatrical ding-dongs, but I thought we were trying to like ENGAGE and you all don't even watch the movie!

GEESE.
WHAT AM I FIT FOR *NOW?*

AYŞAN. *(To CHARLIE:)* I resent the implication that—or maybe implication is too strong a word, but say innuendo of blame that's—I mean, Colleen and I have been doing some pretty serious research.

COLLEEN. Yah I figured out how to disable the spy software.

AYŞAN. Listen: "Down" is the soft underfeathering often plucked out of live geese. Plucking the geese causes them considerable pain and distress. After the last plucking, the geese have five weeks to grow more feathers before they are sent through a machine that plucks their longest feathers. From there they go to the slaughterhouse. They kill them.

DAMIAN. That's not research that's spite. Spite does not count as research.

COLLEEN. It's not spite. It's fact. Fact does not count as spite.

DAMIAN. And excuse me "plucked out of live geese," that's *my* point. They shear them.

AYŞAN. And *then* they kill them

DAMIAN. After they've lived a *full life* with occasional unpleasant plucking, jeez—but if you ladies want to go like call up Kim Basinger and go throw some red paint at the US Ski Team be my guest—

AIMÉE. Is this conflict becoming gendered? Because I am so not cool with that.

DAMIAN. And look: Brian, Charlie, and I have been busy too—Brian?

BRIAN. Okay, this bit is from Bill Lishman's book *Father Goose,* Charlie—

BILL LISHMAN. Looking back, I could see the geese flocked about the plane, but I didn't see one goose fly up over my left wing until I heard a "brap blap" as it went through my starboard propeller. I was only about ten feet in the air when the disaster happened. The prop exploded, but there was no problem setting the aircraft back down. The sad thing was that the goose was decapitated. That was a black day.

BRIAN. Ayşan, get the rubber chickens. *(Pause.)* Please get the rubber chickens.

AIMÉE. No. The rubber chickens are cut. I'm cutting the chickens. I hate the chickens. This show is about geese.

DAMIAN. And this is Terry Kinney. I heard he played some part in *Fly Away Home* though I haven't seen it yet—

AIMÉE. You can't just conflate wildlife and poultry—

DAMIAN. —but Colleen talked to him—he's a friend of Carolyn's…

TERRY KINNEY. When we were filming the scene at the Canadian border, this one goose just took off on his own. Just turned straight around and went right into this truck. And the director, he's like this nature movie guy, you know he made *The Black Stallion* too, and he's like, "That fucking goose! Wha—that fucking goose!"

AIMÉE. Excuse me but did I just fall into the cone of silence? Can anyone actually hear me?

CHARLIE. Shush. Right and Canada Geese are a big problem at airports. They get sucked into the jet engines and then the planes blow up.

(AIMÉE exits. AYŞAN enters with rubber chickens.)

BRIAN. This is Bruce MacKinnon, he's a world expert of some sort on bird strikes—

JENNY. *(Who's been drinking with KRIS over at the piano:)* Birds on strike?

BRIAN. No, bird strikes. Birds striking airplanes. Or airplanes striking birds. Basically, bird slash airplane conflict.

COLLEEN. Hey, nice chickens.

(COLLEEN and AYŞAN start playing with the chickens, surround BRIAN and make the chickens do a sexy disco chicken dance.)

BRUCE MACKINNON. Most jet engines are designed to withstand striking an eight pound bird—the problem here, the problem with the Canada goose is this is a large bird. A large heavy bird, and you're encountering a flock. There's only so much you can do. And Canada Geese like airports, because it presents a vegetation mosaic that they find very attractive. But there are things we can do to discourage them. The most effective method is pyrotechnics—your bangers, exploders, flyers and screamers mostly—

(BRIAN snatches the chickens.)

DAMIAN. And this is Randall Watt, he's like an airplane windshield tester—

COLLEEN & AYŞAN. Chicken Cannons!

DAMIAN. Right, yeah. This guy Randall launches the chickens— *(Then, simultaneous with* GUY WHO RENTS AIRPLANES:*)* Would you stop that. I was— Okay, this is Randall Watt: A supersonic chicken hitting a stationary windshield simulates the effect of a fast-moving jet hitting a slow-moving bird. It gets a little messy. After all, our standard bird package is traveling at up to 600 miles per hour when it hits. There's not much left.

(BRIAN and JENNY have brought a translucent panel on stage. AYŞAN and COLLEEN crash chickens into the wall.)

GUY WHO RENTS AIRPLANES. They did try to get a bald eagle before. They wanted to film a bald eagle flying in the desert. But the US government wouldn't give them bald eagle eggs. So they found this guy, he had a seventeen-year-old bald eagle and they rented it. And then, something— happened with the plane and that bird went straight into the prop. I remember that because they had to pay out $42,000 in insurance.

(AIMÉE has entered. She hits CHARLIE with a pillow until she's distracted by COLLEEN making a screaming chicken impact on the clear panel. AIMÉE drops the pillow, gets the chickens and drop kicks them off stage. BRIAN and JENNY remove panel.)

AIMÉE. This woman I know. Her sister became a lesbian separatist, changed her name to Hawk Madrone and founded this like lesbian ranch.

(CHARLIE and DAMIAN hit AIMÉE. AYŞAN lobs chickens back to COLLEEN.)

AIMÉE. And she named the ranch, "Fly Away Home."

(Big Pillow fight. AYŞAN is suffocating herself. BRIAN and DAMIAN stab each other's hearts with chickens.)

COLLEEN. *(A la Honey from "Who's Afraid of Virginia Woolf?":)* Violence! Violence! Violence!

AIMÉE. She totally lives off the land, no electricity, phone, or men of any kind!

ONLINE QUESTION. I have a question for Anna Paquin. Do you have a favorite goose out of all the geese?

ANNA PAQUIN. To be honest I can't tell them apart.

(Pillow Fight resumes. All text except ANNA PAQUIN *text is simultaneous, overlapped at the "/". DAMIAN then AIMÉE do Ninja chickens.)*

COLLEEN. Hey, didn't Anna Paquin win an Oscar for *Fly Away Home?*

(Theme from The Piano.*)*

RANDALL WATT. We buy our chickens from the same source as Kentucky Fried Chicken, then the birds are gassed to death and popped / into a regular, homestyle freezer, where they are kept fifty or so at a time until a new windshield prototype has to be tested. We can shoot this launcher up to 1,200 feet per second, slightly supersonic.

BRUCE MACKINNON. But yeah, there comes a point when the problem gets so great—not only from an aesthetic perspective, but there comes a point/ when the numbers are so great that they become a threat, then we have to take more drastic action—but it's done humanely, and the food is turned over to the needy.

COLLEEN. Hey check this out—this is Graydon Carter in Vanity Fair. November 2001. "The city, for the first time in its long history, is destructible. A single flight of planes no bigger than a wedge of geese can quickly end this island fantasy, burn the towers, crumble the bridges, turn the underground passages into lethal chambers, cremate the millions."

(Theme from The Piano *stops.)*

AYŞAN. I'm sorry, "cremate the millions" did I miss something?

(Everyone freezes in mid-fight.)

ONLINE QUESTION. Are there any films of 1996 that you really enjoyed?

ANNA PAQUIN. I liked *Independence Day, Twister, Die Hard with a Vengeance.* It's a GREAT film.

ONLINE QUESTION. What's your all-time favorite film?

ANNA PAQUIN. *Die Hard with a Vengeance.*

(Now, pillow fight free-for-all, feathers start spilling out. Everyone does text simultaneously—some character from Long Lake. The Long Lakers end in a back-and-forth chant: "Go with the Geese." "Feet Don't Fail Me Now.")

POOR LITTLE FUCKING GOOSE

COLLEEN.
POOR LITTLE FUCKING GOOSE
ALWAYS STUCK ON THE ICE
LOOKING AT THE STARS
SITTING IN YOUR OWN SHIT

DO YOU HAVE TO FOLLOW THE FIRST FUCKING THING
YOU SEE?
YOU THINK A BEACHBALL IS YOUR MOTHER!
I MEAN, GET OFF THE FUCKING RUNWAY!
I MEAN, GET SOME GODDAMN DISCRETION.
CAN'T YOU TAKE ANY RESPONSIBILITY FOR YOUR
OWN FUCKING ACTIONS?
YOU FUCKING GOOSE!
YOU'VE MADE YOUR DUVET, SO LIE IN IT.
POOR LITTLE GOOSE
POOR FUCKING GOOSE
POOR LITTLE GOOSE
POOR FUCKING GOOSE
AAAAAAAAAAAAAAH!
WILL YOU JUST GET A FUCKING PLAN AND EXECUTE
IT.

*(Feathers settle down. Everyone's flopped about catching his or her breath. Song
begins slowly.* AIMÉE *translates.)*

ALLEZ AVEC LES OYES (PIEDS, NE ME RATEZ PAS)

THE MEN.
LES DEUX FILLES AVEC LES OYES
The two girls with the geese
ELLES RESTENT TOUJOURS,
They have to stay
C'EST LE LOI
It's the law

C'EST PAS TRISTE
It's not sad
QU'ELLES N'AVAIENT PAS CHOIX
That they have no choice
ELLES ONT LEUR TRAVAIL, ET JE CROIX
They have work to do, and I think

QUE SI JE POUVAIS FAIRE COMME JE VOUDRAIS
That if I could do what I wanted
JE SUIVIT LA VOIX QUI DIT:
I would follow the voice that says:

WOMEN / MEN.
VA AVEC LES OYES!
PIEDS, NE ME RATEZ PAS!
GO WITH THE GEESE!
FEET DON'T FAIL ME NOW!

VA AVEC LES OYES!
PIEDS, NE ME RATEZ PAS!
GO WITH THE GEESE!
FEET DON'T FAIL ME NOW!

(From this, a spotlight.)

BRIAN.

FLYING IN FORMATION DOWN THE RIVER
AND WE'RE GOING HOME.

ALL.

FLYING DOWN THE BYWAY,
IT'S THE HIGHWAY RIGHT TO WHERE WE'RE GOING
FLYING, GOING MY WAY,
BUT WE HAVEN'T MADE IT DOWN THERE YET
WATCH OUT FOR THAT COMMERCIAL JET!

FLYING DOWN THE HIGHWAY
AND I CAN'T SAY JUST WHERE WE WILL ROAM TO:
RIO, GUAM OR ROME
BERMUDA, ECUADOR OR NOME.

WE'RE TRYING TO GET BACK—
WE'RE TRYING TO GET BACK—
WE'RE TRYING TO GET BACK—

(Somehow The Civilians have arranged themselves in a precarious perfect V formation. BILL LISHMAN in the center, flying his ultralight. Sound of wind. Over the next monologue, the soundscape will fill in as he describes the various sights of New York.)

BILL LISHMAN. In the late Fall of 1999, there came a phone call. One of Jacques' film crews was in northern New York State with a flock of aircraft imprinted Canada geese and two special ultralight aircraft. Their plan was to bring the geese to New York City and film them against the backdrop of the Manhattan skyline, and they needed help.

(Sound: Morning Harbor.)

Monday, November 8th, 6:30AM. We're tied to the dock at the boat launch ramp at Liberty State Park in New Jersey. Off to the east in the pre-dawn gray, is the distinctive silhouette of the Lady of Liberty. Behind her, stand the equally distinctive towers of lower Manhattan. The plan is to lead a flock of French raised Canada geese around the Statue of Liberty and then across the Hudson and up the East River. Jacques' son Mathieu will fly with me and film Manhattan from a bird perspective with flying geese in the immediate foreground. The take off will be to the west. The geese, already ferried out on one of the boats, are released. Away we go.

(Sound: Take Off with Geese, followed by wind, flapping.)

I sit back, take a breath and look around. Our altitude is about shoulder high to the Lady. Breaking away, I climb to the northeast toward the Battery and pass over the Staten Island Ferry. The geese string off in close formation.

(Sound: a helicopter.)

A news helicopter stands off to the south. Every few minutes, a jet passes a few thousand feet above us. How privileged I feel to have bird freedom around this outcrop of architectural wonders.

(Sound: Closer and closer to the ground, earthly details.)

My memories of New York stretch back forty years. For a few minutes as we round the Battery and head up the East River. I remember the Spring of '63. I was visiting my sister who lived on the Lower East Side in a five story walk up. The apartment was just wide enough for the bathtub which doubled as the base of the dining room table. Then in '96, I flew to Manhattan for the premiere of *Fly Away Home*. I was chauffeured around "Hollywood Style" in a limousine. But I was able to break away for a few afternoon hours and have the gritty experience of accompanying a detective friend on his rounds.

(Sound: The city fades, leaving only the sounds of flight.)

And now, here I am, over the East River, almost at the Brooklyn Bridge. At this altitude with some of the floors of buildings at a higher altitude than our passage I am awestruck by the shards of glass layered upon each other. What keeps this collection of skyscrapers afloat I do not know. They stand arranged on a gridwork flowing yellow with taxis. The whole protrusion seems precariously top heavy—anchored in the current of reality only by the most minimal filigree of bridges. Compacted into this geometry of outsized crystalline forms are millions of beings. I grope for the reality of it all as we buzz its periphery like a mosquito in a world of surreal wedding cakes.

I have seen The Big Apple from the goose's eye.

(The TWO FRENCH GIRLS *appear. And another* TWO FRENCH GIRLS. *And another* TWO FRENCH GIRLS. *Someone gives* BILL LISHMAN *a yellow raincoat and beret. The sounds of taxis, car horns and other city noises fade up. Someone honks a horn. Goose honking. Car honking. So much fabulous honking. An infinity of honking. Yellow feathers fall from above. The stage is engulfed in yellow. Music: "Let the Sun Shine" from the French production of "Hair.")*

End of Play

GONE MISSING

written by Steven Cosson
from interviews by the company*

music and lyrics by Michael Friedman

"Interview with Dr. Palinurus" by Peter Morris

Gone Missing was created with Damian Baldet, Trey Lyford, Jennifer Morris, Brian Sgambati, Alison Weller, and Colleen Werthmann.

INTRODUCTION

A friend of mine's daughter once came to him in a panic and asked quite stricken, "Is this it?" She was five at the time and not necessarily so precise, so my friend asked her to clarify. "THIS," she said with a gesture meant to encompass a great deal—life, the present, reality, "All of this. Is this all there is?" And then she wept, inconsolably. Perhaps she was paraphrasing Peggy Lee's classic song of life as a series of disappointments, "Is that all there is?" Hearing this story struck a chord with me. I felt like I'd been asking myself the same question—consciously or unconsciously—since I was about...five.

I don't know if it hit me with the force of an epiphany, as it did with my friend's daughter, but somewhere around age five I realized that existence was not an infinitely expanding universe of wonder and possibility but was instead a concrete, structured daily experience of time, space and predictability (not to mention other people's horrible children). And around this time I have my first memories of genuine sadness, of feeling a sense of loss that was more than just ice cream falling on the sidewalk. This feeling told me that from now on, consciousness would be a constant struggle between the possibilities of the imaginary and the disappointment of actual living. And this grieving for lost possibilities is something that has replayed itself throughout my life in different forms. Sometimes it's attached to the breakup of a relationship. Sometimes it's the memory of a particular landscape or simply a lost object. Whatever the stimuli, the emotional experiences are largely the same, varying in intensity, but always familiar. It's a feeling of suffering but also a sensation of being awake again, back in the world, fully myself and connected to other people. It is a seeming contradiction. In this state of grief, aware of the temporary nature of all things, I somehow become fully alive again. To quote Dr. Palinurus from *Gone Missing*, "It is both a pleasure and a pain." I think that's part of why we treasure our losses despite the suffering, or more accurately, because of the suffering.

Each of us at some time has that special loss. We tell ourselves stories about it, and that at least gives an outline to the absence. Our stories provide some dotted line around the thing that's missing, the life that could have been, the love and tenderness that somehow turned into pain and anguish. In creating *Gone Missing*, I wanted to find a way into that space. I wanted to learn if the mechanics of loss and grief were significantly different in other people. Or do we instead all just have different names and objects tagged to the various holes in hearts, with the nature of the holes themselves being more or less the same? And is there a way that we as a society remember lost things that can tell us something about how we live now? Could these holes somehow make a map of absences that would describe the territory that encompasses both "all there is" and "all there might have been?"

These were some of the questions I had in mind when I began working with The Civilians to create *Gone Missing*. The rules were simple. Each company member conducted a series of interviews and listened to other people's stories about lost objects. No stories of lost people were allowed. Pets were ok. The other rule was that the thing had to have truly "gone missing," meaning that there was some question or mystery connected to the loss. A sock that disappeared in the laundry could count. An apartment that was destroyed by fire wouldn't.

Over a period of several months, the members of the company gathered stories first hand in coffee shops, at bus stops, in retirement centers. Some of the subjects were relatives, some are friends, but most were complete strangers. We also interviewed "finders," the people who have to deal with all the lost stuff. These interviews became the text for the show, and the actors of the company play the people they've interviewed. It's important to mention that as a part of this process we didn't take notes or record anything during these interviews. Whatever's spoken is committed to memory and written down later, and the words are inevitably altered somehow by the listener. So we don't identify anyone by name, as the character is not exactly them. It is an impression of them interpreted by a performer, as accurate as possible but—like all perceptions—subjective.

Responding to these interviews, composer Michael Friedman and playwright Peter Morris wrote original material resulting in the nine songs of *Gone Missing* and the radio interview between our host Teri and Dr. Alexander Palinurus, author of *Losers Weepers: A Cultural History of Nostalgia*. While the NPR-esque radio interview is a fiction, the facts are true and somehow all of these questions of loss and memory are indeed intimately connected to the life-cycle of the eel. I don't know why.

As a maker of theater, I am predisposed to being curious about other people. Perhaps it's merely schadenfreude, but I love listening to other people's problems, especially strangers. I'm fascinated by how people talk, how they move, how they tell a story. This is the basic premise behind the work of The Civilians. All of our projects begin with that first step of going outside of oneself and seriously considering the existence of another human being. It's almost always a surprising experience. When you sit down and let someone reveal themselves to you, you realize that people are never exactly what they seem. Your perceptions open up and in this moment the "possibilities of the imaginary" side of existence scores a point against the "disappointment of actual living." That's a big part of why I create our shows, to have this opportunity to get a glimpse into another person's life and remind myself that what I think I know is much, much narrower than the real phenomena of existence in all its sad, sweet, cruel and strange beauty. And hopefully, by glimpsing into other people's losses and looking at what's "gone missing," we might think that we in fact do not bear our various holes and hurts alone. And that perhaps this empty space we carry inside is not something that will ever be completely filled or satisfied, but it is in fact part of what it means to be alive in the world and may be a quite necessary ingredient of living compassionately. And that perhaps this is indeed "all there is."

—Steven Cosson

ACKNOWLEDGMENTS

Gone Missing received its World Premiere by The Civilians at The Belt, New York City, October 9, 2003, and was premiered in London by The Civilians at The Gate Theatre, February 5, 2004. It was directed by Steven Cosson with the following cast:

Damian Baldet
Maria Dizzia
Michael Esper
Trey Lyford
Jennifer R. Morris
Alison Weller

Musicians:

Andy Boroson, Piano
Ernie Adzentoivich, Bass
Richard Huntley, Drums

And the following production staff:

Stage Manager...Terence Dale
Assistant Director ....Isaac Butler
Assistant Director ....Jonathan Spector
Graphic Design...Abby Weintraub
Associate Producer .... Hillary Cutter
Managing Director .... Leslie Graham
Set Design.. Takeshi Kata
Lighting Design .... Thomas Dunn
Sound Design..Ken Travis
Choreographer...Jim Augustine
Costume Design ....Sarah Beers

The play subsequently received its Off-Broadway Premiere, produced by Scott Morfee and Tom Wirtshafter at the Barrow Street Theatre, in association with The Civilians, June 24, 2007. It was directed by Steven Cosson with the following cast:

Emily Ackerman
Damian Baldet
Jennifer R. Morris
Stephen Plunkett
Robbie Collier Sublett
Colleen Werthmann

Musicians:

Andy Boroson, Piano
David Purcell, Drums
Steve Gilewski, Bass
Music Direction: Andy Boroson

And the following production staff:

General Management ....2 Step Productions
Production Manager ....Jason Reuter
Production Stage Manager.............................Robert Signom III
Press Representative ....O & M Co.

For The Civilians:
Steven Cosson, Artistic Director
Kyle Gorden, Producing Director

Additional interviews conducted by: Quincy Tyler Bernstine, Matthew Francis, Winter Miller and Charlie Schroeder.

Emily Ackerman, Stephen Plunkett, Colleen Werthmann, Jennifer R. Morris,
Robbie Collier Sublett, and Damian Baldet
in *Gone Missing*

Barrow Street Theatre, New York City, 2007
Photo by Sheldon Noland

GONE MISSING

The company enters. Sounds of underwater bubbles.

OLD MAN. You lose something in New York, it don't come back.

POSTER.
Lost Dog
Please call—we miss her!
NAME IS "KIRBY"
has one eye plus red harness.

POSTER.
Lost Back-Pack
Valuable Contents:
2 Beanie Babies
and a toy dolphin
mostly needed back
If found please call.

POSTER.
Found Bird
If you think it's yours please call
This is not a picture of the actual bird
But one that looks very much like it.

MUM. There was the teeth. Well my mother, she had three gold teeth and they disappeared. She would leave them in a little dish, you know, she'd take them out and they disappeared.

OLD MAN. A ring, your wallet, my glasses—who'd want my glasses? She never lost nothin. She was a schoolteacher.

HIS WIFE. I never lost nothin. I had laser surgery.

OLD MAN. Yeah, they say it's a snap, it don't hurt, but it ain't true—

HIS WIFE. It ain't true. That's why I wear these glasses. I had laser surgery.

MUM. Well, I figured Stubby took them. To sell them. For the gold, you know. Now that I think about it…Stubby…Stubby L'Engle, not Stubby *Wood*. Stubby *Wood* is the guy Fred shot in the forehead with a bee bee gun. But I'm pretty sure Stubby *L'Engle* had a hand in the teeth.

COP. My first DOA—this guy had disappeared down this big elevator shaft. It was filled up with three, four feet of water. And the smell! It was something awful. His body had spread out all over the place, and it was my job to find all the parts and get them into the body bag, and I started to get *(Eyes bug out indicating "sick")* and the guys are yelling down to me, "Hey rookie, how you doing?" and they're laughing, "your first DOA!" They're laughing. You gotta laugh.

43

POSTER.
Lost
Picture of my father sitting in a field of daffodils
Great sentimental value
If found please call.

PEARL RING WOMAN. Could I talk about losing a husband? Because I would certainly have a lot to say on that subject.

OLD WOMAN. No? You don't want to hear about people? Well, sorry honey, after you've lost as many people as I have you don't care about material things. They simply don't matter at all.

LOONY BIN.
"Things I have lost"
(in the loony bin 1994)
I've lost my toothbrush
my sweater
all my socks
my sense of humor
the plot
any sense of self-worth
the will to live

GONE MISSING

WHEN I WAS 8 I LOST MY INNOCENCE
PLAYING DOCTOR, IT WAS TENSE, BUT I FOUND OUT
    THAT EXPERIENCE IS GREAT
WHEN I WAS 8.
WHEN I WAS 17 I LOST MY VIRGINITY
YOU KNOW IT REALLY WOULDN'T BOTHER ME IF
    AFTERWARDS I HADN'T BEEN SO MEAN
WHEN I WAS 17.

GONE, GONE MISSING
GONE, GONE MISSING

WHEN I WAS 29 I LOST MY WAY
MY MOTHER THOUGHT THAT I WAS GAY, BUT I THINK
    I WAS JUST WAITING FOR A SIGN
WHEN I WAS 29.
WHEN I WAS 33, I LOST MY COOL
I WAS TEN YEARS OUT OF SCHOOL, AND AS OLD AS
    JESUS CHRIST WOULD EVER BE
WHEN I WAS 33.

GONE, GONE MISSING
GONE, GONE MISSING

WHEN I WAS 42 I LOST MY MIND
MY FRIENDS ALL TRIED TO BE KIND, BUT I SAW THAT
    BEING CRAZY WOULDN'T DO
WHEN I WAS 42.
WHEN I WAS 61 I LOST THE WAR
I CAN'T RECALL WHAT IT WAS FOR BUT I REMEMBER I
    HAD NEVER HAD SUCH FUN
WHEN I WAS 61.

GONE, GONE MISSING
GONE, GONE MISSING
GONE, GONE MISSING
GONE, GONE MISSING

*(*FRENCH LESBIAN *alone on stage.)*

FRENCH LESBIAN. Well, umm, it is kind of hazy, I keep blocking it out, but I think it was between 1993 and 1995, or it was 1993 or 1995, and I had this scarf that I had borrowed from my sister and never returned it. I loved this scarf it was an Agnes B. scarf. I don't even think she knew I borrowed it. But one night I took my girlfriend to this bar, Henrietta Hudson. I think it is on Hudson. And we had put all of our bags and things on this pool table. And then this big crowd came in after us and they took over the pool table and one of them picked up my scarf, I think it was by mistake but uhhheeck, this softball dyke took my scarf. It really pisses me off that this really beautiful scarf, it was an Agnes B. scarf, fell into such uncouth hands. It like *gnaws* at me even today. You know where I picture it? Balled up with a cat on it. Or worse. In an SUV. In an SUV balled up with a cat on it. That's where it is. I hate softball. I mean I hated softball before but I hate it even more now.

    (Beep. Beep. Beep. Beep. Beeeeeeeep. LAURA *enters. She is leaving a message on an answering machine.)*

LAURA. It's Laura. Hi, um, I called Tom about this embarrassing issue and I'm now calling you. I think I left one of my pumps at PS 122 last night, but um, I'm back in Los Angeles and can't go to the theater myself. And they're like my good shoes and it's embarrassing.

    *(*TOM *enters.)*

TOM. So, do you know Laura? So she was meeting with some big TV people. And she had on this pair of black Gucci pumps and a nice skirt and everything, and after her meeting we were all going out. And somewhere along that night she lost her shoe. One of her Gucci shoes, because she had changed at PS 122 because she felt overdressed. She thinks that she left the shoe in the bathroom. I think she actually lost the shoe later that night, because I think they went out drinking—

    (Beep.)

LAURA. Hi, it's Laura, um I was really hoping that you could have secured the shoe before you left town but apparently you have not, so I've been working with Tom and Tom has gone back to PS 122 numerous times. And I'm leaving numerous messages for the house manager, the artistic director, the director of development to see if they have gotten their act together enough to find the shoe. Um, I am sending a packet of flyers to you, to Tom, to Big Daddy, and to Elizabeth, and I'm sending maps of where I'd like you guys to post the flyers because I'm really hoping if someone sees some—you know—one legged person wearing it–who wears a size six—that uh, it will become clear whose shoe that is and where they need to send it to in Los Angeles immediately. Um, I am working on the flyer, and I've also started an email address: ilostmyshoe@earthlink.net. So, um, I don't know if you have gone back to PS 122 or not—no one there returns my calls and it's really depressing—but I'm really hoping the flyers will stir up some leads!

TOM. Laura sent me jpegs of the shoe and she wanted me to post them around PS 122. "Lost black Gucci pump." But it was just a basic black pump.

(LAURA and TOM exit. A young man who works at a Korean deli enters.)

KOREAN DELI YOUNG MAN. My kitten? No, someone took it. Stole it. It had Korean name. Nabi, it means butterfly. I am very mad at the person who took Nabi. She was my best friend and I was always so happy to see her. I don't think I can get another cat now. I just miss her running around here.

(A woman from the deli enters, young man exits.)

KOREAN DELI WOMAN. What? Oh, the cat. No, no. Cat gone away. I gave it to friend. In deli, it ran around, made me very angry. Always in around food, no good. Now it is in Queens with my friend. It had Korean name, Nabi. It means butterfly so it fly away.

THE ONLY THING MISSING

> I'LL ADMIT I HAVE A PROBLEM HOLDING ONTO
>   THINGS
> A SOCK, A BOOK, A CLOCK, A LOOK, A CHANCE.
> AND THE MOMENT THAT A FELLA
> LENDS ME HIS UMBRELLA
> IT'S JUST ANOTHER DOOMED ROMANCE.
> I'VE LEARNED TO NEVER WORRY ABOUT LOSING
>   THINGS.
> A CAR, A PIN, A STAR, SOME GIN, A BET.
> BUT THEN YOU SAID THAT WE WERE THROUGH
> AND SUDDENLY I KNEW
> THERE WAS ONE LOSS I'D REGRET.
> I'VE LOST DIAMONDS AND PEARLS
> LOVE LETTERS FROM EARLS

AND MORE SUITORS THAN GIRLS USUALLY DO
BUT FROM THIS GREAT LIST
I WILL HAVE TO INSIST
THAT THE ONLY THING MISSING IS YOU
I HAD BARBIES AND THEN
MY MOM CALLED AND MENTIONED
THEY'RE ALL AS THE FRENCH SAY PERDU
EVEN BARBIE HAD KEN
BUT I'M LEFT WITH RIEN
'CAUSE THE ONLY THING MISSING IS YOU.
AND SILLY AS IT SEEMS
I LOST ALL MY DREAMS
WHEN WE SAID ADIEU
AND I THINK YOU WILL FIND
THAT I LOSE MY MIND
WHEN I THINK OF YOU
AND NO ONE HAS SOLVED
THE CASE THAT INVOLVED THE REVOLVER
IN MY GAME OF CLUE
WELL I'VE STILL GOT THE KNIFE
BUT WHAT GOOD IS MY LIFE
THOUGH WITH ALL THAT I'VE LOST
NO I DON'T MIND THE COST
THINK WHAT MY NEPHEW CHRIS
JUST LOST AT HIS BRIS…
AND YOU'LL HAVE TO ADMIT THAT IT'S TRUE
THAT THE ONLY THING MISSING
DO YOU MISS THE KISSING?
THE ONLY THING MISSING IS YOU.

COP. We get a lot of DOAs. And sometimes they're badly decomposed. Sometimes they're partially mummified, if it's summer, with the heat. I don't know why this is, but a lot of times old women—and I'm not saying anything—but we'll find old women and they'll be naked! I don't know why this is. It's just, you know, it's summertime and it's warm. I mean, I do it and I'm sure you do too, you walk around with no clothes on. But that's, you know, that's not the way they want to be found.

(NPR-style theme music. TERI and DOCTOR PALINURUS enter. This is a radio interview.)

TERI. Welcome back. For those of you just joining us, we're talking to Dr. Alexander Palinurus, author of "Losers Weepers: A Cultural History of Nostalgia." Doctor, before the break, you mentioned Atlantis.

PALINURUS. That's right, Teri.

TERI. Which is, what, a continent?

PALINURUS. Well, Teri, if it was a *continent*…how'd we lose it?

TERI. That's a pretty big thing to lose.

PALINURUS. Right. It's not, like, a toothbrush. Or a little box of cookies.

TERI. Now is this a—a myth, Doctor?

PALINURUS. I'd prefer to call it a literary fiction. Because we have an original source for the story, in the work of Plato.

TERI. The philosopher.

PALINURUS. Yes. Plato, in his dialogues, told the story of a fantastic island. He says it was bigger than all of Asia Minor, and it lay beyond the Pillars of Hercules…what we would call today the Straits of Gibraltar. Which would place it in—

TERI. The Atlantic Ocean.

PALINURUS. Right. The so-called Atlantic.

TERI. And we call it the Atlantic because—

PALINURUS. Yes. But what I'm fascinated by, Teri, and I crave your indulgence here, but: Plato uses Atlantis for a philosophical argument. Because what do we know about Plato's philosophy? That the things in this world are inferior, they're shadowy imperfect versions of some kind of ideal—

TERI. Platonic Ideal—

PALINURUS. Right. And so there is some kind of ideal, I dunno, justice-with-a-capital-J. But everything on earth that we call justice is kind of an imperfect copy of that.

TERI. So how does this take us to a lost continent?

PALINURUS. Well, that's what I'm saying, Teri. Atlantis didn't get lost. What we're talking about is a specific locus for our nostalgia, some lost paradise. The Garden of Eden. In the classical world, it's the Golden Age, or Atlantis. Mythic places like this. Xanadu. Shangri-La.

TERI. Brigadoon.

PALINURUS. One of the funny things about Atlantis, though, is many people think it was situated in the Sargasso Sea.

(Transition into "La Bodega" begins, interrupted by KHAN.*)*

KHAN. Well, I lost my job. I lost all my money. I had nothing left. But you don't want that. Right. Only things. Like I lost a something…I'll think about it.

("La Bodega" sets up. The singer announces the song.)

BODEGA SINGER. "La Bodega"

LA BODEGA

SE ME PERDIÓ LA BILLETERA
QUIZÁS LA DEJÉ EN LA BODEGA
NO ME HICIERA FALTA
SINO QUE LLEVABA ADENTRO
LA ÚNICA FOTO
QUE YO TENÍA DE TI
LE PREGUNTÉ AL SEÑOR DE LA BODEGA
PERO ÉL SE ENCOGIÓ DE HOMBROS
ME VENDIÓ UNOS CIGARRILLOS
Y UN CARTÓN DE LECHE

¿TE RECUERDAS DE LA NOCHE EN ESE HOTEL?
¿CUANDO TÚ NO PUDISTE ENCONTRAR TU BOLSA?
Y ESTABA ESA SEÑORA EXTRAÑA
LA QUE USABA PELUCA
Y ELLA NOS DIÓ COMIDA
SIN COBRARNOS NADA

AHORA TE PIENSO EN LA BODEGA
CADA VEZ QUE COMPRO CERVEZA
PERO SIN TENER ESA FOTO
OLVIDO COMO TE PARECES
Y QUIZÁS UNA PERSONA CUALQUIERA
QUIÉN VA A ESA BODEGA
AHORA TIENE TU FOTO
Y CON ELLA, MI BILLETERA
Y CON ELLA, MIS SUEÑOS DE TI

(Three women enter.)

PEARL RING. Could I talk about losing a husband, I would certainly have a lot to say on that subject. No, but I do have a story about losing something—

SILVER RING. It was a silver ring with a gold buckle and I had it for years. It was a manly ring. It was manly. But wait. Here's the thing. This is it—

SAPPHIRE RING. My uncle saved his entire life, you know, lived through the depression, saved old rubber bands. Well, I opened up my wedding gift from him—there was a big saffron…s'phire—jewel, right in the middle. It was like this *(Gesture meaning half an inch)* surrounded on both sides by two small diamonds. I was like—whoa!

SILVER RING. Yes. It was like a talisman. I wore it for eight or nine years. It was a small thing but it was big because I loved it.

PEARL RING. When I was a little girl about eight years old or so—this was in the forties—I got a very special present from my mother and father or from Santa. That's who I thought it was at the time. Santa. What did I know I was a kid. This was just after the Depression so this was a very special ring. I wore it everyday, never took it off.

SAPPHIRE RING. I wore it all the time for the last forty years, never took it off, but I lost one of the small diamonds—it fell out—and I wanted to get it fixed, so I put it in my purse to get it fixed—

> *(Everyone joins in on the chorus.)*
> ¿TE RECUERDAS DE LA NOCHE EN ESE HOTEL?
> ¿CUANDO TU NO PUDISTE ENCONTRAR TU BOLSA?
> Y ESTABA ESA SEÑORA EXTRAÑA
> LA QUE USABA PELUCA
> Y ELLA NOS DIO COMIDA
> SIN COBRARNOS NADA
>
> SE ME PERDIÓ LA BILLETERA EN LA BODEGA.
> *(Bodega singers exit, back to the three women.)*

SAPPHIRE RING. And about six months later I remembered I'd put the ring in that purse, but the purse just wasn't there anymore. Maybe I gave it to the Salvation Army or the women's shelter.

SILVER RING. It went down the drain when I was in the shower, but I didn't realize it. I remember thinking, "My ring is coming off." I could feel it slipping, but you know, it was the shower and I think it was DENIAL. Because I'm in the shower and everything is FLOWING and it was, well, because I'd had it for eight or nine years so how could it fall of now?

PEARL RING. Years later, I was out with my future husband. He had taken me to a party. Well, it couldda been a wedding, it couldda been a party, it couldda been a lot of things. The point is—I had to go to the bathroom. I asked him to hold my ring so that when I washed my hands it didn't fall into the drain. I gave it to him and said, "Hon hold this." I remember he put it in the breast pocket of his white shirt. After the party we went out to the park—well, it couldda been a park, couldda been a car, couldda been a lot of things—the point is, we had a make out session. So I certainly wasn't thinking about the ring then, that much I can assure you.

SILVER RING. You know what they say about married people that when they first get married the engagement ring feels very present, like a reminder of the commitment and a ring leaves an indentation. So, the indentation was there but no ring and I just hadn't realized it.

SAPPHIRE RING. This was soon after my uncle died in 2000—he was ninety-eight and very frugal—well, I got a nice inheritance from him and put it into the stock market in 2000 and it just went *(Gesture meaning down the drain).*

PEARL RING. Next day I realized he had the ring. Back then you just didn't call people at the office like you do now. I had to wait until after five. Well, he had already taken the shirt to the cleaners. The cleaners didn't have it.

SILVER RING. I looked down and I saw it was gone and I was like, "Oh, it must have come off in the shower." And I never saw anything like it again.

SAPPHIRE RING. My uncle, he probably knows somehow that I've let him down, that all his money is gone and the ring, it's just so irresponsible on my behalf. It's so sad, the irony of this frugal man saving everything and I turn around and lose it all: the ring, ninety percent of his money. I feel like I've erased him, like every last bit of him has vanished.

(Bodega singers return, but this time the text is spoken, intimate.)

BODEGA SINGER. "The Bodega"

> MY WALLET LOST ITSELF FROM ME
> PERHAPS I LEFT IT AT THE STORE
> I WOULDN'T HAVE MISSED IT
> EXCEPT THAT IT CARRIED WITHIN
> THE ONLY PHOTO
> I HAD OF YOU
>
> I ASKED THE MAN AT THE STORE
> BUT HE SHRUGGED HIS SHOULDERS
> HE SOLD ME SOME CIGARETTES
> AND A CARTON OF MILK
>
> DO YOU REMEMBER THE NIGHT IN THAT HOTEL?
> WHEN YOU COULDN'T FIND YOUR PURSE?
> AND THERE WAS THAT STRANGE WOMAN
> THE ONE WHO WORE A WIG
> AND SHE GAVE US DINNER
> WITHOUT CHARGING US ANYTHING?
>
> NOW I THINK OF YOU
> EACH TIME I BUY BEER
> BUT WITHOUT HAVING THAT PHOTO
> I FORGET WHAT YOU LOOK LIKE
> AND PERHAPS A PERSON WHO COULD BE ANYBODY
> WHO GOES TO THAT STORE
> NOW HAS YOUR PHOTO
> AND WITH IT, MY WALLET
> AND WITH IT, MY DREAMS OF YOU

PEARL RING. That ring really meant so much to me. I never told my parents I lost it. I just couldn't. I felt so awful. Knowing what it meant for them to buy it for me. I was so ashamed. Years later, my husband bought me another pearl ring. But it wasn't as nice. First of all, it was white gold and it was set with two diamonds. Not as beautiful as that simple pearl ring. That was so many years ago now, but I still feel emotional about it.

(Transition, KHAN *interrupts.)*

KHAN. Well I lost my job. Oh no it was terrible. Everything was gone. I had nothing left. But you don't want that. Only things. Like "I lost something." I will think about it.

(Transition completes.)

HIDE AND SEEK

SEEMS TO ME I ALWAYS USED TO PLAY
HIDE AND SEEK
AND I WOULD WAIT SO PATIENTLY
FOR SOMEONE TO COME AND LOOK FOR ME.
AND I CAN'T REMEMBER JUST HOW LONG I'D SIT
    THERE,
I'VE FORGOTTEN SEEMS I CAN'T HOLD ON TO ANY-
    THING AT ALL
I LOST THE FOURTH GRADE JOURNAL
AND THE SWEATSHIRT THAT WAS RUINED
WHEN I HID INSIDE THE CLOSET
AND KNOCKED MY MOTHER'S PERFUME FROM THE
    SHELF
AND SMELLED FOR WEEKS LIKE I WAS GOING SOME-
    WHERE.
SEEMS TO ME I'M ALWAYS SPILLING SOMETHING,
LOSING SOMETHING, SEEKING SOMETHING, HIDING
    SOMEWHERE
IN MY MOTHER'S PRETTY BLOUSES WAITING 'TIL THEY
    COME AND FIND ME.
BUT THEY'RE NOT COMING.

THEY'RE NOT COMING.
SO I'M WAITING IN THE DARK,
FEELING JUST LIKE ALICE ADAMS
WHEN SHE TRIES TO THROW A PARTY
BUT NOBODY COMES.
SEEMS TO ME I ALWAYS USED TO PLAY
HIDE AND SEEK
AND I AM SEEKING SOMETHING OTHER
THAN WHATEVER THERE IS NOW
IF I COULD FIND SOME SORT OF MEMORY
TO GIVE ME SOME CONNECTION
AND I WONDER, WHY IS NO ONE SEEKING ME?

(KHAN *is back.*)

KHAN. Well, I didn't lose anything. But my friends found a dinette set. Table and chairs. Nice. Wood. We were four guys living in the same apartment and we would eat sitting on the couch or the endtable, you know. So with the table, we would all meet once a week to eat together at the table. No, it didn't make us closer. It helped us eat better. We were already good friends.

(COP *enters.*)

COP. A lot of times we'll be called in because the neighbors smell garbage or gas and then we'll find a body. A lot of times pets will, you know, if a body is left decomposing. Not cats but dogs. And mice and rats—a lot of times when we find a DOA we'll throw a book at it and you'll see the mice and rats run out. Eels too. If we have a DOA that's a floater, a lot of times you'll have eels that crawl into the orifices, then you fish the body out and the eels slither out of the body.

(*Theme music.* TERI *and* DR. PALINURUS *enter.*)

TERI. Now where is the Sargasso Sea, exactly?

PALINURUS. In the Atlantic Ocean. It's not a sea, per se. It's a region, of the Atlantic. And would it spook you if I said that it overlaps with the so-called Bermuda Triangle?

TERI. Another place where things go missing.

PALINURUS. Precisely. And that's the funny thing about the ocean. When you throw something in, you don't generally get it back. And before we had stories about the Bermuda Triangle, we had stories about the Sargasso Sea. But the Sargasso Sea is not a place where things get lost. It's a place where things get found.

TERI. Flotsam and jetsam.

PALINURUS. *Everything.* What gets lost in the ocean, well, it turns up there. This was the folk-belief. You read the Captain Nemo, the—

TERI. Jules Verne.

PALINURUS. *Twenty Thousand Leagues Under the Sea,* yes, and when the submarine, the Nautilus, takes its tour of Atlantis, first he describes the Sargasso Sea, and how it is full of all this—lost stuff. Simply because it is full of seaweed. A type of seaweed that the Portuguese sailors called "sargazo." And this seaweed does collect driftwood, cork, things like that. It also, this is one of the big mysteries of the Sargasso Sea…it collects eels.

TERI. Eels.

PALINURUS. Yes. Those slippery fellows. Well known to the Japanese gourmet as unagi.

TERI. Yum.

PALINURUS. My sentiments exactly. Now this is one of those scientific facts that sounds stranger than the myth or the fiction. But every eel in

Europe has to swim there to mate. And the baby eels are born. Then they—and this is still a mystery, we don't know *how*—but then the eel larvae find their way back to Europe. From the Sargasso Sea.

TERI. Are those eels nostalgic?

PALINURUS. Who can say? But if everything we lose ends up in the Sargasso Sea, maybe the eels are going to…you know, like rummaging around at the Salvation Army.

(Beep. LAURA is back, leaving another message on an answering machine.)

LAURA. Are you there? It's Laura. Ok. um, you know I went to Brazil, right, and, uh, I flew to Rio and I'm taking a taxicab from the airport to go to my hotel and what do I find on the floor of the taxicab? Are you sitting down? What do I find on the floor of the taxicab? I'm not fucking kidding you I find my shoe. Ok. I lost the left shoe. Left Gucci pump. And I found a left Gucci pump. And I'm shaking because I feel like I'm in a fucking time machine black hole sci-fi movie like *Logan's Run* because there's no way that this could fucking happen at all. And then I go through my bag and notice that all of this stuff in my bag is gone. And then it was like a *Lion Witch and the Wardrobe* kind of thing, and then I realize that the stuff that had disappeared had gone into this like crevice of my bag it's got this like weird back pocket, and the shoe was in that pocket and then like, the bag opens, the shoe fell out, the other stuff fell in and I'm thinking I'm in a tesseract. *Wrinkle in Time*. Remember that book. Madeline L'Engle. So…

(BEEP. End of messages. TOM enters.)

TOM. Yeah. I heard that Laura found her shoe. She'd been carrying it around with her the whole time. I think she thinks that's funny. I don't think that's funny.

(LAURA and TOM exit. SECURITY GUARD, DANCER, MOMMY, and DAD enter. MOMMY has a Midwestern accent. SECURITY GUARD has a Caribbean accent.)

SECURITY GUARD. Well, I loss my palm pilot.

DANCER. I left my cell phone in the cab when I got out.

MOMMY. So, this is the story of the loss of Sniffle.

DAD. Kyle, come get this dog, it's biting my leg, and it just smelly-farted, it might have to go outside.

MOMMY. We were, Dad and I, and you three girls, on a car trip in Iowa. It was during Easter vacation and we went to see the Amana colonies in Iowa, with all of the Amish people living there. Right, darling, where the Amana refrigerators come from. Exactly. You were in, maybe, fourth grade, and the twins were in first grade. And there was that horrible snowstorm, and we were stuck in Grinnell, Iowa, on the way down? And we stayed in a motel in Grinnell, and when we could finally leave, the next day, the drifts were eight feet high, and we were very excited to get out of *(Laughs)* godawful Grinnell!

And we were in the car for about a half an hour, and Ingrid suddenly asked, very worried, "Where's Sniffle?"

DAD. Yeah, well, this dog here is a Boykin Spaniel, but our first dog, Boone, was a hunting dog, a chocolate lab. He was amazing at escaping. I had to build a brick bottom pen for him so that he wouldn't dig his way out and I put an electric fence around the bottom perimeter but that dog would endure any amount of pain to escape. He had bloody gums and abscesses from biting through the wire and once I saw him reach over the fence and pull the cyclone with his teeth and there was a blue arch going from the generator to his face for a long period of time and he pulled on that until the wire was busted and then he pulled it upwards so that he would be able to climb under. And then he dug a hole and tried to squeeze out sustaining a shock for at least thirty more seconds while he climbed under the wire. Well, anyway, we had a call from my sister in South Carolina that Boone had escaped and they hadn't seen him for a week.

DANCER. So later I was soooo exhausted, so I just totally spaced on the phone you know? I called the number later, when I got home and nothing and I called and called and called and I just kept getting voice mail voice mail you know? Then finally the phone picks up and I hear these girls talking in the background, you know. This one girl is like "Girl, you and that stupid phone you found" or something, and I could hear rustling and stuff because the phone was in her pocket or something and so I started screaming you know I was like "Heeeeeey!!! HeeeeeeeeeeeeY! Hellooooooooooooo!" You know and I was making all this high pitched noise you know, so she would hear me so I'm like "Ooooooooooooooooooooo! Heeeeeeeeeyyyyyyyyyyy!!! This is my phone HEEEEEEEEEEEY!" And I am so fucking exhausted dude. I'm just so tired. *(Weakly:)* "Heeeeeeeeyyyy this is my phone." And then I hear it just like rustled and shut off. And I'm like FAAACK!

MOMMY. Now, SNIFFLE was this tiny sock doll. A little doll made from a nylon anklet, and stuffed with some kind of pillow filling, With little ball-shaped arms and legs, and little embroidered eyes and a mouth. You girls each had one, yours was red, and Allison's was yellow, and Ingrid's was light blue. And neither you nor Allison were particularly attached to yours, but Ingrid LOVED hers, and she named it Sniffle. And we're in the car, and Sniffle has disappeared. And poor Ingrid is hysterical. And Dad guessed that maybe Sniffle had been left behind in the hotel room, and we drove back and talked to the lady at the front desk

DAD. I guess another three weeks passed and I just got to the place in my heart where I knew he must be dead and so I stopped praying and asking God to bring him back. And I told the boys and we drove the twelve hour drive back to Louisiana.

DANCER. I had this image of these two girls fucking hanging out in Central Park, walking through the park in school uniforms with my phone in their backpack. No, they're not sexy, just, you know, regular school uniforms. And I mean this image is soo clear to me. And I'm like FAAACK! And I call back and they don't answer!

MOMMY. And you girls were all huddling around Dad and me, and then the lady said that everything in the rooms that got left behind got thrown away and was probably in the dumpster outside in the back, and Ingrid began SOBBING. And then you and Allison started to cry because you felt so sad for Ingrid. And the poor lady felt so bad. And I was trying to quiet you all down, which didn't work at all, of course, because you were all devastated by the loss of Sniffle. And Dad was quiet for a few seconds, and then he asked the lady if he could take a look in the dumpster. So I took you girls to the car, and Dad got on his ski pants and his big Sorrel boots and he climbed in there. And you girls became very quiet all of a sudden. The dumpster was absolutely enormous, and every now and then you could just see the top of Dad's hat as he rummaged around in there. He must have been in there for about twenty minutes. It was freezing cold outside, and we kept wiping off the windows because they kept fogging up from our breathing.

DAD. But right when I got home, I got a call from my sister saying that someone had found Boone.

DANCER. So a couple of days later or something I try again and this woman answers and I'm like "HELLO HELLO this is my phone and I lost it in a cab please don't hang up!"

MOMMY. And then, Dad's arm shot up above the top of the dumpster— and there was Sniffle, in the palm of his hand. And Ingrid CRIED.

DAD. I got back in the truck and drove another twelve hours right back to South Carolina. And when I saw him, you could just see every bone in his body and he had lost all his hair, just like a sack of bones and he didn't want to eat. But the amazing thing is that Jake, my sister's ten year old son, when we had all given up our prayers, he didn't stop praying and he kept believing that Boone would come back and he didn't give up until he showed up.

DANCER. And she was like, "Yeah, I just got out of this rehearsal. I'm a dancer. Do you know where Capezios is?" you know and I was like "I'm a dancer too!" So she left it for me at Capezios.

MOMMY. It turned out that Sniffle had been in a pile of some awful kitchen garbage, or something, and he was covered with all these dark smudges. Dad didn't want Ingrid to have Sniffle until he could wash him off, but Ingrid was desperate to hold Sniffle. And she rocked back and forth, with such love.

DAD. We brought Boone back to Louisiana and got him eating again, and he lived a good life for another—no what was it—I guess it was really close to three more years. We didn't have a funeral, I'm not real big on that, cuz I don't think animals have souls. The Bible doesn't mention that so I don't think that there will be dogs in heaven. The Bible does talk about all the magnificent creatures that are in heaven, seraphim and angels, but I just think of dogs as good friends that I have for a while and then they live on in my memory.

DANCER. Oh and the worst part of this whole story is that two hours after I got it from Capezios, I was fucking running up the stairs and I tripped and fucking cracked the whole phone. It was in my pocket and I—my hip landed on it and broke it. I had that huge fucking bruise.

MOMMY. And your father was all covered in coffee grounds *(Laughs gently.)* and all sorts of horrendous stuff. And it was a very beautiful experience, when I think back on it now; of course back then, it was probably smelly and exhausting and stressful. *(Choked up:)* But I can still remember Ingrid's face, all red and swollen from tears, as she hugged Sniffle. *(She recovers.)* Would you like another glass of wine darling?

SECURITY GUARD. I loss my palm pilot runnin from Worl Trade. I work at Battry Park Autority an Worl Trade at night. When na firs plane hit, my boss ee say, go secure da baseball fiel for da secret service comin. I was checkin IDs and, you know, secure da area for the secret service comin wit a helicopter, goin land in da fiel. So, I rode my bike to da baseball field. The palm pilot, it must have fall out of my pocket.

When the first building fall, I see da cloud comin', and we can see below it, but not above level. So, we all fall on da ground, and when we got up we was all covered like ghost. An I foun a hose and spray on my face, on my head, I was in charge of the fiel, so I know where everyting was.

When second one fall we all start runnin into Stuyvesant High School.

Tracy fin it. Da police fine my Palm Pilot and Tracy see it was mine an she say she know me and she call. So...I got it back.

(They exit. SOCIAL WORKER *enters. The other women set up for the song during her speech.)*

SOCIAL WORKER. In my case, I lost all my possessions and then I lost my mind. I gave everything to a maharaja. He was sixteen. In New York, not in India. We would meditate; the goal was to become egoless. You know, so by giving away all of your earthly goods you become egoless. There was this place, a store sort of, where you'd bring all of your stuff. And God only knows what they did with it then. And they gave me, you know, like a skirt to wear. But there are still some things that I'm sad I gave away. One was this little wooden tugboat that my mother gave to me and, like, her mother gave it to her, and hers to her, and like I'm sure it had been in the family for generations. But that was a crazy time.

I GAVE IT AWAY

BEEN THINKING ABOUT THE WAY YOU LEFT
AND ABOUT THE THINGS YOU USED TO SAY
SAID YOU HAD GIVEN ME YOUR HEART
SAID WE WOULD NEVER BE APART

NOW YOU CALL AND ASK TO COME ON BY
SAY YOU LEFT THINGS BEHIND AND
I COULD
GIVE YOU ALL YOUR THINGS BUT
WHY SHOULD
I WHEN YOU,
YOU MADE ME CRY?
WOULD YOU GIVE MY HEART BACK TO ME?
SO IF YOU'RE MISSING THE CLOTHES YOU LEFT BY THE
    BED
I GAVE THEM AWAY
AND THOSE OLD BOOKS THAT YOU READ
I GAVE THEM AWAY
YOU CHOSE TO PLAY WITH MY HEAD

AND IF YOU'VE LOST ALL YOUR POWER TO SLEEP AT
    NIGHT
YOU'VE LOST YOUR BELIEF THINGS WILL BE ALL
    RIGHT
YOU CAN'T FIND YOUR STRENGTH AND YOUR WILL TO
    FIGHT
WELL I GOT ALL THAT TOO, AND I'M NOT GONNA
    GIVE IT BACK.

SOCIAL WORKER. I had some pretty amazing hallucinations from meditating. I remember one where this guy I was with, his head like turned into a flame, sort of going up, elongated, like whoosh, and this voice said, "If the face of God frightens you, don't look." Pretty far out stuff. But then I had this car accident. I was lucky because you know, sometimes, I'd drive around with my eyes closed, you know, only the blind can see, yadda yadda. And I got into this accident, went through a stop sign. But the accident was like IT for me. I was like, what are you doing? I had done the sex and the drugs and the rock and roll and Europe and anarchy and now religion. Then I went back to school and met certain people, like my husband. And you get on a different track.

SO IF YOU'RE MISSING THE SHEETS YOU BOUGHT
    WHEN WE MET
I GAVE THEM AWAY
THE DOG YOU LEFT AT THE VET

I GAVE HER AWAY
YOU LIED SO THAT'S WHAT YOU GET

AND IF YOU'VE LOST ALL YOUR POWER TO SLEEP AT
    NIGHT
YOU'VE LOST YOUR BELIEF THINGS WILL BE ALL
    RIGHT
YOU CAN'T FIND YOUR STRENGTH AND YOUR WILL TO
    FIGHT
WELL I GOT ALL THAT TOO, AND I'M NOT GONNA
    GIVE IT BACK.

(COP *enters.*)

COP. But back with the lost things. Sometimes with organized crime we'll find a body and it'll be missing…something. Head, fingers, something. And a lot of times that's a sign, a signal. We'll find a body in the fields or whatever without a head or hands. It's a signal. And a lot of times—now I've got nothing against homosexuals or the gay COMMUNITY—but a lot of times in those cases when a homosexual will kill another homosexual, a lot of times the genitals will be missing. And that's a sign, too. That's a signal.

(*Exits.*)

ICH TRAUMT DU KAMST AN MICH

ICH TRAUMT DU KAMST AN MICH
UND SUSSLICH MICH GEGRUSST.
DU SAGST, "ICH LIEBE DICH"
UND HERZLICH MICH GEKUSST

AB' TRAUME SIND NICHT WAR
ICH BIN ALLEIN HEUT MORGEN.
DU BIST GAR NIMMER DA,
MEIN HERZ IST VOLLE SORGEN.

(Translation:
I dreamt that you came to me
And sweetly looked at me.
You said "I love you."
And kissed me deeply.

But dreams are never true
I am alone this morning.
For you are never there
My heart is filled with grief.)

(COP, PET PSYCHIC, *and* DISPOSEAPHOBIC™ *on stage.*)

COP. We get a call from the super of this building. He finds a partially mummified human head in a paper bag in the garbage! And he doesn't know what to make of this! Turns out, a woman in the building, her husband died and she's been dragging him around the apartment for weeks, dragging him around by his HEAD! By his HEAD!

PET PSYCHIC. Sure I'll find lost things. Lost pets. People will call and say, "I've lost Fluffy can you help me find her." I'm a people psychic as well as a pet psychic. I took a class back in the eighties. At a community college. It was called Consciousness Frontiers. I trained myself. Anyone can do it. You can do it. You CAN. I used to be a stockbroker.

DISPOSEAPHOBIC™. Where are you? Manhattan? Brooklyn? I only ask because we deal with a lot of disposeaphobics™ in the Village. I'm in Queens. Exit veintetres right near the Long Island Distressway. The Long Island Distressway.

COP. And she's dragged him around so much—his head pops off! And she doesn't know what to do. So she puts the head in a paper bag and puts it out front with the garbage. And the super finds it! It's crazy, right? You got to laugh. You just got to laugh. But never in front of the family.

PET PSYCHIC. A couple of weeks ago I was talking to this old horse. Just this great old horse. And I asked him how things were and he said "It's been a tough year for rabbits." And I laughed and said "Really what do you mean?" And he said, "Well a lot of them had been dying they go down by the river and drink the water and it was making them sick." And I said, "Well why don't you tell the rabbits?" And the horse just said, "Well, you can't tell a rabbit anything." I love that.

DISPOSEAPHOBIC™. Disposeaphobics™. They collect things they find on the street—anything from cat hair to rocks. It's all about emotional attachment. They are attached to these things they collect. These people are not stupid. They're not well, but they're not stupid. We get lots of lawyers and teachers. Lots of teachers. Lots of women teachers. I did a seminar at the Learning Annex on How to Rid Your Life of Clutter Forever and I can't tell you how many teachers showed up. The people who showed up were of two types, either they were there so I could teach them how to file. Literally, "Don, how do I file?" And I said this is NOT what this seminar is about. I'm not going to show people how to fucking file. Lots of teachers.

PET PSYCHIC. A friend of mine called me once his brother had been out fishing on a lake and the boat had returned, but his brother was gone. And my friend called to ask me what happened. And I said your brother had a heart attack and fell over the side of the boat. And then he wanted my help trying to find the body. I was on the phone with him and he was on a walkie talkie communicating with the divers. And it was like I was seeing behind the eyes of the divers. I actually saw where the body was but by the time the message got through the diver had turned and he didn't see it. And the dead brother was also sending me little messages. He told me that his son almost made him a grandfather. And when I told his son that he started to cry, because it turned out he had been seeing a girl and she had been pregnant and had got an abortion and that's why they'd broken up. Hm? Oh, yes, I work with the police too. Usually murders and rape cases. But it's completely anonymous. They don't acknowledge I work with them and I don't want them to.

COP. Have you heard of the Colombian necktie? Yeah, that's where they slit your throat and pull out your tongue through the hole. The Colombian drug lords do that. This one time we found—now this is a terrible thing—we found this guy's whole family. They'd been killed by the Colombians. Killed his wife and raped her, raped his twelve year old daughter, sodomized their nine year old boy. Slit their throats, pulled out their tongues and hung their bodies from the shower curtain rod. And you know, shower curtain rods are flimsy things and I'm thinkin'—I ask my superior officer—what the hell kinda shower rod is that you can hang up a whole family? You know, you don't wanna laugh but sometimes you just need to, you know? It's either that or *(Insinuating nod and drinking motion:)* you know?

DISPOSEAPHOBIC™. The worst case I've seen? Well that depends because what are you talking about here? The worst stench? The worst clutter? The worst roaches? The most despicable person? Because a lot of these people are assholes. Serious assholes. They yell and scream and treat you like crap and I'm like, "HEY YOU CALLED ME. YOU'RE ABOUT TO GET EVICTED SO DON'T YELL AT ME." First, I try love. If that doesn't work I use my Nazi approach. My mix between the Nazi and the Russian approach.

How do I do what I do? How do you do what you do? How are you an actor? If someone says to you, "How do you act?" What would you say? COME ON.

Now, most of these people have no sense of time. They've lost touch with reality. I get them to come back to reality by having them look at their watch. If that doesn't work, I have other techniques. I'm also trained in open-eyed hypnosis. I know how to hypnotize people while they're awake. For example if I said to you—DON'T THINK OF A BIG BLUE HOUSE AND DON'T THINK OF A GREEN BARN BEHIND IT. What did you think of? You couldn't help but think of those things. I'm trained in techniques like that.

What causes this? OCD, Depression. We all get depressed. I get depressed. You get depressed. Don't you? Don't you get depressed? WHY ARE YOU AN ACTOR? HUH? WHY? So you get to act like you're happy ninety percent of the time.

PET PSYCHIC. Oh. Oh. This one man had this beautiful Chattahoochee Leopard Dog and he wanted me to ask the dog what he really enjoyed. And the dog said, "A hot poop on a cold day." Now how am I supposed to tell this man that? Well, I guess what else does the dog have to worry about.

COP. Well, I hope that helps you out. Here, let me get that for you. No, no it's on me. Come on. No, I insist. Listen, life had been very good to me. If I can help out some young people, I will.

(Somewhere in the city outside, we hear a man talking to a cop, both played by the same actor.)

DRIVER'S LICENSE. I don't have it sir. I lost it. I don't have my ID. I was just going to get some cigarettes…come on man…I was just on my way to get some cigarettes…I was just going to get some cigarettes…come on man…come on man…come on don't do this to me man, I was just going to get some cigarettes…please, come on don't do this to me… sir… Michael Smith, sir… come on man, please don't do this to me… I don't have it sir I lost it…I lost it…I'm just going to get some cigarettes I'm staying at my girl's around the corner…please don't do this to me man. *(The cop:)* If you don't shut the fuck up not only are you going to fucking jail but you'll be going to fucking Bellevue. *(Back to the man:)* Come on please I was just going to get some cigarettes…

(Singer enters.)

LOST HORIZON

I WANT TO LIVE IN SHANGRI-LA
WITHOUT YOU
ABOVE THE MOUNTAINS WHERE THE SNOW FALLS
    DOWN
I WANT TO SAIL AWAY AND FIND LOST CITIES
UNDERNEATH THE OCEAN FLOOR
I WANT TO LIVE IN XANADU
WITHOUT YOU
WITH KUBLAI KHAN SO I CAN SMOKE MY PIPE AND
    DREAM OF YOU
I WANT TO SAIL AWAY AND LEARN WHAT SIN IS
IN SODOM AND GOMORRAH
IMAGINARY CITIES THAT LIE UNDER THE OCEAN.
AND DID YOU SAY
I SEEMED SO FAR AWAY
AM I OK?
WHY COULDN'T I STAY?
MY BOAT IS SINKING IN TO THE WIDE SARGASSO SEA
THIS IS MY LOST HORIZON
THIS IS MY LOST HORIZON
I'M GONNA FIND ATLANTIS.

I WANT TO LIVE IN BABYLON
WITHOUT YOU

IN HANGING GARDENS WHERE NOBODY TALKS THE
    WAY YOU DO
I WANT TO SAIL AWAY AND FIND LOST CITIES
ALL FULL OF TROJAN HORSES
IMAGINARY CITIES
THAT LIE UNDER THE OCEAN
AND DID YOU SAY
I SEEMED SO FAR AWAY
AM I OK?
WHY COULDN'T I STAY?
MY BOAT IS SINKING IN TO THE WIDE SARGASSO SEA
THIS IS MY LOST HORIZON
THIS IS MY LOST HORIZON
THIS IS MY LOST HORIZON

(Theme music. TERI *and* DR. PALINURUS *enter.)*

TERI. Why don't we take a call. This is Linda, from Wilmington, Delaware. Linda?

LINDA. Yes. Hi, Teri, Hi Professor Palinorotz.

TERI / PALINURUS. Hello.

LINDA. When you're talking about this, uh, psychology, I wonder, does Freud have anything to say about this? And I'll take my answer off the air.

TERI. Well, that's a good question. Doctor Palinurus, is there a Freudian Atlantis?

PALINURUS. If you want to see those eels as phallic symbols, maybe. *(Laughter.)* Actually, I'm glad the caller asked that. Because of course Freud has something to say about loss. Say you lose something. I don't know. A little box of cookies. Well, Freud says, maybe there's some *reason* why you lost the cookies. Maybe your mother has told you that you need to lose weight. Or maybe these cookies were a particular favorite of someone you loved very much. And you feel guilty enjoying such cookies when she can't.

TERI. Even when we don't know it, our actions make sense.

PALINURUS. Yes. But what I'd like to ask back is: *nostalgia.* Literally, in Greek, this means a kind of *pain. Algia:* is *pain.* And *nostos,* the Greek word, means homecoming. So nostalgia is the pain you get from going home again. But why do we use this word to refer to thinking about things we lost? Because it's not a pain. It's a pleasure. We enjoy this. And one thing you might say, if you like Freud, is: sometimes we need to lose something before we can enjoy it. Or maybe we enjoy it better. I could say to you, Teri, that I wish I had some cookies now, to dip in my cup of tea. But the cookies taste better in my mind than they would if you gave me cookies. Is that Platonic thinking? Is that Freudian thinking? I don't know. But that's *nostalgia.* Although Freud doesn't use the word.

TERI. We're a long way from Atlantis now.

PALINURUS. Well, actually, funny you should mention it. Do you know how Freud became a scientist? His first job, he received a university grant to do graduate work, to find the testes of the eel.

TERI. So there is a connection!

PALINURUS. Yes. Their missing testes. Which weren't really missing…it's not like, oh dear, what did I do with my eel gonads. Nobody could find them. The reproduction of the eel is still a mystery. We know *where* they do it—

TERI. Atlantis.

PALINURUS. Sargasso Sea, yes, but even now, when we think science has solved so much, there's still this little bit of mystery.

(ENGLISHMAN *enters. Note: the* ENGLISHMAN *should use the name of whatever actor is playing him.*)

ENGLISHMAN. Trey… Hello, how are you? then. So *(Breathes deep)* I was living in Fulbourn. This was in 1976. I had just divorced my first wife and I was *(Breathes)* incredibly depressed, sleeping with anyone I could and drinking and doing drugs and…

And so…this is the bit. I woke up in this room in some college in Cambridge. I didn't know who I slept with or who was next to me in bed and so I stumbled out of bed and… *(Breathes)* I got dressed and started to walk to Fulbourn, which was about an hours walk. It was the beginning of dawn, so the light… and I…the sun was coming up and I remember thinking…there was a lamp post and the thought I had, I mean I remember what I wanted to say, "The sun has come up and the lamp post is still on" But when I got to the word "lamp" I couldn't think of the word. The word was missing. But it wasn't like I had forgotten what the word was. I'm not explaining this very well. Look, Trey, they didn't exist then of course, but it was like my mind was a computer and the word had just been deleted. I was racing my mind, trying to get the word out before it was deleted from the other side.

I was walking along the railroad and there was a big fence and I'd think, "Well, that's a big _____." Or I'd look down and think "I can see my _____." Shoe.

Yes, that's it. Yes. Like I'd never been told the name of it. But I knew what it was, what it did. Just not what it was called. And by the end of the walk to Fulbourn, I had lost all words.

I sat around the house with my friends and they…I remember just going about my normal everyday business, eating, sleeping. But I wasn't talking. And…

(Long silence.)

And later when I woke up, my language had returned.

(Sounding like he felt used:) Is that what you wanted? Good. All right Trey. Good. Good Luck.

Bye.

ETCH A SKETCH

ONCE I WAS A LOCKIAN TABULA RASA
I SOAKED UP INFORMATION
LIKE WEDDING INVITATIONS
I KNEW THAT THE CAPITAL OF THE CONGO WAS KIN-
    SHASA
AND EVERY OTHER NATION
WHERE FRIENDS OF MINE VACATION

I'M AN ETCH A SKETCH (BUT NOW I'M ALL SHOOK UP)
I'M A PIECE OF WAX (BUT NOW THE IMPRINT'S LOST)

THE WORKS OF TROLLOPE
THE PERIODIC TABLE
AND WHERE TO BUY MEN'S SUITS
OR FASHIONABLE BOOTS
THE SETTING AND THE MORAL OF EACH OF AESOP'S
    FABLES
ALL KINDS OF FOREIGN FRUIT
AND HOW TO PLAY THE FLUTE
LATELY THOUGH I FIND THAT I'M NOT QUITE AS ABLE
TO COME UP WITH SQUARE ROOTS
AND TRIVIAL PURSUITS

I'M AN ETCH A SKETCH (BUT NOW I'M ALL SHOOK UP)
I'M A PIECE OF WAX (BUT NOW THE IMPRINT'S LOST)

NOW I CAN'T REMEMBER THE THINGS THAT I WAS
    THINKING
LIKE WHEN DO CHICKENS BASTE
OR HOW A KISS SHOULD TASTE
WHO WAS THE PRESIDENT WHO CAME AFTER LIN-
    COLN?
MY BLACKBOARD'S BEEN ERASED
MY BLACKBOARD'S BEEN ERASED.

(GREAT AUNT in a chair.)

GREAT AUNT. Well. Because of my situation I've lost everything that was valuable to me. Just remember unless it's nailed on you or hanging off of you hold on to it because it all goes. The HYPOCRISY of these people who would come to help. They would come in the morning and say "Oh, what a lovely _____ Mrs. Weller" and then it would be gone. There were so many people helping that I couldn't pin anything on any one person. And I'm glad. I made a crocheted blanket. It took me weeks to make it. Because I'm sitting around all the time, so I can do this. And it wasn't the kind with you know, all the circles. I HATE those. And I went into the hospital and I thought, I should put this away before I go. Someone might want it. I should tuck it away. And I folded it up and put it right into the closet. I know exactly where I put it. And when I got out of the hospital I kept it there because I still was worried that someone might take it. Then, when it was time to come here, it was gone. GONE.

You have to defend yourself until the day you die. Until you just can't anymore, because who else is going to do it for you? Because they'll take anything. Not necessarily china, because who has the room for it any more. Everyone lives in these one bedroom apartments. Nothing lasts. And silver, they wouldn't know what to do with it probably. They don't know beans about polishing it or using it or what to do with it. People should just buy from the five and dime.

(OLDER WOMAN joins her, sits.)

OLDER WOMAN. Well, first let me start by saying that I put things places all the time and I don't remember where I put them. And you have to talk slow, it's not just the volume of your voice, but you have to talk slow and clear, it's the speed I process the information at.

Okay, that said, my mother had a very thin necklace, not silver, not white gold—platinum! With three diamonds all in a line. Mother didn't like jewelry; she thought people who wore a lot were *(Points to head.)*. So, she gave it to me. Well, I had jury duty downtown and I was on the way there, I was walking, and three boys were across the street and they were laughing. I was eighteen at the time and they were laughing. So, I reached in to make sure I was wearing a slip—women wore slips under their dresses at that time, you see. So I reached in to make sure. And I walked, and a few minutes later I felt for the necklace and it was, it was gone. When I had reached in to check for my slip, I must have snapped the chain. It was so thin.

I don't remember if Mother was mad. You see, I always wanted Mother's approval, I always wanted her to like me, to love me. And she was not a good person, and not a very good mother. And I have blocked out the bad things about her, I don't remember them, and I only remember the good things. So, I don't remember if she was mad. But if she was true to form, she really let me have it.

STARS

WHEN I LOST MY KEYS YOU TOLD ME THE WORDS OF
    PLATO
THAT OUR POSSESSIONS ARE ONLY SHADOWS ECHOES
    OF FATE, SO

THE THINGS THAT YOU LOSE, YOU NEVER POSSESSED
YOU'RE ONLY REMEMBERING
ONLY REMEMBERING

AND ALL WE SEE IS STARS
FALLING FROM SO FAR AWAY
THE THINGS THAT WE SEE ARE JUST MEMORIES OF
    THE THINGS THAT USED TO BE

SO I KNOW THAT YOU UNDERSTAND THAT NOTHING
    WE HAVE IS REAL
WE'RE JUST TRYING TO GET BACK TO A PLACE WE
    KNEW BEFORE
SO WHEN I LEAVE YOU YOU'LL KNOW, I'M JUST A
    SHADOW, AN ECHO
YOU NEVER POSSESSED ME

NEVER POSSESSED ME
AND ALL WE SEE IS STARS
FALLING FROM SO FAR AWAY
THE THINGS THAT WE SEE
ARE JUST MEMORIES OF THE THINGS THAT USED TO
    BE.

(We hear TERI's *interview with* DR. PALINURUS *on the radio.)*

TERI. And that's your argument, is…

PALINURUS. …is that, yes, it is mysterious. How we lose things. How time only goes in one direction. And memory. Put it this way: I'm an old man, Teri, my memory's not so good anymore. This happens. But when I first came to this country, to America, I was very surprised. Because people here, the memory is very short.

TERI. So you think we have a—it's like a goldfish culture, with a five-minute memory?

PALINURUS. I was like that once.

TERI. I think we all were.

PALINURUS. But let me tell you a famous story, Teri. There was a poet, in ancient Greece. Simonides. And he is invited to perform at a banquet where the host, a King, has offended the gods. But Simonides is a poet, he praises the gods, the gods like him. So after he has performed for the King and his guests, a messenger comes, and says, there is somebody here to talk to you, Simonides. He goes outside. There is no one there. But at that very moment, the banquet-hall collapses.

TERI. The gods were on his side.

PALINURUS. Yes. But the *story,* Teri. Because there were so many people at the King's banquet. And all of them lost when this hall collapses. And the bodies were so mangled that the relatives who came to take them away for burial could not tell which was which. But Simonides closed his eyes, and remembered his performance, remembered singing his poetry to every person there, and he remembered the place-settings at the banquet, and thus he could tell the grieving families which were their dead. The Greeks called Simonides the inventor of the art of memory. For this reason.

TERI. What an evocative story.

PALINURUS. Yes, Teri, yes. And it is no accident that he was a poet. Because nostalgia? Is just how you feel about the things you lose. We use words to do it. Literary fiction. Like a poet. To hang on to what we lose. It's a way of keeping those things, by recollecting, by, uh, commemorating.

TERI. Big things, too. Continents.

PALINURUS. Anything. Big things, little...like I said, car keys. Are important too. My wife, Madeleine, used to say, and she's been dead now for six years, come December...she was fond of saying to me, "Sascha, this world is made of little things. What is important...is to see them largely."

TERI. And I think you've helped us to do that, Doctor.

PALINURUS. Well, I hope so, Teri. Just a little.

End of Play

(I AM) NOBODY'S LUNCH

(A CABARET ABOUT HOW WE KNOW WHAT WE KNOW WHEN NOBODY KNOWS IF EVERYONE ELSE IS LYING AND WHEN SOMEONE OR SOMETHING WANTS TO HAVE YOU FOR LUNCH)

written by Steven Cosson
from interviews by the company*
music and lyrics by Michael Friedman

*(I Am) Nobody's Lunch was created with Andy Boroson, Daoud Heidami, Christina Kirk, Alix Lambert, Matt Maher, Caitlin Miller, & KJ Sanchez. Additional interviews contributed by Maria Dizzia, Jennifer Gillespie, Jen Taher, Amy Waschke and Chris Wells.

Playscripts, Inc.
website: www.playscripts.com
email: info@playscripts.com
phone: 1-866-NEW-PLAY (639-7529)

INTRODUCTION

(I Am) Nobody's Lunch came about as a response to a time in America when it seemed that the country had lost its mind. The years surrounding the invasion of Iraq felt like watching a slow train crash from somewhere inside the train, with the conductors calmly announcing that everything is ok (or occasionally screaming "The train is crashing!") It did not feel much like democracy. Feeling utterly powerless, we tried to at least follow the story. And the story went something like this: "We are not _____. Actually we are _____. We are _____ for your safety. What you thought was _____ has been redefined and now we are no longer _____ and it is unpatriotic to keep asking questions about _____."

In response to all this, the company wanted to do something more expressly political. Figuring out how to do so however posed some challenges At such a time, the strongest impulse was to shout "That's a lie!" "Here's the truth!" But the problem wasn't really that the truth was censored. It was readily available. The problem was that the truth had lost its power to affect reality. Furthermore, shouting the truth violated one of our working principles. We had decided that any project had to be driven by an open-ended question, some sort of inquiry for which we couldn't presuppose a result. What's the point, in other words, of making a show about what we already know? After much deliberation, we came up with a question. Essentially, we wanted to know how everyone else was sorting out the mess. If a democracy depends in part on there being some common understanding of what is actually taking place in the world, then we wanted to know if in fact if such a consensus existed, and if not, then just how are people parsing reality?

As with *Gone Missing*, the company conducted wide-ranging interviews and Michael Friedman wrote songs at the same time. We found words of wisdom from all sorts of unlikely corners (like the Pleiades). And in the end I think we discovered some helpful thoughts for difficult times.

—Steven Cosson

ACKNOWLEDGMENTS

(I Am) Nobody's Lunch received its U.S. Premiere by The Civilians at 59E59 Theaters, New York City, January 19, 2006. It was directed by Steven Cosson with the following cast:

Quincy Tyler Bernstine
Matt Dellapina
Brad Heberlee
Daoud Heidami
Caitlin Miller
Jennifer R. Morris
Andy Boroson

And the following production staff:

Piano .... Andy Boroson
Choreographer .... Karinne Keithley
Set Designer .... Andromache Chalfant
Costume Designer .... Sarah Beers
Lighting Designer .... Marcus Doshi
Sound Designer .... Shane Rettig
Stage Manager .... Catherine Bloch
Dramaturg .... Jocelyn Clarke
Dramaturg .... Jim Lewis
Dramaturg .... Janice Paran
Illustrator .... Josh Neufeld
Associate Producer .... Kirsten Bowen

The play subsequently received its London Premiere by The Civilians at Soho Theatre, September 6, 2006. It was directed by Steven Cosson with the following cast:

Matt Dellapina
Daoud Heidami
Brandon Miller
Caitlin Miller
Lexy Fridell

And the following production staff:

Piano .... Andy Boroson
Choreographer .... Karinne Keithley
Set Designer .... Andromache Chalfant
Costume Designer .... Sarah Beers
Lighting Designer .... Marcus Doshi
Sound Designer .... Shane Rettig

Stage Manager...Robert Signom III
Assistant Directors...Dyana Kimball,
Donya Washington
Dramaturg...Jocelyn Clarke
Dramaturg...Jim Lewis
Dramaturg...Janice Paran
Illustrator...Josh Neufeld
Associate Producer...Kirsten Bowen

The initial development of the play was supported by a residency at The Public Theater (George C. Wolfe, Artistic Director). An earlier version of the play opened in September 2004 and was produced by The Civilians and presented by Performance Space 122. Development of this final version was provided with the assistance of the Sundance Institute (Philip Himberg, Artistic Director), and was premiered by The Civilians (Steve Cosson, Artistic Director; Kyle Gorden, Producing Director) in New York City, February, 2006.

Jennifer R. Morris, Brad Heberlee, Quincy Tyler Bernstine,
Matt Dellapina (on table), Caitlin Miller, and Daoud Heidami
in *(I Am) Nobody's Lunch*

59E59 Theaters, New York City, 2006
Photo by Leslie Lyons

(I AM) NOBODY'S LUNCH

A cast member enters and speaks to the audience. The stage is bare except for a small duffel bag.

PERFORMER. Oh hi, gosh wow, hi everyone. So…before we start our show, *(I Am) Nobody's Lunch (A cabaret about how you know what you know when nobody knows if everyone else is lying and when someone or something wants to have you for lunch),* I just want… Look here's the thing. We did some focus groups and some of our previous audience members expressed a feeling that…that our show was well, confusing. So—that is NOT what we want to do to you, is that clear? So here's the basics. We interviewed people and asked them how they know what they know—today. How they know what's real, what's true and then we'll play the people we talked to… Yeah? And we started interviewing in what like 2003 and then we just keep going back for more.

Ok you get the idea? Great. That's great. So yeah remember 2003? "Weapons of Mass Destruction" "Shock and Awe" "Mission Accomplished" yeah that was 2003. "Mission Accomplished." What else…2003. Uh…Tom Cruise was with Penelope Cruz. And uh Private Jessica Lynch— Do you know who she…? She's not the one with the leash and the *(Does thumbs up gesture like Lynndie England in the Abu Ghraib photos.).* Jessica Lynch, US Army, captured by the Iraqis, then the BBC did an expose about the US rescue how it was sort of staged for the cameras. Like this. A stage. Oh right— Also! Last thing. This is a *cabaret,* ok? So there's no plot. No. Plot. As in story. I mean there are plots… there are plots against people aren't there? So, right.

(ANOTHER PERFORMER peers out onto the stage, looking at the small duffel bag.)

ANOTHER PERFORMER. Hey. What is—THAT?

PERFORMER. Huh. Excuse me is this somebody's bag? Did anyone leave this bag here?

(She moves towards the bag.)

ANOTHER PERFORMER. Chht.

PERFORMER. What? It's just a—right. You're right. *(To the audience:)* Hey this is no time to be leaving…*bags*…laying, lying, laying…about. *(Calling offstage left:)* Is this someone's—

ANOTHER PERFORMER. *(Calling offstage right:)* Is this someone's bag? HEY!

(The rest of the cast peers out and sees the bag.)

PERFORMER. There is a *bag* on the *stage.*

(Everyone looking like it's not their bag.)

It's not…? No one…?

THIRD PERFORMER. *(Moving towards bag:)* Well why don't we just—
    (Everyone gathered round the bag.)
FOURTH PERFORMER. Stand back!
    (Flinching.)
THIRD PERFORMER. Jesus Christ.
FOURTH PERFORMER. I mean just stand back a little. You don't want your face so close when we open it.
FIFTH PERFORMER. I really don't think we should open it or move it or touch it.
ANOTHER PERFORMER. She's right.
    (Actors stuck.)
PERFORMER. *(To audience:)* We are so sorry about this.
THIRD PERFORMER. Hold on. It's just a bag.
    (Picks up the bag.)
ANOTHER PERFORMER. Go ahead…
THIRD PERFORMER. I'm just gonna…
FIFTH PERFORMER. Sure. Ok.
    (As THIRD PERFORMER *exits there's a meow from inside the bag.* THIRD PERFORMER *pauses, then exits.)*
PERFORMER. So then. On with the show!

THE TELEPHONE SONG

(Text indicated with a "—" is spoken.)
(Ring.)
—Why are you asking me this? Whatever, you have your reasons, right?
—You're not taping this are you? What was that sound? Is someone else on the phone?
    (Ring.)
—I think the news is mostly just highlighting nonsense.
—I have friends who work for ABC, CBS news who say they've been given tapes by the government, pre-cut tapes and they're just running them without editing. I mean I don't want to buy into the *(Uses his hands to say "conspiracy theories.")*.
—I mean I'm not sure just hearing about things is real. The radio sings about love, for instance, but love's something you have to experience for yourself to know it… That's true. Or at least I think that's true!
SOLO.
        SINCE WE'VE BEEN GOING OUT I'M SEEING ONE
            THING CLEARLY
        YOU NEVER EVER SAY A WORD TO ME SINCERELY

WHEN WILL YOU COME INTO FOCUS
AND SHOW ME THE WAY

CHORUS.
DON'T YOU WANT TO BE IN LOVE?
DON'T YOU WANT A LOVE THAT'S TRUE
DON'T YOU WANT TO FEEL IT'S TRUE IN YOUR HEART?

SOLO.	**CHORUS.**
AND THOUGH I'M WAITING TO BE IN YOUR ARMS ENVELOPED,	WOULDN'T IT BE GREAT TO BE YOUNG?
YOU'RE LIKE A PHOTOGRAPH THAT'S NEVER QUITE DEVELOPED	WOULDN'T IT BE GREAT TO BELIEVE?
WHY WON'T YOU COME INTO FOCUS	WOULDN'T IT BE GREAT TO BELIEVE
AND SHOW ME THE WAY?	FROM THE START?

(Ring.)

—Why are you asking me this?

—I read the paper and I'm like—all of this is lies! I mean, I don't remember feeling this before—that it was all a lie.

(Ring.)

—What do I need a President who's going to entertain me? I don't need a whole… *(Gesture meaning "song and dance.")*

—We were lying in my bed and Kate's holding me and she said to me "I love you more than anyone does. More than your Mother loves you, more than your Father loves you, more than anyone." And then she broke up with me a week later.

SOLO.
HOW DO I KNOW WHAT I KNOW?
HM…I GUESS I DON'T THINK I KNOW… WELL…I DON'T KNOW, WAIT…
I KNOW A LOT ABOUT A LOT OF THINGS…WAIT…I KNOW…WAIT…
I KNOW A LOT ABOUT A LOT ABOUT A LOT OF THINGS…

SOLO.	**CHORUS.**
BUT I DON'T KNOW A LOT ABOUT ONE THING…	WOULDN'T IT BE GREAT TO BE YOUNG?
NO, WAIT. I KNOW—	WOULDN'T IT BE GREAT TO BELIEVE?
NO. I *DON'T* KNOW A LOT ABOUT *ONE* THING,	WOULDN'T IT BE GREAT TO BELIEVE
BUT I KNOW A LITTLE	

ABOUT A LOT OF THINGS.   FROM THE START?
PATHETIC. I'M PATHETIC.

SOLO.

> WHAT ARE YOU SO AFRAID OF?
> WE'RE GONNA FIND AN ANSWER
> IT'S JUST AROUND THE CORNER AND I KNOW...
> WHAT ARE YOU SO AFRAID OF?
> WE'RE GONNA FIND AN ANSWER
> IT'S JUST AROUND THE CORNER AND I KNOW...
> *(Ring.)*

—Why are you asking me this?

—I think there are two reasons why 911 happened

—Do you think Tom Cruise is gay?

—YES.

—Why do you ask that? Who cares?

—I've heard from a ton of different sources, different people. One of my friends her father is an agent and he's always telling us things about people.

—Doesn't he have a wife now and like four kids or something? ...He's a terrible actor.

—He's a very good actor! He is!! Top Gun!! I love his moves. He's a prick but I still love his movies.

—How do you know he's a prick?

—I don't know. I've read interviews with him. I've seen him on talk shows. He's just really arrogant.

—You know, why don't you just ask me the questions. She's my wife. I'm sure I'd know how she'd answer.

—That's why I always end up staying in bad relationships. I can't leave.

CHORUS.	**SOLO.**
DON'T YOU WANT TO BE IN LOVE?	TOM CRUISE IS DEFINITELY GAY
DON'T YOU WANT A LOVE THAT'S TRUE?	TOM CRUISE IS DEFINITELY GAY
DON'T YOU WANT TO FEEL IT'S TRUE IN YOUR HEART?	TOM CRUISE IS DEFINITELY GAY
	THAT'S WHAT MY HAIR DRESSER SAYS AND HE KNOWS

CHORUS. *(Simultaneously.)*
>WOULDN'T IT BE GREAT TO BE YOUNG?
>WOULDN'T IT BE GREAT TO BELIEVE?
>WOULDN'T IT BE GREAT TO BELIEVE FROM THE START?

SOLO. *(Simultaneously.)*
>TOM CRUISE IS DEFINITELY GAY
>TOM CRUISE IS DEFINITEY GAY
>TOM CRUISE IS DEFINITEY GAY
>THAT'S WHAT MY HAIRDRESSER SAYS AND HE KNOWS

SOLO. *(Simultaneously.)*
>WHAT IS HAPPENING WITH THE BAG?
>IS NOBODY CONCERNED ABOUT THE BAG?
>WHAT ARE WE DOING WITH THE BAG?
>DOES NOBODY ELSE CARE ABOUT THE BAG? OH, GOD!

CHORUS.
>WHAT ARE YOU SO AFRAID OF?
>WE'RE GONNA FIND AN ANSWER
>IT'S JUST AROUND THE CORNER AND I KNOW…

>WHAT ARE YOU SO AFRAID OF?
>WE'RE GONNA FIND AN ANSWER
>IT'S JUST AROUND THE CORNER AND I KNOW…

>WHAT ARE YOU SO AFRAID OF?
>WE'RE GONNA FIND AN ANSWER
>IT'S JUST AROUND THE CORNER AND I KNOW…
>*(RING.)*

JESSICA LYNCH OPTOMETRIST. Hello, yes this is Jessica Lynch. Yes, this is Oregon, Portland Oregon. Ok. I'm an optometrist. Ok. What *I* think happened to Jessica Lynch? Are you serious? Ok. Well I know, you know, what was on TV. Her convoy was on a mission…or something…and…she …got stopped *(Implied male voice in background:)* What? Oh, ambushed. Yeah, that's the word ambushed *(To male:)* I know, I just said it. Ambushed, by the Iraqi army. And then they went in for her, you know with *night* goggles and the big rescue…God Yeah. You know, I hear that people think it was like, all for show that the rescue was like all for show but…not one of my friends, my family, not ONE person I know has ever mentioned anything of the sort. And now the media's saying too that there was, you know, no weapons of mass destruction and…no reason, and I…I…I don't believe that. But really, as far as this subject goes, I haven't given it that much thought, because I don't really…um…care…

(A sad long meow from offstage. Performers enter and set up the next scene. Sad meows of a trapped cat.)

PERFORMER 1. Should we…?

PERFORMER 2. Not now.

PERFORMER 1. But it sounds like there's a—

PERFORMER 3. Right. Probably that's true, but

PERFORMER 2. I think it's stopped.

NONAGENARIAN. *(Scolding a barking, growling toy poodle:)* Sweetie! Sweetie! She's not going to hurt you. You just stop it! Stop it Sweetie! Stop it! *(To audience:)* This dog is so dramatic. My younger daughter, she decided to get a poodle too. But her poodle is as big as a horse. It's beautiful. It's beautiful. It looks like a prime minister. But it's huge. Do you like dogs?

BOY. Something is real when it's living and something's not real when it is not alive. Sponge Bob is not real. And neither are witches. Oh! I have to tell you this great story. There was a place, a long time ago, where people thought other people were witches and they'd throw them in the water and if they swam they were witches and if they drowned they weren't witches. Isn't that ridiculous?

NONAGENARIAN. I love my dog. She's spoiled. But that's my fault. But I'd be lost without her. Aside from that I read. I read everything. When I was younger, I used to read this slightly…quasi-communist paper. It just seemed more, much more…questioning. But you had to be careful, because of this Senator McCarthy. He was checking into teachers, because they were generally left-leaners. It was very frightening for me, because you could lose your job.

BOY. I get afraid if I'm alone. If I'm alone here at the house I can get scared, and we have Penny now, and I feel less afraid. She can't do anything, but she barks. We have a cat too. She's huge. We took her to the vet to get, um to get de-clawed because she was scratching up the screens. And when she came back she was really depressed and she never moved, she just ate, so she's fat. But it turns out she wasn't the one clawing at the window. It was the other cats from outside, trying to get in. We ruined our cat.

NONAGENARIAN. Now I'm feeling unhappy about my country because I do not understand the president I have. Presidents have been inadequate. Presidents have been crooked. Presidents have been whatever…not behaving well. (Oh I can't forgive Clinton. He should have had better taste.) But this man is really incredible. I'm afraid…I'll tell you that as a child of immigrant parents, who lived during McCarthy, I'm afraid to send a letter to the editor of *The New York Times*. I'm afraid to say something negative about Bush because someone will come down on me and I'm just too old now to handle it. And I'm very disappointed in the Democrats. I've always thought they were more concerned with the general population. They used to go out in the streets with papers and say, "This is not good. This is what's really going on." But now…I don't know what people care about. It's like people have forgotten how to feel pain. And those are the type of people that don't have dogs.

(*Cat meows from offstage. The pianist brings the bag out on stage. Performers figuring out what to do.*)

PERFORMER. Just give us a minute.

(*One Performer takes the bag out of the theater and gives it to a* HOUSE MANAGER.)

PERFORMER. No it was just there. It's not ours. It just showed up. Could you just—take care of it? Thanks so much.

OTHER PERFORMER. We're really sorry about this.

SOMEONE TO KEEP ME WARM

I USED TO THINK THAT I WAS INDEPENDENT
MY LIFE WAS MINE
MY LIFE WAS FINE.
ALWAYS THE PLAINTIFF NEVER THE DEFENDANT
BUT THEN THINGS CHANGED
LIFE REARRANGED,
AND I JUST WANT TO SIT BACK AND BE TOLD
TO BE CONTROLLED
TO BE SECURE
SO NOW THE ONE I'M SEARCHING FOR IS—

SOMEONE TO KEEP ME WARM
SOMEONE TO GUARD ME
SOMEONE TO BEAR THE STORM
TO PRINT AND CARD ME
NOT JUST SOME STAGE DOOR JOHN
WHO'LL VENERATE ME
THE ONE I'M SET UPON
WILL DOMINATE ME.
HE'LL TELL ME WHEN I'M GOOD
AND HE'LL GOLD STAR ME
IF I DO WHAT I SHOULD
HE'LL NEVER SCAR ME
AND THOUGH I'M FRIGHTENED
AND THOUGH HE'LL SOMETIMES SCARE ME
I'M MORE ENLIGHTENED
AND IN THE END HE'LL SPARE ME
I NEED TO FEEL HIS POWER
EACH DAY AND EVERY HOUR

> DON'T TRY TO CHANGE MY MIND
> 'CAUSE I CAN'T HEAR YOU
> HE'S TOLD ME OF YOUR KIND
> AND NOT TO FEAR YOU
> AND IF HE'S BIG AND STRONG
> I'LL LOVE HIM RIGHT OR WRONG
> HE BEATS ME BLACK AND BLUE
> THEN I DESERVE THAT TOO
> WHAT OF THE CHILD I WAS?
> WHAT OF THE LIFE I HAD?
> I NEED TO FEEL HIM NEAR ME
> I NEED TO FEEL HIM HURT ME
> I NEED TO FEEL HIM NEED ME
> I NEED TO NEED TO NEED HIM SO…
> SOMEONE TO KEEP ME WARM.

CHANNELER. Okay well, what will happen is that I'll take a minute to empty my thoughts and get centered—maybe less than a minute, but maybe a minute, and then you can ask him whatever you like. This is sort of an informational down-load, right?

I now declare myself a clear and open channel this day. I declare that only that which is in conscious service to the light shall speak to me or through me this day. I declare that all that be brought forward be for the highest good of all those involved. Amen.

(The entity arrives in the CHANNELER's *body.)*

ENTITY. All right. Hmm. Tell me your name my boy. Hello *(Name of actor).* Where would you have me begin speaking or would you like to ask me questions? I see. Go ahead.

I am from the Pleiades. Do you know the Pleiades? It is a star system not far away from your planet. Yes of course I am there now, but I am also here. If you saw me now as I really am you would imagine that I am, mmmm… sleeping. All right, what is your next question?

I see, you are wondering about fear. I will give you an assignment. Go to the news and count the number of times you hear words of caution in a single hour: "Fear. It is feared that it is caution oh be warned it's dangerous the world is dangerous!" So everyone is always worried about getting stabbed in the street or losing their jobs and starving to death or the whole world blowing up.

(Loud knocking sound, tires screeching and a car driving away.)

HOMELAND SECURITY. I started working here, just before September 11th so two years now. Yeah. And see my department after 9/11 was made part of DHS—Department of Homeland Security. Right. And I'm in charge of policy for student visas. So now I'm five away from the President. And completely alone. Ideologically. Yeah. I'm twenty-four. *(Giggles.)* I stay in things way after when I should have gotten out. Like I always end up staying in bad relationships. Like this job. My friends all tell me to save myself and get out but I can't leave. Because ideologically I'm the only one here. Yeah, I'm seen as the Trojan liberal. And, yeah, I'm working fourteen hour days. I got today off because I told them I would quit if I didn't. Yeah, I had the day off except I had to go to a meeting from twelve to four-forty. Yep, that's a day off. *(Giggles.)*

(Phone rings.)

EGYPTIAN GRADUATE STUDENT. *(On the phone:)* Yeah hello.

HOMELAND SECURITY. When are you doing this piece? Because what I tell you depends on... Ok, I can tell you. There's this deadline of August 1st, you know, when the student visa tracking system would be up and running. Right, for foreign students—

EGYPTIAN GRADUATE STUDENT. Salam aleikem. Ok. I'm from Egypt. I'm working on my PhD. I'm a computer Engineer. Yes, you know I came here in 2001 so yes two years in San Diego. And where are you now? *(Pause.)* You live in New York? Oh... Are there a lot of black people? Oh...I love black people. Black women are my weakness.

HOMELAND SECURITY. I've been saying for a year that this tracking system, it's not gonna be ready. But the politicians would never budge on the deadline. Anyway, this date... Well, we're just not gonna make it. So, the tracking system will be up but because it doesn't work all these students on valid visas are gonna try to get back into the country after summer break and they're gonna be denied. Tens of thousands of foreign students stuck at the borders.

EGYPTIAN GRADUATE STUDENT. Yeah, I had to go downtown to register as a foreign student. Oh the guy was very nice, but he asked me a lot of personal questions. I didn't know if he was just that nice, or was being nice to try to get more private information from me.

HOMELAND SECURITY. So the President calls us in and says, "I don't want to look bad so by August 1st you have to do whatever you have to do to fix this. Do something—ANYTHING." Yeah, so that he doesn't get blamed for the failure of the system we've got to somehow let the students get back in the country without the public finding out we're breaking our own enforcement rules and then thinking that we're possibly letting terrorists right back in the country. That was my day. I've had a bad day

EGYPTIAN GRADUATE STUDENT. He asked me how many credit cards I had and what the numbers were,

HOMELAND SECURITY. It's that—all they care about is appearances.

EGYPTIAN GRADUATE STUDENT. My email address, where do you live, do you live in a house or apartment,

HOMELAND SECURITY. Only two of the terrorists were on expired student visas.

EGYPTIAN GRADUATE STUDENT. Who is your roommate, is he from Egypt as well?

HOMELAND SECURITY. The rest were on visitor visas. But nothing has been done with the visitor visa situation

EGYPTIAN GRADUATE STUDENT. Questions that I think are private.

HOMELAND SECURITY. Nothing

EGYPTIAN GRADUATE STUDENT. And very trivial.

HOMELAND SECURITY. The level of manipulation / of information…

EGYPTIAN GRADUATE STUDENT. I felt very embarrassed and stupid.

HOMELAND SECURITY. The obvious, out there, blatant manipulation is…

EGYPTIAN GRADUATE STUDENT. What? Oh, ok. Well, when Saddam invaded Kuwait, the U.S. intervened and stationed many American troops in the region. This was Bin Laden's turning point—he felt the U.S. was taking on Islam and the holy city. *(Pause.)* I don't want to talk about this over the phone. I think Arabic people's phones are tapped. I think the U.S. is watching all the Arabs. No. No. I don't want to talk about this anymore.

HOMELAND SECURITY. What am I afraid of? *(Thinks.)* I'm afraid of the whole world. I'm afraid of our government, I don't think they're protecting us. I'm afraid of the lack of democracy. I'm afraid… I mean, I do feel safe in my tiny world: my boyfriend, my parents, my fifteen D.C. friends. But no, I don't feel safe. I'm not afraid that our building is going to blow up. I'm afraid of the whole world—

(Sounds of Grand Central Station.)

SOLDIER AT GRAND CENTRAL. Yeah, we talk about this stuff in the platoon. We never debate though, no. That's the rule. Lieutenant. I've been at Grand Central two weeks now, after this I'll be somewhere else.

No, I don't really believe what they tell us in the news. The trick is to look at what they're not telling you. For example, they tell you they've got a tape of Bin Laden talking but it's probably a fake. They didn't translate it. He's not speaking in English. What's the voice saying? We don't know.

(A passenger asks for directions.)

Hold on. What train? Down that corridor take a left.

No. I don't vote. They're all crooks anyway. But you notice, all during Clinton, two terms in office, no problem. Then Bush gets in office—wham. 9/11 happens. Is that an accident? What? 9/11? Well I'm just saying, I wouldn't be surprised if that was us. You get what I'm saying? Yeah, us. I'm not saying that's true or that's not true. I just wouldn't be surprised. If it was.

Sure, go ahead. *(Laughs quietly.)* Well, I don't know. I think he's probably bisexual, but I don't think he's gay...

(Loud knocking, sound of a door opening. Two teenage Baptists are outside.)

BAPTIST 1. Um, hi I'm from the Ridgecrest Baptist Church on Vaughn, and I just wanted to ask if you would participate in a short survey? Um, first of all what is your name? Hi, Maria. What do you do for a living? Ok. Um how often do you go to church? Ok. If you were to die today do you think you would go to Heaven? Ok, well I can tell you how you would be sure. All you have to do is ask God and he will get you there. Would you like to ask God for his salvation? OK, well, take your time. You have all our information there.

BAPTIST 2. Maria, I don't want to interrupt, but sometimes people don't know how easy it is. We Christians are always yelling about this or that and sometimes people don't understand how easy it is to get into Heaven. Like, I'll use an analogy: if I had a million dollars in my hand, and I wanted to give it to you, it was a gift. Everybody likes the money. As an actress, what would you have to do to get it? *(MARIA responds: As an actress?)* You, as a person. No, you could just take it. It's a gift and that's what God is doing. It's scary how easy it is.

(Several car doors slam shut. Tires screech as the car drives away.)

IT'S SCARY HOW EASY IT IS

IT'S SCARY HOW EASY IT IS
IT'S SCARY HOW EASY IT IS
IT'S SCARY HOW EASY IT IS

THE ROSENBERGS JUST GOT LIFE WITHOUT PAROLE
KISSINGER ADMITTING THAT HE HAS NO SOUL
PATTY HEARST SHOOTING FROM THE GRASSY KNOLL
ALIENS GIVING PEOPLE BIRTH CONTROL
I WOULDN'T BE SURPRISED,
OH, NO
I WOULDN'T BE SURPRISED,
OH, NO
I WOULDN'T BE SURPRISED,
OH, NO
I WOULDN'T BE SURPRISED,
OH, NO

ENTITY. You want to know why there is so much fear in your society now. Now think, are you not more secure and less violent than you have ever been? I will tell you a hundred years ago in the city where you live people carried guns on their hips and shot each other with impunity. Your people are in fact in less violent now, but still you are very afraid. Yes? So then— Why?

> PRIESTS TOUCHING ALTAR BOYS IS NOT OK
> CASTRO NEVER COULD GET OVER CHE
> MY BOYFRIEND WAS EXPOSED BY THE CIA
> BUT HE NEVER REALLY LOVED ME ANYWAY

> I WOULDN'T BE SURPRISED,
> OH, NO
> I WOULDN'T BE SURPRISED,
> OH, NO
> I WOULDN'T BE SURPRISED,
> OH, NO
> I WOULDN'T BE SURPRISED,
> OH, NO

(Phone Rings.)

JESSICA LYNCH MIDDLETON. Hi. Yep this is Jessica. What? Look, I really don't know, OK? I didn't watch any of the war coverage or anything, on TV or anything. Uh, I didn't watch ANY of the news. I just, don't care to be involved with that. And if…LOOK. THIS IS REALLY WEIRD. THIS. This QUESTIONING. Well, I think it's really WEIRD. What, what are you… You're just calling EVERY Jessica Lynch in the phone book. Is that it? What does it matter what I think, I'm not her. It's a common name. There are two more in MIDDLETON, even. THAT I KNOW OF!

ENTITY. And it is so easy to encourage you to feel this panic in your body because you think you are all on your own yes? And who will protect you? This would not happen if you still lived in a tribe. Because tribe is about survival. But for you, your tribes are now so very small, first nuclear families and now mere couples. This is too small a tribe. If you remove one member of a two member tribe there is no tribe. You understand? Yes.

> JOHN F. KENNEDY'S A MAJOR WHORE
> WAR AGAINST THE NAZIS WAS A RIGHTEOUS WAR
> DIPLOMATIC POLICY'S A REAL BORE
> WE DON'T DO THAT SORT OF THING ANYMORE

JESSICA LYNCH MIDDLETON. Wait, WHAT?!? Who said that? I have never heard anyone say it wasn't true. Wait, are they saying there was no Jessica Lynch AT ALL? Or, oh, just that it maybe didn't happen the way they said it did. I don't know. I've never heard that. But, you know, I wouldn't be surprised.

IT'S SCARY HOW EASY IT IS
IT'S SCARY HOW EASY IT IS
IT'S SCARY HOW EASY IT IS

ENTITY. Fear is a highly energetic emotion. Now let us say that you are a being who is not physical, but has an energetic body, you understand? You would have to eat energy, yes? The Annunaki feed off the energy of fear. They are creatures of pure energy and to them our fear is like food? You understand? *(Implied: No. The WHAT?)* The Annunaki. No, my boy, they are invisible to you. They were left behind on your planet by a compendium of beings from other star systems. You see the Annunaki were meant to assist humankind by giving you certain technologies and so they have, but they misused their position. They say here come and plant your crops in one place don't gather and hunt, you understand? Then they said oh come and live in these little towns—you call them cities we call them corrals. All of these are mechanisms to simply generate mmm when you have a cow now you give them hormones to make them milk more. Think of it like that. They are farming you.

(The door of the theater opens. HOUSE MANAGER *returns with the bag. Leaves it on stage and exits.)*

PERFORMER. But—

(PERFORMER moving the bag around from place to place backstage, other Performers ejecting it. Finally PERFORMER brings the bag to the audience and places it in front of the front row.)

PERFORMER. *(To someone in front row:)* Thank you. Thanks so much. *(To the backstage:)* Ok!

(Performers set up the next scene.)

PERFORMER 1. Yeah. So now we're just going to read a bit of, uh…this is something we found in *Newsweek. Newsweek* magazine.

(PERFORMER 2 reads Newsweek *magazine:)*

"Khaled el-Masri had a hard time getting people to believe him. Even his wife didn't know what to make of his abrupt, five-month disappearance last year. Masri, a German citizen of Lebanese descent…taken off a bus in Macedonia while on holiday," etc. etc. "Says he was then flown to Afghanistan, where at a U.S. prison facility he was shackled, repeatedly punched and questioned… released months later, the still-mystified Masri was deposited on a deserted road, where he brokenly tried to describe his nightmarish odyssey to a border guard. The guard responded by saying: 'Don't tell that story to anyone because no one will believe it. Everyone will laugh.'" etc. "The CIA…" etc. "clandestine interrogation facilities" etc. "Global 'ghost' prison system," etc. And well, then there's more…

PERFORMER 1. And this is from Cathy O'Brien she wrote *Trance Formation of America The True Life Story of a CIA Mind Control Slave* by Cathy O'Brien. We found her book on the internet and we're quoting–

PERFORMER 3. Probably I'll paraphrase a little—

PERFORMER 1. But—right—but quoting basically. *Trance Formation of America*...

(PERFORMER 3 *reads Cathy O'Brien.*)

"At that time, I was a 19-year-old mind-controlled programmed sex slave in the CIA Project Monarch Freedom Train operation." And moving ahead...

"President Bush claimed to be a hybrid between a lizard-like alien and humans. And during my prostitution in the oval office he changed into a lizard right before my eyes which was terrifying at the time, but now I know he'd just activated a hologram inside my mind..." OK, then...

"Jimmy Buffett told me to me to take the duffel bag full of drugs to the CIA agent and then I was to come back to the Inn and join the buffet. But first Buffett unzipped his shorts and said to me "Do you like a buffet? I have a Buffett buffet for you now."

PERFORMER 1. Ok, so the story from *Newsweek*... This is a more recent update from *The Washington Post.*

PERFORMER 2. A federal judge yesterday threw out the case of a German citizen...Khaled el-Masri... ...The judge stated that the remedy cannot be found in the courts. Masri's "private interests must give way to the national interest in preserving state secrets."

PERFORMER 1.

—Do you think Khaled el Masri's story is true?
—Do you think Cathy O'Brien's story is true?
—Do you think we can talk to aliens?
—Do you think the CIA is kidnapping people?

(*Explosions.*)

WATCH OUT LADIES

DIIRU BAALKUM YA SITAT
Watch out ladies
IR-RAJUL IL-GHARIIB
The alien man
HUWA BITGHAZA `ALA KHOOFKUM
Is feeding on your fear

DIIRU BAALKUM YA SITAT
Watch out ladies
IR-RAJUL IL-GHARIIB
The alien man

BIDDU YAGHIISH JIWATKUM
Is going to inhabit you
IR-RAJUL IL-BRIZGA IL-'IMLAQ
The giant lizard man

STUDENT. You mean Guantanamo? I think they might do what *they* think is torture. You know, things that *they* feel are torture—I mean they think that they feel are things that are torture.

SOLDIER. Let me tell you something about Guantanamo. They get hot meals, showers, it's air conditioned. That other crap that's just the news. Trust me, I've seen it. I know.

INTABIHU YA SITAT
Beware ladies
HUWA JAY
He's coming
YIMKIN HUWA HOON
Maybe he's already here

DIIRU BAALKUM YA SITAT
Beware ladies
HUWA JAY
He's coming
HUWA BIDDU YA KHAWWIFKUM
He wants you to be afraid
IR-RAJUL IL-BRIZGA IL-'IMLAQ
The giant lizard man

MAN WITH AUSTRALIAN ACCENT. Once someone gets out like my brothers they tell me they poured hot water on their heads. They stuck a nail in between their fingernails pulling on their polly wacker and hitting the shit out of it with a stick you know on top of the table…oh yes oh yes

LATINO TEXAN IN NEW YORK. Look we only know what the media gives us. We didn't see it so we can't know these so-called torture victims are innocent. We didn't see these detainees *not* do anything. So now, post 9/11, there's a necessity to hold people until they are proven, without a doubt that they are innocent—

TIGHRAFEE WHEN IBNIC
Do you know where your child is?
TIGHRAFEE WHEN UTITIC
Do you know where your cat is?

LA, LA, LA, LA, LA, LA.
La, la, la, la, la, la.

WOMAN IN NEW YORK. But if America says it stands for human rights, then I don't think they can just justify torturing people? But I feel both sides.

I feel bad for the people being tortured, but then my patriotism kicks in, and I wonder how we could do these things without a good reason. The government must know that they know something. Hopefully, they're really sure that they know something.

> DIIRU BAALKUM YA SITAT
> *Beware ladies*
> HUWA JAY
> *He's coming*
> HUWA BIDU YA KHAWWIFKUM
> *He wants you to get freedom*
> IR-RAJUL IL-BRIZGA IL-'IMLAQ
> *The cheerful and free man*
>
> LA, LA, LA,LA, LA, LA.
> *La, la, la, la, la, la*
>
> *(Meows from the bag. PERFORMER retrieves bag from audience. Horrible, sick, angry cat sounds. Then, silence.)*

PERFORMER. It's quiet now.

> *(Pause.)*

Do you think that means it's…?

OTHER PERFORMER. *(About to play* ENTITY:*)* I don't know.

PERFORMER. Or…

> *(*PERFORMER *shakes bag to test, nothing.)*

Oh god.

> *(Seems that the cat is dead. No one opens the bag.)*

ENTITY. Each time that the Annunaki have given you a new technology that generates fear there has also been a sweet cookie at the end of it. Because the Annunaki are very wise farmers. So what appears in American homes literally in coincidence with the atom bomb? The television. The television when it's introduced it is not full of mayhem and war it's full of Ozzie and Harriet and Milton Berle and it's very entertaining very fun a place for the family to gather but then soon within a few years there is a newscast then two a day then three a day four a day and now you have stations that only play news. And how does the news make you feel? Yes, you understand.

TEENAGE ASPIRING PIERCER. Yeah. Ok. Sixteen. So what do you want to ask me?

SPECIAL ED ASSISTANT. I work in special ed in a public high school. A lot of the work I do is just physical, manual labor, like opening doors for wheelchairs or helping the kids move around. I think I am going to try and go to law school though. I'm too confrontational and analytical to be dealing with kids. Besides, dealing with kids with special needs—their lack of progress is…just boring. I live in Queens too, the high school is just down the block from my apartment. No, I don't want to talk about my roommates. My apartment is, like, my own personal Guantanamo.

TEENAGE ASPIRING PIERCER. Ok. Well, we're all gonna die someday, if it's going to be some stupid terrorist fuckface who cares? Like my boyfriend he just thinks we should bomb them all, kill them all. Afghanistan, Iraq, whatever, he thinks we should just kill them all.

SPECIAL ED ASSISTANT. Remember Cheney had that secret energy task force? And, there were, apparently, documents and papers that discussed the fact that we are running out of oil so I think they used 9/11 as an excuse to occupy a country that is oil rich. Yeah, of course Iraq backfired. I know that but I don't think they knew that it would. Are you purposefully being adversarial?

TEENAGE ASPIRING PIERCER. I'd like to be a body piercer. You can make a lot of money that way. *(Pointing to ear:)* I did all of these myself. Yeah, I have four more. They're in supersecret places.

SUPERSECRET PLACES

I'M STARING UP AT THE TV SCREEN
FLASHING BLUE, AND RED AND GREEN
SOMEBODY SAVE ME
I SEE THEM TELLING ALL THE THINGS WE'VE
    LEARNED
ALL THE CITIES THAT HAVE BURNED
SOMEBODY SAVE THEM
I HAVE SEEN THE PHOTOGENIC FACES
I HAVE SEEN THE SPEEDING HIGHWAY CHASES
I WISH I COULD EVER KNOW WHAT GRACE IS
WILL I KNOW
WILL I KNOW
I WANT TO DIE FOR SOMETHING
I WANT TO DIE FOR SOMETHING
I WANT TO DIE FOR SOMETHING
CAUSE THERE'S NOTHING FOR ME HERE.

(Cell phone rings.)

TEENAGE ASPIRING PIERCER. Hold on. Sorry. Hey. Yeah. Nothing. I'm not. What? I'm not. I'm not. I'm not. I'll tell you when you get here. I'm being interviewed. I'll tell you when you get here. *(Hangs up.)* That was my boyfriend. He said I sounded like I was pissed about something.

SPECIAL ED ASSISTANT. Look, I'm not a pacifist. I think that there are times when torture is justifiable but only after the person is tried and convicted. Like, maybe, after the Nuremberg trials, I might have condoned the torturing of Goering and Hess.

(He starts to cry.)

Why are you asking me this?

I don't know if I want to continue talking about this.

I don't know, I don't know. I think I just have to be psychologically prepared to talk about torture.

I think I am drunker than I thought I was.

(Sung by PIERCER:*)*
I'M STARING UP AT THE TV SCREEN
WAITING IN THE DARK UNSEEN
SOMEBODY SAVE ME
I'M LEARNING SLOWLY HOW TO SEE THE SIGNS
HOW THEY HIDE BETWEEN THE LINES
SOMEBODY SAVE THEM
I HAVE LEARNED TO READ THE EMPTY SPACES
I'VE BEEN PIERCED IN SUPERSECRET PLACES
*(*SPECIAL ED *joins.)*
I'VE BEEN PIERCED IN SUPERSECRET PLACES
(Sung by SPECIAL ED *only:)*
I WANT TO DIE FOR SOMETHING
I WANT TO DIE FOR SOMETHING
I WANT TO DIE FOR SOMETHING
CAUSE THERE'S NOTHING FOR ME HERE.

SPECIAL ED ASSISTANT. It's ok. Yeah what else do you want ask me? What?! I don't give a fuck about Tom Cruise! I mean who gives a shit? He's a terrible actor…although he was okay in Born on the 4th of July. No, actually, he was pretty good in that. He was pretty intense, it's kind of an intense movie, he did give it his all, I guess I'll give him credit for doing that movie. Fuck! Now, you have me obsessing over Tom Cruise!

(Ring.)

J LYNCH. Hello yes this is J Lynch. No, Jacqueline. Jacqueline Lynch. I'm a writer, I'm a ghost writer. Well, I won't answer all your questions. Why don't you just start and I'll answer what I, you know, what I think is appropriate. I don't feel comfortable telling you what I write. I'm a ghost writer. What do you mean 'my information?' What do you mean by that? I try not to watch the news lately because I am recovering from cancer and I need to focus on getting well. And I don't believe hardly anything I read in the newspapers. Well, because you can't—everybody's got an opinion. They're writers. It's like when you're writing, you just…*go*. Sometimes you got it, sometimes you don't, and when you got it it just comes. It just comes outta ya like a *dancer*. No I'm not afraid at all. I don't have time for all those negative thoughts. I meditate. I read my Bible. It's bad enough being poor, what do I want to walk around afraid on top of that? And you're in a theater company? What? Off-Broadway? Broadway? Well, I hope it's very successful. Just keep thinking positive thoughts and you'll get through it! Ok, bye!

ENTITY. My dear boy I will tell you something important which you must share with your audience. You humans are too easy with your guidance. You go to the Ouija board or whatever listening to the spirits, to whatever energy with no idea who you are talking to, whether they mean you good or ill. You notice before we started she said, "Only positive energies may speak through me" whereas most of you humans merely say, "Somebody talk to me."

(A panel with three panelists: REMOTE VIEWER, SOLDIER, GUY IN LA.*)*

REMOTE VIEWER. Well, this is a remarkable thing. With Remote Viewing you can find the absolute truth. Whatever you want to know, we call that the "target." I was trained in TRV—technical remote viewing—which is a technique that was originally developed in the military about twenty years ago to find out things like what the KGB was up to.

SOLDIER. I'm in the National Guard. Yeah. We're posted here to look for terrorists. I can't tell you that. Well, this is my post, Penn Station. We're also at Grand Central, Times Square, you know anywhere that's a potential target. Could I ask you something? Why'd you choose me? Are you just interviewing anybody? Oh, so I should feel special. You know, to be honest, we're basically here just to instill confidence in people, to get them out using public transportation, going out to public buildings. I'll tell you something, this gun isn't even loaded.

REMOTE VIEWER. Ok, you want to know how it works? So, say some guy has a lost cat, OK, let's say the cat's name is Wendy, he'll write down the word "Wendy" and maybe the word "lost", and then he'll put that in an envelope. That's called "setting the intent," and on the front of the envelope he'll write down a series of eight random numbers, and then he'll file that envelope and give me that target and I'll do a session. No, I won't get the name of the cat. All I know about the target is the eight random numbers. Right, just the numbers. You can't be given any specifics about the case, otherwise that will interfere with the universal consciousness. When you're in a session, at first I'll get a lot of sounds and images and colors, umm, maybe textures. Say Wendy was lost in the desert you might get "flat, brown, hot, gritty," umm, "HORIZONTAL." But see my physical self is still doing the exercises. Hm? Because you have to keep the imagination at bay. Like here's an example, my mother disappeared back in 1980. It was categorized as a homicide, but the case is still open—

SOLDIER. Hold on. He doesn't think I should be talking to you. He says you could be taping it. Well, when we talk to people usually it's not like this. We're not supposed to get too in depth with civilians.

(He exits. Awkward silence.)

REMOTE VIEWER. And well this one time, this friend of mine and I agreed to trade targets, so I sent him my mother. And when I went into a session, about fifteen minutes into it, I realized that he'd sent me the exact same target I'd sent him. Yeah. I started getting this image of skeletal shoulders and a skeletal neck. And then I got a face and I just knew it was my mother. Oh no, I wasn't upset at all. I thought it was really neat. But see that's the thing as soon as I realized it was my mother, all my preconceived ideas about what had happened to her started coming in, and I had to stop.

GUY IN LA. My friend went to a private screening at his house of *The Last Samurai*. There were only six people there at the theater that he has in his house. So they are all watching the film and at the end when the lights came up, Tom Cruise, who had apparently been watching from behind them came down to the front and he had taken his shirt off and he was all sweaty and he was crying and he made that motion that he made during the couch jumping Oprah incident, where he kneels down on one knee and pulls his fist down from the air in front of his face and then he says "I just get so pumped!" No one knew where to look. I mean it wasn't a public appearance or anything. It was his house! What are you supposed to say after that?

SONG OF PROGRESSIVE DISENCHANTMENT

I ONCE HAD A FRIEND NAMED SALLY,
WHO ENDED HER LIFE IN AN ALLEY.
SHE BELIEVED IN NOTHING AT ALL
SHE BELIEVED IN NOTHING AT ALL.
YOU COULD SAY THAT HER LIFE WAS, WELL, SCREWED
    UP.
EVEN SHE SAID, "AH, HOW I'VE BEEN CHEWED UP."
SO I ASKED HER, "SALLY, WHAT DID YOU DO?"
I SAID "SALLY, WHAT THE HELL HAVE YOU BEEN
    THROUGH?"

AND SO SHE TOLD ME WHAT HAPPENED…

AT FIRST YOU SEARCH FOR THE TRUTH
IT STEALS THE BLOOM OF YOUR YOUTH
YOU TAKE YOUR GIN AND VERMOUTH CHILLED WITH
    A TWIST.
WHEN YOUR LOVER SAYS "I'M RIGHT" HE'S RIGHT,
WHEN HE WANTS TO SPEND THE NIGHT HE SPENDS
    THE NIGHT,
WHEN THE BARMAN SAYS "YOU'RE TIGHT" YOU'RE
    TIGHT.
YOU DON'T RESIST.

AND ALL THE KNOWLEDGE
YOU GOT IN COLLEGE
KEEPS YOU PRISTINE
YOUR HANDS ARE CLEAN.
(UNTIL YOU WAKE UP PREGNANT AND STINKING OF
    DEWARS.)
AND NOW YOUR YOUTH, GONE.
AND THE VERMOUTH, GONE.
WHERE IS THAT TRUTH YOU TRUSTED SO?
JUST WAIT YOUR TURN, PET
AND SOON YOU'LL LEARN PET,
YOU'LL BE THE ONE TO SAY,
"I TOLD YOU SO."

IN BUDAPEST OR WAS IT TALLAHASSEE?
YOU TOLD ME PRETTY LIES, JOHNNY,
AND BROKE MY HEART INTO SO MANY LITTLE PIECES
JOHNNY, YOU BASTARD
TAKE THAT FUCKING NICORETTE GUM OUT OF YOUR
    MOUTH
CREEP.

ENTITY. My boy, you are distressed because you want to have some magic way to know the truth and so you suffer because you see there is NO ABSOLUTE TRUTH. There is only *authenticity*.

YOUNG REPUBLICAN. Truth is…is there one truth? Well, I think truth is whatever the majority believes is true. If the majority of people believe that Osama Bin Laden is an evil man—there are some that might believe otherwise, and people are entitled to that opinion. But it does go against the accepted truth. So, right if enough people believe something is true, then it becomes true, to a certain degree.

REMOTE VIEWER A. When I do a remote viewing session I bi-locate— bi-locate, that's what we call it, because one half of you is in the room doing the exercises and the other half of you is off in the matrix gathering information.

   (In the following the underlined sections indicate a phrase that is shared by two or more actors.)

REMOTE VIEWER B. <u>If you think that the universe</u> is like a giant library, then I just find the right <u>book and open it up!</u>

REMOTE VIEWER A. It's all based on the Jungian system. <u>Have you heard of gestalt?</u>

YOUNG REPUBLICAN A. I believe that. I believe there is a <u>reasonable case</u> for

YOUNG REPUBLICAN B. weapons of <u>mass destruction</u>.

REMOTE VIEWER A. Umm, Well, I try to <u>avoid politics</u>, umm, you know,

REMOTE VIEWER B. because the <u>thing</u> about <u>politics</u> is

YOUNG REPUBLICAN A. Think of it this way: <u>Do you believe Hitler existed?</u>

YOUNG REPUBLICAN B. Do you? <u>You do</u>. Why?

REMOTE VIEWER B. I'm more <u>interested in morals</u>. And to me, life is about

REMOTE VIEWER A. being <u>alert</u> and <u>awake</u> and <u>present</u>

YOUNG REPUBLICAN A. We never found his body. We only have <u>pictures of him</u>, records of things

YOUNG REPUBLICAN B. he did. So are we to suppose that he <u>might not have existed?</u>

REMOTE VIEWER A. You know after 9/11

YOUNG REPUBLICAN A. It's the same with weapons of <u>mass destruction.</u> We <u>had photos.</u>

REMOTE VIEWER B. we tried to figure out where the next <u>terrorist attack would be</u>

YOUNG REPUBLICAN B. Why would we <u>assume that they</u> are no longer there?

REMOTE VIEWER A. and I found those sessions very <u>draining</u> and very <u>depressing</u>

YOUNG REPUBLICAN A. And <u>I don't mind about the Patriot Act.</u>

REMOTE VIEWER B. So I try to <u>avoid politics</u>

YOUNG REPUBLICAN B. I want the government checking up on people who go to *internet sites* where people can learn to <u>make bombs.</u>

REMOTE VIEWER A. and just concentrate on the <u>present</u>, and what it means to <u>alive</u>.

YOUNG REPUBLICAN A. I mean, have your civil rights been violated? <u>No. Me neither.</u>

SONG OF PROGRESSIVE DISENCHANTMENT PART II

AND SO I SAID SALLY AFTER THE TRUTH WHAT NEXT?
SO THEN YOU LOOK FOR THE LIE,
YOUR LIFE GOES FLYING ON BY,
YOU TAKE YOUR GIN VERY DRY, AND JUST ONE SHOT.
WHEN YOUR LOVER SAYS "I'M RIGHT" HE'S NOT,
WHEN HE WANTS TO SPEND THE NIGHT, YOU SAY "I'D
    RATHER ROT."
WHEN THE BARMAN SAYS "YOU'RE TIGHT" YOU FIGHT,
    IT'S ALL A PLOT!

AND YOU ENJOY THE
NEW PARANOIA
IT FEELS PRISTINE
YOUR HANDS STAY CLEAN.
(UNTIL YOU LOOK AROUND AND WONDER WHY
    YOU'RE SO ALONE.)
AND NOW YOU DARE ADMIT
THAT YOU DON'T CARE A BIT
WHAT OF THOSE LIES YOU TRUSTED SO?
JUST WAIT YOUR TURN, SWEET.
AND SOON YOU'LL LEARN, SWEET,
YOU'LL BE THE ONE TO SAY,
"I TOLD YOU SO."

IN SIDI BOU SAID, OR WAS IT TALLAHASSEE?
YOU NEVER CAME, JOHNNY
YOU'RE STILL THE SAME,
TAKE THAT FUCKING GUM OUT OF YOUR MOUTH YOU
    DOG!

ENTITY. My boy yes of course there is no absolute truth but still you must insist on the truth. You must participate in the truth. And this is not something you can do by yourself, yes? You understand? Do you understand?

FORMER CULT GIRL. Yeah, Tom Cruise is definitely gay. He is gay, he is totally gay. Well, he's in a cult too, right?

CABBIE. The other day, I saw Ethan Hawke and his girl, I picked em up, he's not with his wife—yeah, his kid looks old enough just about to understand

FORMER CULT GIRL. Or maybe he's bi. With Nicole Kidman…I'm sure he felt some measure of attraction towards her. And they had two kids.

CABBIE. You know, your marriage is shitty, but you gotta have two kids just to be sure before you break up. Fuckin mess, yeah. I gotta kid—and she's got me over the balls cuz she knows how much I love this kid. She's a sick fucking bitch. The kid's one and a half, so I figure I got till she's three then I can get the hell out.

FORMER CULT GIRL. Oh, they're adopted? I didn't know that. Well, there you go.

CABBIE. Do I think what's over? Being scared? Nah. See the thing we gotta worry about now is the germ warfare.

FORMER CULT GIRL. But it's just like Bush! He's still totally snorting coke and a complete alcoholic. Sure! Apparently he's still throwing all these parties at his ranch. He's still doing coke. I mean, look at him. He can't even wear a suit he's like (*Mimics George Bush awkwardness.*).

CABBIE. But in Israel, the reason they don't use biological <u>germ warfare</u> is cuz it's right next door. You're not gonna spread <u>smallpox</u> to your <u>neighbor.</u> Like, that's why I'm not gonna kill my wife, cuz if I <u>kill my wife,</u> that's gonna <u>affect my kid,</u> and if it <u>affects my kid,</u> then it's gonna <u>affect me.</u>

FORMER CULT GIRL. And Laura Bush is a total pothead. Yeah! It's insane.

CABBIE. But, I tell you, if anything <u>happened to my kid,</u> I wouldn't <u>care what happened to</u> *me*—I'd sacrifice myself, kill myself. Probably what's gonna happen <u>if I leave her, or she'll leave me</u>—cuz that is one <u>sick bitch,</u> man, <u>sick bitch.</u> And, I was so careful for so many years. And now I got a <u>kid with this insane bitch.</u>

FORMER CULT GIRL. America's a brand. America has branded itself. And we're trying to sell this brand <u>to the rest of the world.</u> Who believes in any of this <u>crap they're spewing?</u> God! <u>It's like a film!</u> But who's the film going to be shown to? <u>Ourselves? The world? Have you ever read Noam</u> Chomsky?

SONG OF PROGRESSIVE DISENCHANTMENT PART III

SO FINALLY YOU JUST UP AND QUIT,
THERE'S NO REASON TO PAY ATTENTION TO THIS
    SHIT,
YOU DRINK YOUR GIN AS YOU LEARN TO KNIT AN-
    OTHER SWEATER.
WHEN YOU LOVER SAYS "I'M RIGHT" YOU SAY, "I
    WOULDN'T BE SURPRISED"
WHEN HE WANTS TO SPEND THE NIGHT YOU SAY "I
    WOULDN'T BE SURPRISED"
TO THE BARMAN YOU SAY,
"GIVE A ME A WHISKEY AND DON'T BE STINGY, BABY,
    THE MORE THE BETTER."
YOU TAKE FOR GRANTED
THAT YOU'LL BE DISENCHANTED.
YOU'RE FAR PAST 30.
YOUR HANDS ARE DIRTY.
(AND NOW YOU LOOK AROUND AND WONDER WHAT
    YOU HAVE TO SHOW FOR IT ALL.)
AND THOUGH YOU'VE TRIED THINGS
YOU'VE STAYED OUTSIDE THINGS.
AND WHAT YOU REAP YOU'RE SURE TO SOW.
WHAT DID YOU LEARN, LOVE?
NOW IT'S YOUR TURN LOVE!
TO HEAR ME SAY TO YOU,
"I TOLD YOU SO."

ENTITY. The Annunaki are not good or evil, they are merely hungry, you understand? And yes, you are being manipulated by them but what can you do? I will tell you my boy. All beings have free will. And so if you refuse to be afraid they will have to live off some other kind of energy. If all of your cows died you would have to learn how to live on pork. And so it will be with you and the Annunaki. But you must exert your free will. So the next time you feel this anxiety, this fear energy in your body you must stop and say out loud, "NO. I am nobody's lunch today."

(ENTITY *leaves the* CHANNELER's *body.*)

CHANNELER. Trippy, huh?

(FORMER HOMELAND SECURITY *and* EGYPTIAN FORMER GRAD STUDENT.)

FORMER HOMELAND SECURITY. I left Homeland Security in, let's see…Spring 2004.

(*Ring.*)

EGYPTIAN FORMER GRAD STUDENT. Yeah Hello.

FORMER HOMELAND SECURITY. When did you interview me?

EGYPTIAN FORMER GRAD STUDENT. Salaam aleikem. What? No. I'm not dating anyone now.

FORMER HOMELAND SECURITY. A LOT has changed since then! (*Laugh.*)

EGYPTIAN FORMER GRAD STUDENT. My girlfriend and I split up about six months ago.

FORMER HOMELAND SECURITY. I'm getting married! That's the big one. And I'm in grad school now, /studying public policy.

EGYPTIAN FORMER GRAD STUDENT. Ah, ah, ah I finished my PhD last year. Shukran habibi. My parents are very proud.

FORMER HOMELAND SECURITY. Yeah. (*Laugh.*) It's a little different from when we last talked. When I started crying more than two or three times a week /I knew it was time to go.

EGYPTIAN FORMER GRAD STUDENT. I think you have to be hopeful…otherwise what's the point?

FORMER HOMELAND SECURITY. Wow. I do have hope now. Not for the U.S. Things in the US are even worse and I see no end in sight, but working with communities outside of the U.S. has given me a lot of hope.

EGYPTIAN FORMER GRAD STUDENT. OK…OK…listen I have to go…yes…yes…Inshallah…Maisallame

FORMER HOMELAND SECURITY. I'm working with people who don't know where their next meal is coming from. For example, the Gabbra Tribe? G. A. BB. R. A. They live across the southern Ethiopian and Northern Kenyan border? They're a nomadic community living between two not terribly tolerant states. And they have become so creative in dealing with their crisis. They set up mobile schools, and they're writing grants to fly in nomadic communities from Iran to teach them...well...this new way...to make cheese balls. So that their food supply lasts longer. Yeah.

(*Question.*)

Oh, of course the US is torturing people. There've been a number of indicators for quite a while now, that people haven't paid attention to. Well, when information is available and people don't respond in a way that creates a demand for more, it just disappears.

YOUNG MAN IN NEW YORK. I hate Bush. I hate him. I think that he is mean, but I have a secret confession to make and this has nothing to do with how I feel, but I think that Bush is gorgeous-looking. He is a hunky villain, and I have to say that he is manly, he has a good body build, and he dresses very well. I hate him. I hate his guts. I can distinguish the outside from the inside and one has nothing to do with the other, but he is a hunk of flesh.

I told you I have a very hard time with reading comprehension. Asperger's people are more left-brained than right-brained which means we're very good at anything that involves rules or language and not so good at things like reading comprehension, social clues and world knowledge. Like I'm not good at inferring things. For some reason it's not the same with entertainment news. I pick it up; it's in the air around me. But see what I am trying to do now is to learn how to distinguish the language of *Melrose Place* from the language of the real world.

Ok. Here's an example of truths. Learning that you are not the center of the universe. That's a truth that's very hard to learn. One night I woke up and I was thinking to myself we are one small planet surrounded by eight other planets and all these other galaxies, and I am as a grain of sand. And that scared me. That scared me for a very long time. It was just a mood. I'm not saying it haunted me for years or whatever. The idea that I am just a little mosquito. A little mosquito or a grain of sand. Although it did haunt me for a good few years.

AMERICA

YOU TOLD ME YOU'D TAKE ME UNDER YOUR WING,
YOU TOLD ME WHY ALL THE CHRISTIANS SING,
YOU TOLD ME I HAD TO DO SOMETHING IT WAS NO
    SIN...
YOU SAID I FELT SO YOUNG INSIDE,
YOU TOLD ME WHY LENNY BRUCE HAD DIED,
YOU TOLD ME TO JUST OPEN WIDE, AND LET YOU IN.

YOU ASKED ME, DO YOU UNDERSTAND?
YOU ASKED ME, DO YOU UNDERSTAND?
YOU ASKED ME, DO YOU UNDERSTAND?
AND OH AMERICA, OH AMERICA, OH AMERICA, YOU
PROMISED LAND.

YOU TOLD ME YOUR WAY WAS THE ONLY WAY,
YOU TOLD ME THAT TOM CRUISE WAS GAY,
YOU TOLD ME IF I DIDN'T STAY THAT IT WOULD WARP
US.
YOU TOOK ME AS THEY MARCHED ON SELMA,
YOU TOOK ME AS WE WATCHED SCOOBY AND VELMA,
YOU TOOK ME AS YOU OVERWHELMED MY HABEAS
CORPUS.

YOU ASKED ME, DO YOU UNDERSTAND?
YOU ASKED ME, DO YOU UNDERSTAND?
YOU ASKED ME, DO YOU UNDERSTAND?
AND OH AMERICA, OH AMERICA, OH AMERICA, YOU
PROMISED LAND.

YOU LEFT ME AT THE BERLIN WALL,
YOU LEFT ME WATCHING LUCY BALL,
YOU LEFT ME IN THE MEN'S ROOM STALL WITHOUT
WARNING.
I WAITED FOR YOU TO COME INTO SIGHT,
I GAVE UP WHEN THE DAWN TURNED WHITE,
AND NOW I SEE THE COLD CLEAR LIGHT OF THE
MORNING.

I'M ASKING, DO YOU UNDERSTAND?
I'M ASKING, DO YOU UNDERSTAND?
I'M ASKING, DO YOU UNDERSTAND?
AND OH AMERICA, OH AMERICA, OH AMERICA,

I LOVED YOU AT THE TRAIL OF TEARS
I LOVED YOU ON THE SET OF CHEERS
I LOVED YOU FACING ALL MY FEARS.
WASN'T THAT YOU?

(Ring.)

JESSICA LYNCH MISS NEW YORK. Oh. No. It's so funny you should ask because. Do you know who…? I'm Jessica Lynch. I just won Miss New York. Thank you! I'm really excited. I've actually been thinking of writing her a letter. Well, you know, I'd express that we are so happy she's returned home safely and, you know, we share the same name but not the same experiences. But that she is a real American hero.

SCHRODINGER'S CAT

MALE SOLO.

I'VE BEEN THINKING A LOT ABOUT PEOPLE IN LOVE
WHY THEY TEND TO BELIEVE THINGS THEY KNOW
    CAN'T BE REAL,
THEY ACCEPT CONTRADICTIONS THAT COME FROM
    ABOVE
WITHOUT QUESTION LIKE INNOCENTS AND THEY
    FEEL THEY'RE STARING INTO FOG
WHEN THEY'RE ONLY SEEING OUT OF FOCUS SO...

I'VE BEEN THINKING HOW LOVE IS LIKE SCHROD-
    INGER'S CAT
LOCKED UP TIGHT OUT OF SIGHT IN A BOX AND HOW
    THAT
MEANS IT'S DEAD AND ALIVE AT THE SAME TIME AND
    SO—
WHEN YOU THINK OF THE BOX IT'S LIKE SEEING A
PHOTO OF A CLOUD OR FOG
IT'S AN OUTCOME THAT REMAINS UNCERTAIN
YOU CAN'T SEE A THING IN ALL THAT FOG
YOU CAN'T SEE A MAN BEHIND THE CURTAIN.

FEMALE SOLO.

WHAT ARE YOU SO AFRAID OF?
WE'RE GONNA FIND AN ANSWER, IT'S JUST AROUND
    THE CORNER AND I KNOW...
WHAT ARE YOU SO AFRAID OF?
WE'RE GONNA FIND AN ANSWER, FIND AN ANSWER...

CHORUS.

DON'T YOU WANT TO BE
    IN LOVE?
DON'T YOU WANT A LOVE
    THAT'S TRUE?
DON'T YOU WANT TO FEEL
    IT'S TRUE IN YOUR
    HEART?
WOULDN'T IT BE GREAT TO
    BE YOUNG?
WOULDN'T IT BE GREAT TO
    BELIEVE?

JESSICA LYNCH MISS NEW YORK. *(Speaks:)* I'm doing an inter view for the WB tomorrow. These questions are so not the questions... They usually ask stuff like "So you're Miss New York, what's it like." The questions I get are, I don't know. Simple. I hate to say it, but they are. It's never like "How do you think Bush is doing?" There's this stereo type of us all that we're just pretty girls and we sit around in our pretty

WOULDN'T IT BE GREAT TO
    BELIEVE FROM THE
    START?

dresses and talk about pretty things. And let me tell you I am not a supporter of this war— *(Phone disconnects.)* Hello?

MALE SOLO.
    BUT QUANTUM PHYSICS DOES NOT, DR. SCHRODINGER SAID,
    CORRESPOND WITH THE LITERAL WORLD THAT WE'VE SEEN
    WE ALL KNOW THAT A CAT MUST BE LIVING OR DEAD

    IT CAN'T BE BOTH AT ONCE, THERE'S A DIFFERENCE
    BETWEEN AN IMAGE MADE OF FOG
    AND AN IMAGE THAT'S JUST OUT OF FOCUS
    WHAT YOU HAVE'S A CAT LOCKED IN A BOX
    AND THERE ISN'T ANY HOCUS POCUS SO…
    I'VE BEEN THINKING ABOUT HOW LOVE LEFT US BEHIND
    ALL THOSE THINGS WE WERE SURE OF BUT LEFT UNSAID
    AND AMBIGUOUS HOPING THAT WE WOULDN'T FIND
    ALL OF THAT TIME THE CAT WAS DEAD…
    WHAT WAS I SO AFRAID OF?
    WHAT WERE WE SO AFRAID OF?
    CAUSE A PHOTO OF A CLOUD OR FOG
    IS NOT THE SAME AS ONE THAT'S OUT OF FOCUS
    AND THE WORLD IS NOT SO FILLED WITH FOG
    THAT WE SHOULDN'T TRY TO SEE IN FOCUS…

    AND I KNOW THERE IS NO TOTAL TRUTH
    BUT I KNOW THAT THINGS ARE VERY BAD
    AND I KNOW THERE IS NO TOTAL TRUTH
    BUT I KNOW THAT THINGS ARE VERY BAD
    AND I KNOW—

    (Ring.)

JESSICA LYNCH MISS NEW YORK. No that's fine. Was that my phone or yours? Oh, good, I thought I hung up on you. God, sorry, I'm so tired, I'm like all over the place. Oh, GOD no! I don't go out. No, I had to sleep on the couch last night. Well, I've been away doing malls and some parades and opening stores, stuff like that. Yeah, it's fun! So I get home and it appears that we have a mouse situation. It's so funny because mice are like my biggest fear. Yeah, so there's like POOP all over. There's poop on the floor, in my dresser drawers. So I just slept on the couch last night. Oh yeah, I told the landlord, but get this I told him, "Uh, we have a mouse in here and

I need you to do something about that." and he said, yeah, "Well sometimes, people THINK they see things, but they're not really there." And I said "Well, I'm sure that's true. Yes, I do agree. Sometimes people do see things. But I see POOP. It's right there!" But it's good to be home.

End of Play

THE LADIES

A TEXT ABOUT GIRLS, AND THEIR FIERCE LITTLE FANTASIES

by Anne Washburn

Playscripts, Inc.
website: www.playscripts.com
email: info@playscripts.com
phone: 1-866-NEW-PLAY (639-7529)

All other inquiries concerning rights should be addressed to the Author's agent: Val Day, William Morris Agency, 1325 Avenue of the Americas, New York, NY, 10019.

The following credit must be printed on the title page of all programs distributed in connection with performances of the play:

> *The Ladies* was initially developed by The Civilians, and was commissioned by Dixon Place with funds from the National Endowment for the Arts, the Jerome Foundation, the Andrew W. Mellon Foundation, and the Lucille Lortel Foundation. The Play was premiered in February 2004 by Dixon Place in association with Chashama and Cherry Lane Theatre and The Civilians.

INTRODUCTION

Anne K became interested in the idea of developing a piece on dictators' wives in 2000 after directing *Mad Forest*, Caryl Churchill's play about the Romanian Revolution and working as assistant director on Jessica Hagedorn's *Dogeaters*—a play about the Philippines. The first Broadway show she ever saw was *Evita*...so she contemplated the connections, added Madame Mao, and approached me.

These were all women with a strong sense of the theatrical—all of them with the exception of Elena had a past, however checkered, in the performing arts, (and you could argue that Elena, who managed with a 4th grade education to pass herself off as an eminent scientist, was nicely in touch with her fantasy life). We were intrigued, inspired, and troubled by their confidence and their ferocity.

We checked out books from the library and settled into the research stage, that wonderful period during which—in contrast to the murky processes of writing and rehearsing—you feel competent and intellectual and cozy. We planned to read as much as possible and to meet periodically for discussions which would help to inform the writing of the play. It was important of course that we have good notes on these important conversations and I suggested that we record them. In the meantime I was beginning to write. Faced with a deadline for a residency, and not enough material, I suggested that we transcribe the tapes and see if there was anything particularly brilliant which could inspire me. It's a sobering exercise, seeing your own conversations laid out for you in black and white. We were fascinated by the clumsy humanness of the dialogues in the transcripts, and the alternate anti-grammars which lie at the heart of colloquial speech. Introducing ourselves as characters opened up the dramaturgy of the play.

We began a series of workshops with the actresses in which we gave them in no way enough time to look at very condensed (but still too long to absorb) write ups on the women's lives, and then gave them a very limited period of time to retell the information. The results were sprightly, and we used recordings of these sessions in the productions for exposition. The tone of these sessions also gave license to a certain strain of girlish hilarity which runs through the work.

—Anne Washburn

CAST OF CHARACTERS

The Ladies is played by 6 actresses in their 20s or 30s.

The actresses playing Anne and Anne are single cast, the other actresses each play the wife of a famous political leader, themselves, and assorted other roles.

> ANNE WASHBURN, Playwright, also plays Jennie Dundas.
>
> ANNE KAUFFMAN, Director, also plays Jennifer Morris.
>
> JIANG QING, also plays Ladies, and Nina.
>
> ELENA CEAUSESCU, also plays Ladies, Quincy, Wang Guang-mei, Hung-Hsi, Pregnant Poor Person.
>
> EVA PERON, also plays Ladies, Striar, Landlord Huang.
>
> IMELDA MARCOS, also plays Ladies and Allison.

Note: Imelda does not speak, but only sings, until she does begin to speak.

Washburn's first name is pronounced 'Anne'; Kauffman's first name is pronounced 'Annie'.

Voiceover Attributions: In developing the script with the actresses they were given condensed histories of the first ladies, and an insufficient period of time to read them. They were then asked to tell what they remembered in an impossibly short period of time, and recordings of these sessions were used in the show. This exercise was repeated at various points in the process over a period of years, during which time several actresses had scheduling conflicts and had to leave the project.

Quincy Tyler Bernstein played Imelda in the first workshop; when she left her role was taken over by Allison Weller. Colleen Werthman played Anne Washburn until the Dixon Place/Cherry Lane production when the role was played by Jennie Dundas. Maria Dizzia played Elena Ceausescu until the Dixon Place production when her role was taken over by Quincy Tyler Bernstein.

So the transcripts of the impromptu histories have been condensed: Colleen Werthman's original comments are given to Jennie Dundas, who also has her own comments; Maria Dizzia's comments are given to Quincy Bernstein and some but not all of Quincy Bernstein's comments are farmed out to Allison Weller.

NOTES

The Script: *The Ladies* combines original written material, transcripted material, and the actual words of the historic first ladies (indicated in the script with quotes).

UNINTELLIGIBLE indicates a word or phrase too garbled to be understood during the transcription process. Where it appears in the script it should be spoken as a word.

A slash mark (/) in a sentence indicates the point at which the next speaker begins her line.

Staging: Staging is as mobile and spare as possible, with minimal props.

Actresses read the Titles.

Staging should include a Spotlight, or Light of History which either illuminates or is illuminated when the actual words of the historical first ladies (indicated in the script with quotes) are said.

Tone: is variable throughout the piece. Much of it is high spirited, but dry, rather than wet. Camp and any kind of obvious satire are to be avoided.

Certain scenes should be played with seriousness of intent, and real emotional commitment:

1) The Model Opera at the beginning is performed with precise movements modeled from the actual model operas which may have paled artistically next to the traditional operas, but which had a great deal of skill, sincerity, and panache.

2) The Red Guard / Wang Guangmei segment is edited from an actual transcript. It should be handled respectfully: Wang Guangmei's plight is real; the Red Guard should not be played as a shrill one-note villain. The "Fish" segment between Anne and Anne, which is interspersed through the Red Guard segment, by contrast, should be played with total unconcern and carelessness.

3) Imelda's monologue should be as genuine as possible.

4) The songs. Have a giddy rampant quality but should have access to perfect seriousness as well. They should be ironic, beautiful, and stirring.

Voiceovers: The Voiceovers include expository material recorded in sessions with the actresses, who were given a very limited period of time to recall a limited amount of biographical material they hadn't been given enough time to read.

In these transcripts both Anne Kauffman, the director, and Jennifer Morris, the actress who plays Anne Kauffman, appear at the same time. Anne Kauffman's brief comments should be played by the actual director of the piece.*

Some of these transcripted sessions should be pre-recorded, and some—the first time each lady is introduced—should be played live. In this case, Anne Kauffman should be played by a live or pre-recorded voice from offstage. Care should be taken that, while intelligible, these sessions have a degree of giddy urgency, as they were recorded under a time pressure.

The Recorded Conversation between Dovie Beams and Ferdinand Marcos: should be recorded with actors who are outside of the production, using a man to play Marcos.

* Who should only be a woman, by the way, unless the piece is played by an all male cast.

Nomenclature: The actresses are referred to by their first names (Nina, Allison, Quincy), with the exception of Maria Striar, who is referred to as Striar, as a reflection of the time when Quincy's role was played by Maria Dizzia; and Jennie Dundas and Jennifer Morris who are both called by their last names for the obvious reasons.

The actresses sometimes play specific first ladies, sometimes play generalized first ladies, sometimes play actresses playing first ladies, sometimes play actresses and sometimes play something or someone falling somewhere in between.

All of the dialogue between Anne Kauffman and Anne Washburn is real, except where it is really really not.

ACKNOWLEDGMENTS

The Ladies received its Premiere at Dixon Place, in association with Chashama and Cherry Lane Theatre in New York City in February, 2004. It was directed by Anne Kauffman with the following cast:

ANNE KAUFFMAN .... Jennifer R. Morris

ANNE WASHBURN .... Jennifer Dundas

JIANG QING (A.K.A. MADAME MAO),
RADIO PLAYER, NINA .... Nina Hellman

ELENA CEAUÇESCU,
WANG GUANGMEI, MODEL,
OPERA ACTRESS, PREGNANT
POOR PERSON, QUINCY .... Quincy Tyler Bernstine

EVA PERÓN, RED GUARD,
TORVALD, MARIA ....Maria Striar

IMELDA MARCOS, RADIO PLAYER,
RED GUARD, NORANNA, ALISON .... Alison Weller

Voice of Dovie Beams ....Maria Dizzia

Voice of Ferdinand Marcos.................................Damian Baldet

And the following production staff:

Sets... Alexander Dodge

Costumes ....Sarah Beers

Lights.. Gwen Grossman

Sound .... Mike Frank

Visual Artist.. Michelle Memran

Choreographer.. Karinne Keithley

Musical Director..Kris Kukul

Stage Manager..Rachel Fachner

Lyrics and Tunes .... Anne Washburn

Musical Adaptation ....Michael Friedman and Kris Kukul

Music of *White Haired Girl* courtesy of Jamie H. J. Guan.

Developed with support from New York Theatre Workshop and the Public Theater through the New Work Now! Program.

Thanks to those who were part of *The Ladies* initial development: Colleen Werthmann, Aimee Guillot, Natalie Griffith and Maria Dizzia.

Alison Weller, Nina Hellman, and Maria Striar
in *The Ladies*

Dixon Place, New York City, 2004
Photo by David Gochfeld

THE LADIES

ACT I

There are voices in the darkness.

KAUFFMAN. Uh, uh, okay, now that you've had 20 minutes to read the material what we want you to do is we want you to tell the life of each woman

QUINCY. Uh huh.

KAUFFMAN. in 30 seconds /

MORRIS. Oh No way!

(General burst of consternation overtalking and shrieking.)

NINA. What?

QUINCY. Oh my God. Annie Annie

(Babble of spirited and giggling objection. Cuts out abruptly.)

(Lights up.)

TITLE: TESTING TESTING

KAUFFMAN. I didn't even know the Village People were gay. And, *(She holds the tape recorder up to speak into it directly.)* Anne Washburn didn't know that Boy George was gay.

WASHBURN. Did you know that Boy George was gay?

KAUFFMAN. Well, I don't think I knew what gay was.

WASHBURN. *(Into the recorder:)* I thought he was imaginative. *(Holds it at a distance.)* Is it working?

KAUFFMAN. Yeah. Look at all the cool red lights.

WASHBURN. But shouldn't they be moving?

KAUFFMAN. It's not a stereo system.

WASHBURN. Oh okay. Okay.

KAUFFMAN. Okay so we're

WASHBURN. We're talking about

KAUFFMAN. We're talking about Madame Mao

WASHBURN. We're—how do you say her name again? How do you pronounce her name?

KAUFFMAN. Zhung Ching

WASHBURN. Jung Ching

(JIANG CHING enters the space, on her way elsewhere.)

KAUFFMAN. There you go.

113

WASHBURN. UNINTELLIGIBLE the Ju? Say 'Zh'

KAUFFMAN. Yeah, and then the Q is a—is a CH

WASHBURN. Zung Ching. Zung Ching.

KAUFFMAN. Zhung Ching.

> *(JIANG QING pauses briefly, listens, shakes her head, and walks off.)*

WASHBURN. Zhung—you're not totally sure are you.

KAUFFMAN. No, I'm—I'm not totally sure but I'm—I'm—it's what did I just say? Zhung Ching.

WASHBURN. Zhung…zhung…

> *(EVA PERON marches through the space briskly, on her way to elsewhere.)*

KAUFFMAN. Zhung Zhung Ching.

> *(KAUFFMAN hails EVA PERON.)*

Can I get another gin and tonic please.

> *(She turns to WASHBURN.)*

Do you want something?

> *(EVA PERON, meanwhile, who has only barely registered the request, continues on her way.)*

WASHBURN. Oh, no. Well, what time is it?

KAUFFMAN. 9:20. What time do you have to be out of here?

WASHBURN. Soon.

KAUFFMAN. Okay.

WASHBURN. I have to be on the lower east side in

KAUFFMAN. In 20 minutes or something?

WASHBURN. Yeah.

KAUFFMAN. You know what can I make, I'm gonna make a quick phone call to Rob to tell him to meet me so he can get his ass on the train before… goddammit. So you were talking about…

WASHBURN. Oh, about this performing arts background thing, about the thing where all the Ladies had this performing arts background and—

KAUFFMAN. Hey Rob? It's Anne how are ya? Good, what's up? Sure. Yeah, I'm I'm it's 9:20 I'm gonna be done in about 20 minutes. And, I'm at I'm at uh I'm near uh the Flea Theater. But I can meet probably you in like, do you wanna meet me in the East Village or something? Because I figure by the time you get

> *(WASHBURN waves at an oblivious IMELDA MARCOS who is just wandering through.)*

WASHBURN. Can we get the check?

KAUFFMAN. It's gonna be so crowded though, don't you think? I know, well let's just I guess let's just meet there. Does that sound good? Excellent. I'll see you there. Bye. *(Wry:)* I hope we got all that on tape.

VOICEOVER. This session is live.

KAUFFMAN. Madame Mao, thirty seconds…go.

QUINCY. She was born in 1914, 'Pure and Simple'

STRIAR. Pure and / Simple

MORRIS. Pure and Simple. Her mother was a concubine of a hard-drinking man named something / like

STRIAR. Tiger Wolf *(Giggles.)*

MORRIS. Tiger Wolf.

STRIAR. Who beat / them both.

DUNDAS. Maybe was a prostitute also.

MORRIS. Yes.

STRIAR. Beat 'em both.

ALLISON. She ran away.

DUNDAS. And then her name was Jung He.

NINA. Bound feet, bound feet.

QUINCY. She was poor

STRIAR. Didn't like those bound feet.

MORRIS. She ripped those bound feet off and they called her Renov / ated Feet.

QUINCY. Renovated Feet.

DUNDAS. They used to beat her up. And then she / ran away.

MORRIS. And then she had to walk for the rest of her life like a / , like, a Quasimodo Walk.

DUNDAS. Funny walk.

STRIAR. She got another name Jung He, or something / right?

QUINCY. Yeah. Which means something about a crane.

KAUFFMAN. 10 seconds.

MORRIS. Her dad flew into a rage, beat the mother.

NINA. She met Mao and 1960 got to be the head of the Cultural Army.

STRIAR. She went to art school with a big headdress.

NINA. Head of the cultural army. She wore khakis.

KAUFFMAN. You guys have 5 seconds.

> (JIANG QING *and* WANG GUANGMEI *at tea. It should seem like an improvisation. The other actresses watch closely.*)

JIANG QING. So I was talking about…

WANG GUANGMEI. You were talking about your past.

JIANG QING. Right. My past Well, Wang Guangmei. What can I tell you about my past *(Stalling:)* There are so many interesting interesting stories…

WANG GUANGMEI. One story that I think is interesting is you could start by talking about how you got your current name: Zhung…

(Little pause.)

JIANG QING. Ching?

(A bit of a pause. They look at each other.)

WANG GUANGMEI. Yes. *(Mini beat.)* Let's say 'yes.'

KAUFFMAN. But okay so wait a minute now you're saying you think Jiang Qing was this great actress?

WASHBURN. Everyone says Jiang Qing was great.

KAUFFMAN. Not everyone says that at all.

WASHBURN. Who said that and also

KAUFFMAN. I heard her Dolls House wasn't so great.

WASHBURN. Who did you hear that from. Where did you hear that. Who told you that?

KAUFFMAN. Who told you that.

WASHBURN. She got good criticism and and that was like that was like New York now like you couldn't Shanghai then was like New York now like what the bitch goddess city or something.

KAUFFMAN. Oh

WASHBURN. Bitch

KAUFFMAN. Right

WASHBURN. Goddess city. Just like New York now let's say. And you couldn't

KAUFFMAN. Well like New York maybe in the seventies

WASHBURN. Yeah like New York in the seventies

KAUFFMAN and WASHBURN. Not now.

TITLE: IF WE'RE TALKING ABOUT WOMEN IN POWER AND WE'RE NOT TALKING ABOUT ALL WOMEN IN POWER WE'RE NOT TALKING ABOUT HILARY CLINTON IS NOT THE SAME THING.

LADY (NINA). Here. We have these biscuits.

LADY (STRIAR). I like what you've done with your infrastructure.

LADY (NINA). Thank you. Would you like to try on my lipstick? I think the shade would be more flattering on you than it is on me. If it looks better on you then you can keep it.

LADY (STRIAR). Thank you. I like these biscuits.

LADY (NINA). Thank you. They are made from the people. *(Mini beat.)* Did I say that correctly?

*(*IMELDA *sings from offstage.)*

IMELDA.
> I DID WHAT I DID WHAT I DID I DID FOR LOVE
> FOR THAT CREAMY DREAMY FEELING WE ALL DIE OF

WANG GUANGMEI. You know I'd love to hear all about your childhood.

JIANG QING. Well, it was very rural. And I was very poor. And my mother may have been a prostitute. And I saw—and it was the end of an era, a time of transition—anyway I saw heads, decapitated heads on the walls of the city, that had been mounted there on spikes. Yes that's right, I remember that.

WANG GUANGMEI. That must have been formative.

JIANG QING. Possibly. And my father—what was my father's name? Tiger...

WANG GUANGMEI. Tiger...

JIANG QING. Not Tiger Woods.

WANG GUANGMEI. No.

JIANG QING. Tiger Wolf!

WANG GUANGMEI. Yes!

JIANG QING. Yes. A hard drinking, cantankerous man. I remember.

WANG GUANGMEI. That must have been difficult.

JIANG QING. I don't think I like sympathy. About my past. I'm sure I don't like to be, um, *pitied*. I bet I hate pity.

WANG GUANGMEI. But even about, I thought you were a hypochondriac. I thought hypochondriacs—

(The actress is transforming into JIANG QING.*)*

JIANG QING. Hypochondriac? What does that mean. Exactly. Wang Guangmei.

WANG GUANGMEI. It means—

JIANG QING. Let me put it this way: I know what it means. What are you saying?

WANG GUANGMEI. Um

JIANG QING. You're not saying that I'm that my symptoms that my uh extreme sensitivity to light, and...noise. And *(To audience:)* insomnia?

WANG GUANGMEI. I'm sure.

JIANG QING. Insomnia.

What were we talking about? Hypochondria...

WANG GUANGMEI. Pity. Do you want pity. Hypochondriacs like they're not quiet about it they want sympathy.

JIANG QING. My symptoms are real. My diseases are actual. Not my past.

(She takes a puff from an imaginary cigarette.)

That's a dream.

(She tosses the imaginary cigarette away.)

NINA and QUINCY. *(Door Slam.)*

TITLE: IT'S ALWAYS VERY SLIPPERY

(They slide off.)

KAUFFMAN. But, my question still is…what…what's bothering me still is, what what I mean what angle are we taking on this. What are we––what are we—

WASHBURN. I don't think…I mean I don't think…I mean I think if we knew that totally at this point it would be really lame. I mean with like four Ladies it can't like it can't be well we know we don't want it to be

KAUFFMAN. Right right right

WASHBURN. and also we know it can't be about their biographies specifically because it's like really really they're a play each and I mean Madame Mao is really is a mini series I mean can you imagine?

KAUFFMAN. Oh I know.

WASHBURN. She would be a great mini series. I can totally see her, like, on a horse.

KAUFFMAN. Okay but so / what about

WASHBURN. That's why I think—sorry, go ahead

KAUFFMAN. No go ahead. I mean / what

WASHBURN. I think you know with all of the research I think we just you know we just pursue the research. We read all of the books.

KAUFFMAN. I really think it's important that Imelda is the only one actually alive.

(A spotlight slowly comes up on IMELDA. *She enjoys it, gleaming demurely.)*

WASHBURN. Oh I know. I mean it's major, it's a major

KAUFFMAN. I mean it's major and there really I think it's really it's important that there be a distinction. Between her and the other ladies. Because it's huge.

WASHBURN. If they start.

KAUFFMAN. It's huge.

WASHBURN. Zombying after her at some point when they realize that she's not, one of them…

KAUFFMAN. Are we sure she's still alive?

(A slight beat.)

(This gives IMELDA *pause.)*

WASHBURN. She's still alive definitely.

KAUFFMAN. Okay good cause I feel like I haven't seen her in the news lately.

WASHBURN. She's definitely, she's definitely still alive *(A tiny moment.)* I mean we could call the Philippine consulate just to double check although that's pretty rude. Colleen works for the U.N. she'd probably know.

IMELDA. *(Singing:)*
> THAT MAN, HE IS SIMPLY MY SUN

WASHBURN. But they *are* in Hell, right. I mean that *is* where you put famous historical figures when you want them to sit around and chat right.

KAUFFMAN. Um, you can put them in Limbo.

IMELDA. *(Continuing:)*
> AND MY MOON AND THE REST OF THE SHIMMERING
> THINGS IN THE SKY

WASHBURN. Yeah. *(A beat.)* I feel like there always has to be a waiter.

(Lurid sudden side light on a lady dressed as a waiter, hand extended menacingly upwards with tray. On the tray a single flaming tea cup.)

(The sound of flames.)

IMELDA. *(Concluding:)*
> HE'S MY WORLD
> AND HE'S MY GUY

(Flames cut out.)

NINA. This is sort of an interesting fact about Mao. Um, and, he was very promiscuous and he didn't like to bathe.

(Muted giggling.)

ALLISON. *(Whispered:)* Oh god.

DUNDAS. "I wash myself inside the bodies of my woman"

NINA. *(Slightly delighted:)* Yes, *(Laughter)* yes.

DUNDAS. That gave me a, not-nice feeling

NINA. *(Reading:)* "His genitals were never cleaned"

QUINCY. His whole life?

NINA. *(Reading:)* But Mao refused to bathe.

STRIAR. He did once swim in the Yangtze river—

JIANG QING. This is the story of Eva Peron, and how she died.

(Everyone assembles around the body of EVA PERON. *They arrange themselves as in the slumber party game* Light As A Feather / Stiff As A Board.)*

ACTRESS (QUINCY). It is a dark evening in winter and you are inside and you are dying There is a wind from the Pampas and as it bangs against the palace window the stars seem to rattle in their sockets. The wind stops. The stars stop rattling. They glitter. Outside in the plaza there are protestors—sorry, not protestors, *mourners:* old ladies and poor women holding babies and candles in jars. All up and down the plaza there are jars and jars of fluttering light, and a terrible wailing you want to roll over but it is too painful. You struggle, you stop. You struggle, you stop. You are too weak. You stop rolling. You breathe heavily. A nurse brings a waterglass to your lips—you did not ask for water! You glare, but she tips your mouth open anyway. You will tell her to roll you over but she is gone. Your stomach is burnt from radiation, your skin is peeling away in black sheets, your sister is going to save a piece of your burnt skin for years; I sort of remember it as if she keeps it in her wallet but I'm sure that's not the case that it's in a drawer somewhere in a box between sheets of pink tissue anyway you know that your husband is standing in the hallway right on the other side of the door. He is standing there, his head bowed, nurses brushing past him as they stream in and out. You're certain of it. If you could just roll over you could stare fixedly at that empty doorway for just the hem of his uniform, or the tip of his shoe. You know that he is standing there, his hands pressed against the wall, his forehead pressed against the wall, his face is set, but there is one tear gliding slowly down his cheek. Oh you know it. He won't come in, no, because he is imagining that you're beautiful, he's remembering you as thought you're perfect, he can't, he won't see you the way you really are. Nothing is more romantic. That is how you want it too. Really. You compose yourself, your mother bends near, and you say your last words and then you expire and you float away from your body and you waft up to heaven.

The embalmer is left alone with you and when he is done your body and the three exact copies made of resins, wax, and fiberglass remain, and will remain, for as long as plastic endures. But now you're dead.

ALL. And now she's dead.

    (Speaking around the circle:)

ONE. And now she's dead.

ANOTHER. And now she's—

    (But she's not dead! She struggles up to life!)

EVA. This is the story of Jiang Qing and how *she* died.

    (The actress playing JIANG QING *rears up and shouts:)*

JIANG. "I am without heaven and a law unto myself! It is right to rebel! I am prepared to die!"

EVA. *(Resuming:)* This is the story of Jiang Qing, and how she died:

    (One of the actresses around the body shouts out:)

ACTRESS (STRIAR). "The chief counterrevolutionary culprit Jiang Qing is an evil star who brought calamity to the country and the people"

JIANG. "I was Mao's dog—when he said 'bite'—I bit!"

ACTRESS (QUINCY). *(Subduingly:) This is the story of Jiang Qing, and how she died:*

> *(Reluctantly,* JIANG QING *subsides into the center of the circle. Everyone else sits around her.)*

MORRIS. I do remember this fact—she tried to kill herself by ramming her head into a wall a number of times

DUNDAS. That is so fucking hard core

> *(Laughter.)*

MORRIS. It really is isn't it?

STRIAR. She ate a chop stick, right.

QUINCY. Oh yeah.

DUNDAS. Or did she? I thought that was some myth.

MORRIS. No I think she ate it.

DUNDAS. Some Orientalist myth.

MORRIS. No no no I think she ate it but she didn't—she *tried* to kill herself that way

NINA. By / eating a chopstick?

STRIAR. How can eating a chopstick kill you?

DUNDAS. Splinters?

ALL. And now she's dead.

> *(Going around the circle…)*

ACTRESS. And now she's dead.

ACTRESS. And now she's dead.

> *(*KAUFFMAN *is next. She bends over and says to* WASHBURN *who is opposite the body from her:)*

KAUFFMAN. I kind of love that thing about the chopstick in her hair and then her sticking it in her mouth.

WASHBURN. You told me that's how she killed herself.

KAUFFMAN. Well she tried to kill herself that way. Later on she hung herself.

WASHBURN. I told people that's how Madame Mao killed herself.

KAUFFMAN. No, she hung herself.

WASHBURN. Did I tell you about the flesh eating computers speaking of things I go around repeating indiscriminately?

KAUFFMAN. No.

WASHBURN. They're developing okay you know how they're developing computers that can clone themselves?

KAUFFMAN. No.

WASHBURN. And improve on themselves.

KAUFFMAN. No.

WASHBURN. This is why you should read the paper. They have a really primitive it's the first permanent—they're developing computers that can design computers.

KAUFFMAN. Well that's not surprising.

WASHBURN. No it's not surprising. But don't you think it's a little creepy.

KAUFFMAN. Yes, very.

WASHBURN. Combined with the fact combined with the fact

KAUFFMAN. Flesh eating.

WASHBURN. they've already developed computers that are powered not by electricity but by the bio chemical electrical impulses created when flesh is digested. They have basically a chamber with acids in it like the human stomach.

KAUFFMAN. SHUT UP

WASHBURN. They're doing it in Australia. Can you believe it? Why don't we just build little human processing centers right now.

KAUFFMAN. Totally you have got to be kidding me.

WASHBURN. I'm not kidding you but I have to get the citation on it because obviously I do. Because all I can say is well it was this guy in a bar. But, it was like I knew him and I knew his friend and

(KAUFFMAN *is looking dubious.*)

he seemed very authoritative and everyone believed him and I just have to get—I have to get hold of the article he read it from. It's the truth.

KAUFFMAN. How can we get that in here?

WASHBURN. We can't. We really can't.

(*Someone goes 'AHEM' and* ANNE *and* ANNE *recompose themselves.*)

KAUFFMAN. And now she's dead.

WASHBURN. And now she's dead.

ACTRESS. And now she's dead.

ALL. Light as a feather, stiff as a board. Light as a feather, stiff as a board. Light as a feather, stiff as a board…

(*They lift her up.*)

NINA. Okay. Do not *drop me!* Do not *drop me.*

(*They lower her gently.*)

ALLISON. This is good:

(She reads:)

"Lan Ping *was* Nora. For the rest of her life she continued Nora's habit of humming to herself when something pleased her, or when she wished to appear *enigmatic*."

MORRIS. And then I heard that she hummed in prison

(Tiny beat.)

DUNDAS. Yeah

QUINCY. She also made / dolls

MORRIS. The dolls

NINA. Yeah she embroidered her name into the dolls

DUNDAS. In a desperate plea

NINA. And then she got caught.

TITLE: I'M LIKE 'YOU HAVE TO GROW BALLS' I SAY THAT AT ONE POINT TO MYSELF I SAY: 'INAUDIBLE, YOU HAVE TO GROW BALLS.'

(JIANG QING steps to the front of the stage and performs "Doll's House." She does Nora's lines full-on, with skillfulness and passion. Torvald's lines are thrown away and used only as place markers.)

(WANG GUANGMEI watches.)

JIANG QING (As NORA). There's something I must do. I must educate myself. And you can't help me with that Torvald. It's something I must do by myself. That's why I'm leaving you.

JIANG QING (As TORVALD). What did you say.

JIANG QING (As NORA). I must stand on my own feet if I am to find out the truth about myself and about life.

JIANG QING (As TORVALD). But this is monstrous Nora! Can you neglect your most sacred duties?

JIANG QING (As NORA). What do you call my most sacred duties?

JIANG QING (As TORVALD). Do I have to tell you? Your duties towards your husband, and your children.

JIANG QING (As NORA). I have another duty, which is equally sacred. *(Beat.)* My duty to myself.

(She breaks pose. WANG GUAMGMEI applauds.)

JIANG QING. Thank you.

WANG GUANGMEI. That's wonderful.

JIANG QING. I'm surprised I still remember the lines.

(ANNE and ANNE are looking at sheaves of paper.)

WASHBURN. What's the UN? Is that—

KAUFFMAN. Unintelligible.

WASHBURN. Oh. Is that like official transcriber terminology?

KAUFFMAN. Yeah we do it—there's more of that in the bar where it was my tape recorder is really crappy. There was a whole section I could hear maybe every other word.

WASHBURN. We have to burn these tapes.

KAUFFMAN. What part is that?

WASHBURN. Where we're talking about—

KAUFFMAN. Oh, yeah. That's hilarious. But we can't use it.

(Beat.)

WASHBURN. We really can't can we.

KAUFFMAN. We really can't. It's really funny though. A lot of this like in their speeches there's a lot you like you made up right?

WASHBURN. No, no. They really said that.

KAUFFMAN. Really?

WASHBURN. Which—which what are you looking at? Well that's not real. That I made up. Do you know what we need? For the actual for the quotes when it's something they actually said, we need a Light of History.

(The Light of History glows.)

KAUFFMAN. Yeah

WASHBURN. What about the Madonna thing?

KAUFFMAN. Having Madonna?

WASHBURN. Yeah because she's sort of—

KAUFFMAN. Well I think

WASHBURN. Or is that too—

KAUFFMAN. Yeah.

WASHBURN. Yeah.

KAUFFMAN. I think that's too—

WASHBURN. Yeah.

KAUFFMAN. But I love the Madonna quote. Did she really say that?

WASHBURN. No.

TITLE: SHE MUST HAVE BEEN REALLY BUSY REVOLUTIONIZING THE ARTS.

(Voiceover:)

NINA. She applied to this experimental arts academy, which was very prestigious, and they needed girls who had long hair to play the parts of saucy maids, and since she had this long beautiful hair she was accepted, but once she was accepted, she cut all her hair off

(For some reason everyone gasps slightly and in unison.)

'cause she was like *(With attitude:)* 'I'm saucy—but I'm no *maid*'

STRIAR. I think, I mean I think she had kind of a fabulous aesthetic code and you know, she shook it up

ALLISON. Shook up the form…

STRIAR. I mean, yeah

MORRIS. Except that she did kill a lot of people

STRIAR. Well yeah, I mean

ALLISON. Not in the opera

(The following is performed Chinese Model Opera style:)

(Enter HUNG-HSI, carrying a wooden pail. She is seven months pregnant, looks haggard, and walks with difficulty.)

(She sings:)

HUNG-HSI.
> SEVEN MONTHS HAVE PASSED—
> LIKE A TWIG CRUSHED BENEATH A STONE,
> I BEAR THE SHAME, SWALLOWING MY TEARS.
> I CAN'T SAY HOW ILL I FEEL.
> THINGS HAVE GONE SO FAR, THERE'S NO HELP FOR ME,
> I'LL JUST HAVE TO BEAR IT AND SWALLOW MY PRIDE.

(Enter HUANG.)

HUNG-HSI. Oh, it's you.

HUANG. *(Wants to turn back.)* Oh, it's you.

HUNG-HSI. You—wait! I want to ask you something…

HUANG. Well but I'm busy now, Hung-hsi…

HUNG-HSI. I'm growing bigger every day, what can I do? People laugh at me and despise me. But I can't die, however much I want to. Tell me, how shall I live on?

HUANG. Er…

HUNG-HSI. Sir, you…

(She weeps.)

HUANG. Now, Hung-hsi don't cry. Er…just keep calm. Keep quiet, Hung-hsi, and don't run about.

(He exits.)

HUNG-HSI. Landlord Huang is my enemy; even if he married me, he would make me lead a wretched life. I understand now. What a devil he is! I'm not a child. He's ruined me, so that I can't hold up my head again; but I'm not like my father! Even a chicken will struggle when it's killed, and I'm a human being! Even if it kills me, I'm going to speak my mind!

(HUANG enters from the other side.)

HUNG-HSI. *(Fiercely:)* Sir!

HUANG. *(Startled:)* Hung-hsi, why are you here?

HUNG-HSI. *(Stepping forward:)* Sir, you…

HUANG. Now Hung-hsi, go back quickly. It doesn't look good if you're seen in the courtyard.

HUNG-HSI. *(Loudly:)* Landlord Huang!

HUANG. *(Startled:)* What! You—

HUNG-HSI. On New Year's Eve you forced my dad to commit suicide! On New Year's Day you got me to your home. Since I came, you've never treated me as a human being, but as dirt beneath your feet! Your mother beats and curses me! *(Coming nearer:)* And you—you ruined me!

HUANG. You…why bring that up now?

HUNG-HSI. *(Coming nearer.)* I'm seven months gone but you're getting married and deceiving me! I ask you, what do you mean by it!

> *(She bites and tears at him.)*

HUANG. *(Throwing HUNG-HSI down:)* You fool! Mad!

> *(He shakes her off and hurries out.)*

HUNG-HSI. *(Getting up:)* I'll have it out with you! I'll have it out with you!

> *(Runs out after him.)*
>
> *(She is almost offstage.)*

JIANG. No no no, Hsi-Erh, what is that?!

> *(The actress playing HUNG-HSI screeches to a halt. JIANG steps forward from the shadows [or, backstage, wherever].)*

What is that?! You look distressed.

ACTRESS (QUINCY). Yes—

JIANG. You look upset.

ACTRESS (QUINCY). I'm very very upset.

JIANG. You look as though you had an upset stomach.

ACTRESS (QUINCY). Well I'm very—because not only myself but the people also…

JIANG. Yes, that is correct. It is not just yourself. The *people* have been wronged. You're standing and making faces like a peasant who is about to be raped.

KAUFFMAN. Okay Nina?

NINA. Yeah?

KAUFFMAN. I like what you're doing. I really like what you're doing.

NINA. Is it too—

KAUFFMAN. I think it's—

NINA. Is it too commentative?

KAUFFMAN. It's commentative. It's pretty, uh—

NINA. It's very angry.

KAUFFMAN. It's cranky. She could be very charismatic.

WASHBURN. And this is also, this is sort of the—do you mind if I just?

KAUFFMAN. *(Disguised irritation at interruption:)* No no, go ahead.

WASHBURN. Even though the way I wrote it it's obviously sort of ridiculous and commentative

NINA. Yeah I think it is commentative, in the writing a little.

(This is a bit of a body check for WASHBURN.)

WASHBURN. A little but it should also be the version of, like, their story. How they want it to be told. It has that aspect to it. Like: why focus on the hundreds of thousands dead, let's look instead at—

KAUFFMAN. You know it's really it's a very significant cultural experiment, in its way, the Cultural Revolution. You know just pulling together all these different forms, from the West and trying to bring in a completely contemporary subject material—I mean she's really avant—I mean she's incredibly—she's totally like a post modern mama. Okay.

WASHBURN. And okay just—sorry, just one more thing—and also it's like this whole dynamic would have been pertinent to her personally, the whole, uh, you know, authority versus girl-trying-to-get-by-in-the-world. I mean she probably would have felt *(Makes gesture)* about it.

(NINA repeats gesture, quizzically.)

(While she's doing that:)

QUINCY. *(To KAUFFMAN:)* So it's like with Elena Ceausescu it's oh no we cut that part.

WASHBURN. *(Responding to NINA:)* Yeah. *(Does gesture again.)*

MARIA. We cut that?

QUINCY. *(Not entirely true:)* I don't take it personally.

KAUFFMAN. Right. Okay. Good. Can we take it from—take it from: um.

MARIA. I liked that part.

ALLISON. Oh that scene got cut?

MARIA. I think we should keep it.

KAUFFMAN. Okay this is not a democracy.

NINA. Can we take it from the beginning?

KAUFFMAN. *(Momentarily distracted; to NINA:)* Yes. Let's take it from. We're taking it from 'You Fool Mad.'

(A pause.)

Okay, from—

HUANG. *(Hastily:)* Right. You fool! Mad!

HSI-ERH. I'll have it out with you! I'll have it out with you!

> *(Runs out after him.)*
>
> *(She is almost offstage.)*

JIANG. No no no, what is that?!

> *(The actress playing* HSI-ERH *screeches to a halt.* JIANG QING *steps forward from the shadows [or, backstage, wherever].)*

What is that?! You look distressed.

ACTRESS. Yes—

JIANG. You look upset.

ACTRESS. I'm very very upset.

JIANG. You look as though you had an upset stomach.

ACTRESS. Well I'm very—because not only myself but the people also…

> *(*KAUFFMAN *starts to get up but* NINA *motions for her to sit down.)*

JIANG. Yes, that is correct. It is not just yourself. The *people* have been wronged. You're standing and making faces like a peasant who is about to be raped. That's not correct is it? No. Remember that you aren't afraid of him. Why? Because you're angry. You're full of anger. A girl might tremble before a man but you aren't a girl, you are a proud farm worker, and he, he is an obsolete part of history an infected appendix and you, you are the surgeon of the revolution. Yes. That's better. Yes. *Bristle* with class hatred. Yes. More. More.

> *(She lights an imaginary cigarette.)*

That's terrible. Do you know why? Because you're only making faces. You're thinking about your pose, your manner, is it attractive, you aren't letting rage consume your body.

> *(The Light of History gleams:)*

"Never forget. Beauty is less important than will and power."

> *(And extinguishes.)*

You must oppose the landlord with your entire strength, all of your inner force—then the audience will look at you—and will have to look away. If you're pretty, if you always have a pretty, little, agreeable expression then the audience will always look at you, and they'll always listen to what you're saying, but they'll never pay attention and they'll never understand. Don't try to be delectable in this world, don't try to be a morsel which is cuddled and nibbled upon, seek to be *blinding*.

It is only when people fall back from you, stunned, that they understand who you really are.

> *(Steps back.)*

Well that's better. Yes. Straighten your back. Good.

KAUFFMAN. And you know a lot of doing this project that we're doing right now, you and I are going to get our asses in gear and we need to grow balls. You know what's interesting about this is that there's actually this section in this book that I'm still reading I swear I'm gonna finish

WASHBURN. Which book is this?

KAUFFMAN. Becoming Madame Mao. There was a point when at the beginning of the Cultural Revolution when um Madame Mao was on stage I'm I'm a little confused about actually the factions within the Communist Party during that whole thing because I didn't believe you for some reason when you were talking about Mao needing to do something to really get back into the into like the sort of thick of it and be seen again and sort of so that this Cultural Revolution was something that he kind of stirred up to get notice or or to somehow

WASHBURN. Reconsolidate power

KAUFFMAN. Reconsolidate power right. And but at one point she just says something here an I it's just really I'm a little bit this is also fictionalized you know so its really hard to know um to a certain extent I guess it really doesn't matter if it's true. But at one point she's on stage trying to um garner support and the crowds are just not responding to her. And Mao actually comes to like is actually called in and all he does is walk across the stage clapping and then he goes off. And, then suddenly they're all

WASHBURN. Right right.

KAUFFMAN. for her

WASHBURN. Right. That's so amazing.

(JIANG QING, *in the Light of History, shouting at the audience.*)

JIANG QING. "Wang Guangmei should be grabbed to make a confession!"

Wang Guangmei is a dishonest person. Before she went to Indonesia, she came to see me. At that time I was in Shanghai, ill. She said she wanted to wear a necklace and flowered dresses on the trip. I said to her that it was right to take several dresses, and I urged black, but that as a member of the Communist Party of China she should avoid necklaces.

Though Wang Guangmei didn't sleep well for several nights after I gave her my advice on dress, in the end she agreed with me and said she would not wear a necklace in Southeast Asia.

"She cheated me! She did wear a necklace!"

(WANG GUANGMEI *enters.*)

WANG GUANGMEI. Mind if I enter?

JIANG. Oh yes, yes, come in, cookie?

WANG GUANGMEI. Thanks. Yes I'll take one.

(*She takes an imaginary cookie from an imaginary tray.*)

JIANG. Tea?

WANG GUANGMEI. Oh I just, no I just I had a cup.

JIANG. You're sure?

WANG GUANGMEI. Yes I am.

JIANG. It's special tea you know, just chock full of all sorts of things, you're certain?

WANG GUANGMEI. Dead certain.

JIANG. I might do the same, I might just abstain.

WANG GUANGMEI. Well not on my account.

JIANG. No, certainly not.

(*A beat.* WANG GUANGMEI *bites into her cookie.*)

WANG GUANGMEI. Oooh—hey, this is great.

JIANG. It's glorious isn't it.

WANG GUANGMEI. It's made with special ingredients, right?

JIANG. It's made with—yes, with a little of this and a little of that. I should imagine. I don't bake them myself, obviously.

WANG GUANGMEI. Oh well no, you wouldn't have time.

JIANG. I used to, you know, of course, in the beginning. And well when that became impossible or bothersome I still I made a point of really supervising but I think now that there is a generalized knowledge of what it is that I want I think it's part now of the kitchen culture.

WANG GUANGMEI. Okay but why I came here today—I actually had a reason.

JIANG. Let's hear it.

WANG GUANGMEI. Because I'm going to a ball, to a party.

JIANG. Uh huh

WANG GUANGMEI. In Micronesia, in—or—Southeast Asia.

JIANG. Well that's—that's sort of a wide area do you think you could maybe you could make it a little more specific?

WANG GUANGMEI. Jakarta. I'm going to a party in Jakarta and because my husband you know he has this big political trip there—well you know all about big political trips of course

JIANG. Do I? I don't actually no because I'm not allowed to accompany the Chairman, really, in any official capacity. That was the agreement, as you know, the Thirty Year agreement under which the Central Committee because they thought I was just some dilettante actress the agreement under which they allowed us to marry that I couldn't, you know, do *anything* really in terms of any kind of political presence or political role or responsibility, you know, for thirty years, apart from maybe summarizing bulky documents for him, something secretarial like that, which is fine for, like, the first 10 years of our marriage when we're living in caves and on the run from the KMT and life is either very dashing or very inconvenient or both but afterwards, of course, now that's everybody's in power and running around Asia Well.

WANG GUANGMEI. Right.

JIANG. I'm afraid it's a bit of a sensitive topic.

WANG GUANGMEI. Of course.

JIANG. Not nearly as sensitive of course as any discussion of—oh, well.

WANG GUANGMEI. As of—what?

JIANG. I would hate to bring it up.

WANG GUANGMEI. Of course you would, you're a delicate person *(She calls offstage:)* Tea!

(A Lady brings on a tea cup.)

JIANG. And really I'm sure it's a series of escalating misunderstandings.

WANG GUANGMEI. Is it?

JIANG. I'm sure your husband is really a very lovely person.

WANG GUANGMEI. My husband.

JIANG. Liu Shaoqi, second in command and successor to the position of supreme leadership. The man whose criticism of the Great Leap Forward and whose resistance to Mao's cult of personality will lead to marginalization and then, during the Cultural Revolution—well—that's all in the future isn't it? Better not to talk about it. It's a little sensitive. Tea! What fun that you're allowed to appear publicly and wave at people! Let's talk about your trip to Jakarta.

WANG GUANGMEI. Right.

JIANG. And what you're going to wear.

WANG GUANGMEI. Right.

JIANG. All right so it's a ball, right?

WANG GUANGMEI. Yes, listen, really, if this—if this isn't interesting to you or if, um, you know if it's at all aggravating we could talk about something else.

JIANG. No no, I'm very interested, so this is this ball, in Jakarta, and you're going to be making an entrance.

WANG GUANGMEI. Well not much of an entrance really I mean I can't imagine that anyone would be looking at me.

JIANG. Oh you'll make an entrance all right. That's very important. I mean I'm sorry if that makes you uncomfortable Wang Guangmei but this isn't just a selfish pleasure trip that you're taking. As you've pointed out it is a political trip and you on this trip you are representing China. And there are many ramifications to that. And one of the ramifications to that is that you it's important you make an entrance and look important and glamorous and self assured. Okay?

WANG GUANGMEI. Okay of course. Right.

JIANG. Because this ain't just about you.

WANG GUANGMEI. Oh well no, I know that.

(*The Light of History flares:*)

"That's why I came to you. Because I know that you read lots of novels and you know what clothes are like and I wanted to make sure that I would look sophisticated."

(*And then dies out.*)

JIANG. Sophisticated.

WANG GUANGMEI. Not like a bumpkin.

JIANG. That's right but what do you mean by sophisticated? I hope you don't mean a cocktail dress or something like that with low cleavage.

WANG GUANGMEI. Oh God no. Of course not.

JIANG. Because you want to send a clear political message.

WANG GUANGMEI. Yes.

JIANG. You want to say that China is strong and that China is modern but not that China is an uncontrollable slut.

WANG GUANGMEI. Of course no I don't.

(*JIANG hums enigmatically for a short period of time while she thinks.*)

JIANG. Okay I have it.

WANG GUANGMEI. Oh you do? That was quick.

JIANG. I have it.

WANG GUANGMEI. That's great, that's great, what is it.

(*The Light of History glows:*)

JIANG. "Like Anna Karenina."

WANG GUANGMEI. Oh?

JIANG. Black Velvet.

(*Beat.*)

WANG GUANGMEI. Oh.

JIANG. In the ballroom scene. She wears a black velvet dress.

(*Reads:*)

"Kitty had been seeing Anna every day; she adored her, and had pictured her invariably in lilac Now now seeing her in black, she felt that she had not fully seen her charm. She saw her now as someone quite new and surprising to her. Now she understood that Anna could not have been in lilac, and her black velvet dress, with it's sumptuous lace, was not noticeable on her; it was only the frame and all that was seen was she—simple, natural, elegant, and at the same time gay and eager." That's what you want. That's who you want to be. Black velvet. That's you.

WANG GUANGMEI. oh

JIANG. "Because that would be elegant, and also beyond the ordinary."

    (The Light of History dims, but continues.)

WANG GUANGMEI. Yes, in that climate, yes, it would be.

JIANG. *(To herself:)* Thirty years…how time flies… *(To* WANG GUANG-MAI*:)* And on the whole…I think it's best to avoid jewelry.

End of Act One

ACT II

KAUFFMAN. Okay Eva Peron, go:

NINA. She got involved in Radio somehow.

MORRIS and ALLISON. Uh huh.

NINA. She got her own radio show where she was doing like the

MORRIS. Great / ladies of history.

QUINCY. Recording monologues?

NINA. Recording monologues of great women in history.

MORRIS. Like Catherine the Great and Elizabeth—

NINA. Yeah.

QUINCY. M-huh.

NINA. And

MORRIS. The / first?

NINA. because she was dating like the head of, or, the advertiser, the main advertiser for the radio /

QUINCY. Who was a Soap Magnate!

NINA. then and then she got involved in like charities, how did she get involved in charities

STRIAR. She made her own ministry of um—the one thing / you can really say for her

NINA. Like she met, she met Nando at an earthquake / relief

STRIAR. Nando?

NINA. No, not Nando, she met whatever his name, is

ALLISON. Oh

QUINCY. Whatsisname

STRIAR. Juan

    (In the darkness a snatch of song.)

IMELDA.
BECAUSE OF YOU…
BECAUSE OF YOUR EXTRAORDINARY SHIMMERING
GLUE…
I'M STUCK TO YOU…
BECAUSE OF YOUR TREMENDOUS PERSONALITY TOO
I FLEE I FLEE I FLEE
BUT I'M STUCK TO YOU

WASHBURN. Whereas Imelda is basically someone who had a good family name.

KAUFFMAN. She did

WASHBURN. Yeah her part of it was the dirt poor living in a garage branch of it but when she gets to Manila there's this sense she's being looked out for and that somebody cares if she lives or dies as opposed to

KAUFFMAN. Eva.

WASHBURN. Yeah, or Jiang Qing and I don't know maybe Elena who knows. Like Imelda like she gets introduced around. I mean I feel like, of all of them, she's the one who actually had a shot at a normal life. Like she actually made a choice. So she's really like a socialite gone wrong. I mean she just

KAUFFMAN. And and did she go wrong? I don't know I mean yeah she did

WASHBURN. Yeah she

KAUFFMAN. she

WASHBURN. went way wrong.

(EVA is holding an empty jam jar.)

EVA. Okay well. I understand you have a problem, And that's why you came to me.

PREGNANT POOR PERSON. I do Ms. Peron.

EVA. Call me Evita.

PREGNANT POOR PERSON. Oh I…yes…I…

EVA. You have a problem.

PREGNANT POOR PERSON. I have all sorts of problems but—

EVA. Pick one.

PREGNANT POOR PERSON. Right Okay.

EVA. Pick one then maybe we can talk about the others.

PREGNANT POOR PERSON. Okay.

EVA. The biggest one. The biggest one first.

PREGNANT POOR PERSON. Okay. Well I think my biggest problem would be that I don't have a house. And I have five kids. Well, six kids soon. Now, mind you, we aren't homeless because we are living in, I guess what you could most accurately describe as an assemblage. There are two walls which are cardboard, and there are two walls which are tin, and then for the roof we have cardboard, and we have a few pieces of plastic sheeting over it which I've sewn together with pig gut so when it rains the roof is okay. We have rocks on top of the sheeting to hold it down when it's windy. Now, the two walls which are cardboard are kind of a problem but my son found a lump of waxy residue in an alley behind a factory and we've smeared that on the sides. So it *is* water resistant.

EVA. But not waterproof.

PREGNANT POOR PERSON. Not entirely.

EVA. Okay, so I see. You'd like a new place to live.

PREGNANT POOR PERSON. Or, I understand also that you give out mattresses. I mean just a mattress would be great because right now—

EVA. No no, I think actually it would be simpler just to give you a house. Okay. So it's you, and five—I'm sorry, six kids. And a husband?

PREGNANT POOR PERSON. Yes. Although he doesn't have legs.

EVA. That's fine. So a room for you and your husband and then maybe three rooms for the kids—they'll each have to share a room but they'll have bunk beds.

PREGNANT POOR PERSON. They'll *love* bunk beds.

EVA. When I was a child I always wanted a bunk bed.

PREGNANT POOR PERSON. Because if you drape a sheet over the top bunk you can play Fort.

EVA. That's right. Or Cave.

PREGNANT POOR PERSON. Those are both very good games.

EVA. There will also be a living room, kitchen, and I think we can arrange a small cement patio.

PREGNANT POOR PERSON. How can I thank you?

EVA. Well you're going to be sad again.

PREGNANT POOR PERSON. Now that I've got this house? No.

EVA. Be realistic.

PREGNANT POOR PERSON. All I've ever wanted is not to be damp and crowded.

EVA. That's sweet but now you'll notice other problems.

PREGNANT POOR PERSON. No, I think that from now on life's going Up Up Up for me…

    (She rises, and prepares to sing.)

(To herself, kind of private:) Life's Going Up Up Up for me—

    (She breaks into song:)

THERE WAS A TIME WHEN I WAS AWFUL SAD
PEOPLE TALK ABOUT THE BLUES
I HAD THE PURPLES HAD 'EM BAD
BUT—

EVA. *(Quietly:)* You're wasting my time.

(The PREGNANT POOR PERSON *sinks back down, tidily and neatly.)*
You're going to have problems. They're going to be big problems. When you have them you're going to cry.

(She hands her the jam jar.)
And at that point here's what you want to do— *(She holds her teacup under the eye area.)* just tip it under here, okay, right under the lid…

(She demonstrates. The PREGNANT POOR PERSON *hesitatingly places the jar beneath her eye.)*
That's right. When you collect a jar-full, send it to me.

PREGNANT POOR PERSON. Okay.

TITLE: THERE'S THAT VANITY FAIR ARTICLE THAT I HAVE TO A. FINISH READING AND B. XEROX.

LADY 1 (NINA). Please, won't you take a cigarette?

LADY (ALISON). *(Looks demure and mysterious and doesn't answer.)*

LADY 2 (STRIAR). Thank you. *I will. (Smokes briefly.)* It's delicious. Is this your tobacco?

LADY 1 (NINA). No, we import it. It's simpler that way.

*(*IMELDA *sings in the dark.)*

IMELDA.
GOT A GOVERNMENT DIRECTIVE TO SIGN
SOME POWER'S YOURS AND SOME OF IT'S MINE AH AH
OOH, OOOH OOOH OOH OOH

LADY (NINA). Here, there's something wrong with your hemline, let me adjust it.

LADY (QUINCY). Thank you. I have a lot of striding to do and I don't like to trip. Later, perhaps, you will show me an historic view.

LADY (NINA). Yes I'd enjoy that. As I said to the Pope:

LADY (STRIAR). I told the Pope: won't you try this? It's made of delicacies, all chopped up.

KAUFFMAN. In a way I mean obviously it's like you know whatever but the thing that I the thing that I'm feeling like these none of these women would ever feel is 'I don't have enough information.' Like these I mean this is what we talk about all the time like these women act on very little information.

WASHBURN. Yes

KAUFFMAN. And they create out of very little information.

WASHBURN. Well and they're able to I mean part of the reason they're able to act and like do all of that is *because* they have very little information

KAUFFMAN. Right

WASHBURN. going in I mean it's like with Elena Ceausescu

KAUFFMAN. Oh it's yeah

WASHBURN. Heading up Romanian science. Which, you know, if you have like a 4th grade education

KAUFFMAN. Oh yeah I mean it's really it's because we were saying that whole that whole arts how the others were all at one time performers or performed I mean can't we say and Elena is the only one who isn't but can't we say that she is really in a sense the greatest performer of all because she of all of them she like reaches farthest in creating a role for herself out of like out of like

WASHBURN. Air

KAUFFMAN. Totally concocted it's like she just decides so it's just it's like I'm a scientist! And I'm head of the Science Institute! And you're all going to do science my way! I mean that's amazing to me that she just has this complete conviction it's like it doesn't seem to even to cross her mind that you can't do that if you aren't actually a scientist.

WASHBURN. I know it's like, the Power of Fantasy I mean my God.

KAUFFMAN. It's complete Meisner.

(The Ladies have gathered around an old style microphone.)

ANNOUNCER (NINA). *(Oddly cursory:)* Starring Eva Duarte in "My Kingdom of Love." Great women in history as penned by leading philosophers and nationalists. Last week Miss Duarte enthralled us all with her Catherine the Great, next week she will appear as the lovely Cleopatra this week as Elizabeth 1 but first a Word from our Sponsors soap ad.

(The ad is sung by the ladies with the exclusion of EVA.)

(It is sung in a weirdly faint and offhand manner, like we're hearing a desultory rehearsal of it from another room.)

LADY (ALLISON).
    IF YOU'RE CLEAN WHEN YOU'RE CLEAN IT'S A... CREAMY GLEAMY FEELING

OTHER LADIES (NINA and STRIAR).
    ...SOFT AND CLEAN...

LADY.
    FIRST YOU'RE WET AND THEN YOU'RE SOAPY THEN YOU'RE CLEAN THEN YOU'RE... SOFT AND DRY... (SOFT

OTHER LADIES. AND

LADY. WARM

OTHER LADIES. AND

LADY. DRY).

(Very offhand:) So *try* it.

> *(Xylophone zing.)*
>
> *(To the 'tok tok tok' of a mallet hitting a wooden block, Chinese Opera style,* EVA *steps up to the microphone in a stylized manner.)*

ELIZABETH 1 (EVA). *(Whirls decisively:)* I will never marry.

> *(A beat.)*

SOME SORT OF LORD (NINA). *(Offstage:)* That's an interesting decision your majesty.

> *(A beat.)*

ELIZABETH 1. I know.

LADY (NINA).

> LATHER UP LATHER UP TO A CREAMY GLEAM, LATHER UP LATHER UP

ALL.   LATHER UP LATHER UP

> *(Two back claps.)*
>
> *(Spoken:)*

LADY (NINA). Yeah we're back now:

> *(The Light of History clicks on full blast.)*

EVA. "Only fanatics do not give up.

I like fanatics and all of history's fanaticisms. I like the heroes, the saints, the martyrs, whatever the cause and reason for the fanaticism.

Fanaticism turns life into a permanent and heroic process of dying; but it is the only way that life can defeat death.

(All the LADIES *join in on this one line:)* Fanaticism is the only force that God gave the heart to win its battles."

> *(The Light of History may switch off now.)*

Those who speak of sweetness and love forget that Christ said: "I have come to bring fire over the earth and what I most want is that it burn!"

WASHBURN. You love them.

KAUFFMAN. No it's well no I don't think it's—

WASHBURN. You *luv* them.

KAUFFMAN. It's because it's because it's not no of course I don't love them but I do I do love them in a way I mean I guess because what it is is that I'm just really impressed by their gumption. They're doers they effect change negative

WASHBURN. But it's terrible

KAUFFMAN. Change.

WASHBURN. Change.

KAUFFMAN. Like I can't I really I mean and it sounds so naive but I really am amazed. I'm amazed at how they just didn't care whether people liked them or not. I mean and that's and how they just said their mind and went after it I mean don't you don't you do you not find something at all impressive.

WASHBURN. Of course I do.

EVA. I have a terrifying affinity for suffering. Whenever I see suffering in one of my people I feel it also in my own body. I think that this is why I am afflicted with illnesses. People who are cold, who do not care for another person, they maintain their body at a cool regular temperature. Me, I have fevers—I love and I hate and I don't forget. I am like the people—they don't forget, they *can't* forget, they can't choose not to suffer. When you have power you can choose not to suffer. Who would not choose not to suffer? Suffering is difficult. One by one by one I see it, I see men rise up to the great heights, the air is rare up there, it is like wine, they become dizzy but they feel wonderful. They are like the deep sea divers who go down to the depths and there something happens to their blood, they become intoxicated, they can't think. They look at the weights on their feet and they think 'Why am I wearing weights on my feet? How silly is that?!' and they unbuckle themselves from the weights on their feet. And their bodies rush upwards through the water too fast, and their brains are crushed and when they arrive on the surface their bones are smashed and they float on the surface like a mangled limp thing. Like the vomit of whales which lies on top of the waves and is called ambergris and is an extremely expensive ingredient in the best perfume from Paris. That is what it is like at the heights; what is most rare, most costly and sought after is really just vomit. And they stand up there and they feel dizzy and they say what is this suffering that I am carrying around my neck. I feel so light and so wonderful and this suffering, the suffering of other people, is weighing me down, it is too heavy and too hot and so they release it, and they don't even watch it fall to the ground beneath them to see if it lands on anyone and hurts them. And then they feel terrific, they feel released. They feel like finally, they are what they always knew they were, deep down in their hearts. Now they are a figure in a fairy story. But they are too light. And at the heights the wind is very strong. Not long after that they lose their balance, and then they fall—falling, they gain a terrible weight. And their bodies lie on the ground in a bloody pulp. That is their fairy story.

End of Act Two

(In the dark a song:)

IMELDA.
> I'VE GOT A LOW-DOWN BURNING FEELING, A FEVER
> FOR

ALL. YOU

IMELDA.
> I'VE GOT A CONFLAGRATION BABY, IN ME IT'S A ZOO

ALL. *(Joining in in a whisper:)* ON FI-RE:

IMELDA.
> THE CHIMPS AND THE CHEETAHS BABY, THE OX AND
> THE

ALL. *(Again, a whisper:)* GNU

IMELDA.
> THEY'RE ALL SHRIEKING AND SMOKING, BABY; BIG
> FUR FIRE-BALLS FOR YOU
> FI-YER, I'M ON FI-YER
> FOR YOU
> I'M WRACKED WITH DESI-YER
> AND YEARNING IT'S TRUE
> YOUR EYES UP ABOVE ME BABY, LIKE STARS IN THE
> SKY
> THEY TWINKLE AND TWANKLE, WHILE I TREMBLE
> AND SIGH
> FOR YOUR SWEET LOVE: THEY'RE PLUNGING LIKE
> COMETS, DOWN ONTO MY THIGH
> I'M BLOWN OPEN BABY, BY YOUR COSMIC RADIOAC-
> TIVIT -AYE

ALL.
> FIY-ER
> I'M A BLAZE AND A PYRE

IMELDA.
> AND A MOUNTAIN OF TIRES ALIGHT
> I'M A COAL-FED COMBUSTION
> UNDERGROUND/OUT OF SIGHT

ONE LADY. *(Whispers.)* But Still Smoking.

> *(Sudden total change in tone, very tender.)*

IMELDA.
> I'M ALIGHT, A LIGHT
> LIKE A CANDLE IN THE NIGHT
> I AM BURNING
> BABY

FOR YOU.

THANK YOU.

MORRIS. She was really into making the Philippines, like, an ideal, like a beacon for the West with like arts

STRIAR. Not making it a backwater

MORRIS. cultural centers. It was like a City on a Hill, if you will.

STRIAR. She had a bad run in with the Beatles, they refused to do a request concert at the Palace and she had them like beaten up.

NINA. We're forgetting about Dovie Beams

QUINCY. Dovie Beams is an American film star.

MORRIS. From Texas.

QUINCY. B movie.

DUNDAS. She was like a B movie actress.

NINA. From Tennessee.

QUINCY. Who had sex with her husband and she recorded it.

ACT III

TITLE: I DON'T KNOW I JUST THINK
SHE WAS A LITTLE HELLHOUND.

WASHBURN. But I think they're all stupid these books. The more I read them they copy from each other they contradict each other.

KAUFFMAN. Right.

WASHBURN. They ca—you know they're all sort of m—they're all so

KAUFFMAN. Exposes.

WASHBURN. UNINTELLIGIBLE suggestive.

KAUFFMAN. Yeah.

WASHBURN. It's just you know it's sucky scholarship it's all just like it's scurrilous or it's froofy.

KAUFFMAN. Uh huh.

WASHBURN. I mean it's just kind of.

KAUFFMAN. Yeah.

WASHBURN. I'm sick of.

KAUFFMAN. Froofy.

WASHBURN. We haven't begun to read all the shit that's been published about Eva and we don't know anything about Elena Ceausescu. UNINTELLIGIBLE black hole of Romanian UNINTELLIGIBLE. We know—

KAUFFMAN. Little Birdie.

WASHBURN. Right. We know she didn't wear underwear as a kid. We don't know why. That's it. That's all we know.

KAUFFMAN. I don't know I just think she was a little hellhound

LADY (NINA). Can I ask you about your hemline?

LADY (STRIAR). Oh sure, certainly.

LADY (NINA). Because it's an unusual length. Is it fashion, or some sort of conviction?

KAUFFMAN. And Bobby knows Imelda. I mean Bobby's father used to work for the um government radio. And then marshal law was declared and he stopped working for them. And apparently she does this wild thing where she doesn't sleep at night. she'll drive around in her limousine and go over to her friend's houses and like call them up and say "you have to come with me". And they'll drive around the city um just talking until until and then drop them off at daybreak.

WASHBURN. Do you know Eva only slept like three hours a night?

KAUFFMAN. I'm so not surprised she died so early.

WASHBRUN. M-hm but you know like all these women like Imelda like the more in power they get.

KAUFFMAN. Oh yeah.

WASHBURN. The less.

WASHBURN and KAUFFMAN. They sleep.

KAUFFMAN. Same with Madame Mao.

WASHBURN. I think it's like I think it's something where if you're really focused but you're not entertaining contradiction—in the way you need to entertain contradiction in order to lead a sane life with other people—but you know that if you really have a strong ideal and you really believe in yourself the more deluded you become and the more effectively insane you become but you also gain this incredible energy.

KAUFFMAN. You're not fighting contradiction. Contradiction's tiring maybe.

WASHBURN. Yeah I think contradiction's very tiring. I mean this what exhausts people like us, and you know for all our kind of self aggrandizing we want to see both sides of the story.

KAUFFMAN. So we're never really gonna make it like the people who can get a full night's sleep are never gonna be really powerful right?

WASHBURN. We're not gonna command nations at this rate.

(Beat.)

KAUFFMAN. You think all those people are waiting for the bathroom or looking at that really ugly art? Cuz I have to go to the bathroom.

(Pause.)

WASHBURN. They do too.

KAUFFMAN. You think?

WASHBURN. M-hm.

KAUFFMAN. There's no telling.

LADY (QUINCY). I like your nails.

LADY (STRIAR). Do you really?

LADY (QUINCY). I like them. They look really strong.

LADY (STRIAR). What do you think of the color?

LADY (QUINCY). I think the color makes you look really strong.

LADY (STRIAR). Oh. Listen. What is that?

LADY (QUINCY). Outside? That's shouting.

VOICEOVER. All in a rush:

NINA. Okay so Imelda wanted to build this cultural center because the Philippines was going to host this international film festival.

DUNDAS. But there was no money allocated for it so she started having screenings of previously banned porno movies to raise the money *fast.*

MORRIS. Right right and they're like it needs to be done by the end of the week so they build this cultural center but they do it really badly and one day while they're working on it, it

NINA. Collapses.

MORRIS. The roof collapses and kills all these workers.

STRIAR. Like / hundreds of workers.

DUNDAS. Like hundreds.

MORRIS. And she's like we don't have time to get the bodies out.

NINA. So pour the cement, just pour the cement.

STRIAR. And they say it's haunted now

DUNDAS. Haunted.

ALLISON. Haunted.

MORRIS. Haunted.

QUINCY. Okay we're going to do the story of Elena's life. I'm going to be in this play somewhere. Elena's life, 30 seconds. Go.

(No one responds. She starts off herself to prime the pump.)

Okay they called her little birdie because she didn't wear underwear as a kid when she climbed trees you'd see her, little birdie.

(They look at her blankly. She continues:)

She had a 4th grade education but when she became first lady she just declared that she was a scientist even though she had no idea what she was talking about, um, she would demand that the real scientists would give her their papers and she would sign her name on them and that really pissed them off. She stole stuff from Queen Elizabeth, she would demand that menus be written in French even though she didn't read French um, ah ah ah it was a total surveillance society they would bug all of the phone lines they would bug ah ah people's toilets people having sex so even when you weren't being bugged you thought that you were—

KAUFFMAN. Okay guys that's enough

NINA. That's really clever. Terrorizing people by just listening to them.

TITLE: AND SHE'S LIKE 'BUILD IT! BUILD IT NOW!'

WASHBURN. The threat of the Dovie Beams thing is that it totally profoundly humiliates Imelda. The threat is that if she were to divorce him because remember she's a large part of his popularity at this point. So it's like part of the deal for her staying in the marriage that after that point it's just like—I mean it's not like he wasn't removing vast sums of money from the country but he was sly about it and he was methodical and like Imelda like after that point Imelda is just marching around in public buying American buildings with suitcases full of cash and he kind of he kind of just can't say boo.

KAUFFMAN. I know but like I just like I don't know that I buy that I mean it's an entire—

WASHBURN. Oh come on hasn't like hasn't Charles ever fucked up in some way.

KAUFFMAN. *(Laughs.)*

WASHBURN. And how do you respond?

KAUFFMAN. Angry. I attack

WASHBURN. Uh huh

KAUFFMAN. him.

WASHBURN. And do you like do you kind of get on him for a while?

KAUFFMAN. Yeah totally.

WASHBURN. And do you then like does he have to do things your way for a while?

KAUFFMAN. Yeah but not like giving me the keys to his like—

WASHBURN. Well you don't he doesn't have vaults to you know he doesn't have keys to give you.

KAUFFMAN. Well that's true.

WASHBURN. And also say you you know something happens with Charles there's a kind of a blow up he really fucks up and you're you know you're really pissed at him and say you go and do something that normally pisses him off.

KAUFFMAN. Right.

WASHBURN. You know that normally he'd call you on.

KAUFFMAN. Uh huh.

WASHBURN. But he doesn't and you you—it's not like you're unaware that he's not calling you on this and you're.

KAUFFMAN. Okay but how many years is this going on? Like you know— if I did something, if Charles fucks up, you know it's like 2 days *(She laughs)* and

WASHBURN. Yeah but that's

KAUFFMAN. And the interests of an entire country are not at stake.

WASHBURN. Yeah and that's because you don't have the interests of an entire country you know it's their country is as your apartment for you. And, you know, Charles has never had an affair with a woman who's made a tape of him having sex with her and talking about how he doesn't sleep with Annie anymore because she's frigid he looooves this other woman and he's singing her like

> *(Singing:)*
> PRETTY LITTLE LOVE SONGS LA LA LA LA
> *(IMELDA emerges from the darkness.)*
> *(This is a peppy smiley song.)*

IMELDA.
> WHEN WE SING SWEET SONGS OF LOVE
> IN THE LAND THAT TOGETHER WE LOVE A-OOOOH

LADIES (NINA, QUINCY).
> SWAYING TOGETHER, TOGETHER IN LOVE
> WE SING WE'LL STAY TOGETHER FOREVER IN LOVE
> *(EVA runs on to join them.)*

ALL. A-OOOOOOH

LADY (STRIAR).
> WE'RE JUST A COUPLE OF CRAZY KIDS TOGETHER

LADY (NINA).
> JUST RUNNING A COUNTRY TOGETHER

LADY (QUINCY).
> RUNNING PELL MELL THROUGH THE POLITICAL WEATHER

IMELDA.
> A NEWSPAPER OVER OUR HEAD A-OOOOOH.

ALL. AND JUST LAUGHING AT THE OVERHEAD
> *(IMELDA peels off.)*

ALL MINUS IMELDA.
> WE'RE LOOPY WITH LAUGHS AND LOOPY WITH LOVE

LADY (QUINCY).
GOT A GOVERNMENT DIRECTIVE TO SIGN
LADY (MARIA).
SOME POWER'S YOURS,
ALL. AND SOME OF IT'S MINE.
A-OOOOOOH, AAAAAAAOOOOOOH

TITLE: I THINK WE DO HAVE TO GO TO
THESE SORT OF VERY DARK EVIL STICKY PLACES
SUCH AS YOU KNOW ROMANCE AND LOVE.

(IMELDA stands, spotlit, in the middle of a darkened stage. She is holding a medium sized tape recorder. She presses play. If we can hear it well enough from the tape recorder, fine, if not, we'll hear it on the overhead.)

(She has heard this recording before. Her expression does not change.)

(The Recording: It is important that DOVIE BEAMS and MARCOS speak without any kind of Texas or Filipino accents.)

DOVIE BEAMS. I'm itchy.

F. MARCOS. Itchy?

DOVIE BEAMS. I've got this rash, look, all over here, it's burning.

F. MARCOS. Let me see. Dovie, look at what you've done to yourself. You need lotion. You need me to rub lotion on it.

DOVIE BEAMS. I took a bath in baking soda. It didn't do any good.

F. MARCOS. *(Getting up and moving away:)* Do you have lotion?

DOVIE BEAMS. No. What is this Nando? Some damn tropical creature did this to me!

F. MARCOS. *(Returning:)* I don't know. I've never seen a rash like that before. Yeah, look at it. That's an American rash. You brought it over with you in your luggage girlie.

DOVIE BEAMS. Nando.

F. MARCOS. Look, it's in the shape of the state of Texas.

(Pause.)

F. MARCOS. Hmmmm.

That feels good?

DOVIE BEAMS. Mmmmh Hmm.

F. MARCOS. Mwh mwh mwh.

DOVIE BEAMS. Ferdie?

F. MARCOS. Mh Hm?

DOVIE BEAMS. This isn't some kind of Philippine sex rash is it?

(Little beat.)

F. MARCOS. If it was I don't think it would be on the *outside* of your thigh my dear.

DOVIE BEAMS. No but I mean—

F. MARCOS. Mwh Mwh

DOVIE BEAMS. I'm serious.

F. MARCOS. You're serious?

DOVIE BEAMS. Mh Hm.

(Little pause.)

I don't know if you have other women. I don't know *how* many girls you have.

(Long beat.)

F. MARCOS. I did have other women. I had a lot of other women. But that was before I met you. Now I only have you.

DOVIE BEAMS. And you have your wife.

F. MARCOS. *(Laughing:)* I can assure you that I haven't passed on to you a sexual disease contracted from my wife.

DOVIE BEAMS. Do you still sleep with her?

F. MARCOS. No. Imelda…she's like ice. In bed she's like ice—
there's only you
my little…popsie poo
my yummy…bitsy—

(Fumbling sound.)

MARCOS. *(Very close to mike:)* What's this?

DOVIE BEAMS. That?

F. MARCOS. Is this on?

DOVIE BEAMS. Oh, is it on? You must have hit it accidentally. With your foot or something.

F. MARCOS. Ah…no, that wouldn't be possible. This has been on the whole time?

DOVIE BEAMS. um…

F. MARCOS. Are there more of these?

DOVIE BEAMS. Machines?

F. MARCOS. Tapes. Or machines.

DOVIE BEAMS. Ten, twelve, something like that. Tapes.

F. MARCOS. Huh.

(Longish pause.)

What were you planning to do with them?

(A beat or two.)

DOVIE BEAMS. I don't know, I don't totally know what I was *planning* to do with them, originally, except that I thought, here you are, you're a very important man, and this is history. I've never been a part of history before— not that I'm not planning to be history on my own, on my own merits as a B movie actress—but anyway I thought, how great: I'll own a piece of history, what a cool souvenir. What I *will* do with them is that later on, when the affair is over and you're being a real jerk, just really standoffish, and Imelda's people are being really creepy and the US Ambassador is being really nasty to me what I'm going to do is I'm going to call a press conference, on the tar-mac or something in November of 1970, just before I step on the plane, and, in what I'm going to claim is for my own protection, I'm going to play these tapes—not these particular tapes because they're made up but the actual tapes in which apparently we make noisy love, and you sing songs to me in your native dialect and say indiscrete things about your wife and I feed you chicken. And reporters are going to make bootleg copies and they'll be played at sophisticated dinner parties and little opposition soirees—including I might add dinner parties given by Benigno Aquino. And during a protest in 1971 students at the University of the Philippines will occupy an administra-tive center and play looped recordings of the tapes out over loudspeakers and the troops who come to arrest them will double over in laughter as they approach the building.

F. MARCOS. Is *that* what you're going to do?

DOVIE BEAMS. Yes, I think so.

    (Long tensifying beat.)

F. MARCOS. You're a rascal.

DOVIE BEAMS. *You're* the rascal.

F. MARCOS. You're a wriggly little rascal.

DOVIE BEAMS. I'm an innocent little Yankee rascal who was *attacked,* by a nasty tropical…*something.*

F. MARCOS. You're suffering.

DOVIE BEAMS. I *am* suffering.

F. MARCOS. I'm going to kiss it and make it all better.

DOVIE BEAMS. No, don't— *(She starts to laugh in dismay.)* Nando don't *kiss* it—you're going to get it on your lips honey.

F. MARCOS. *(Muffled, indistinct:)* I'm making it *all* better.

    (The tape is starting to fade out.)

DOVIE BEAMS. No Nando, honey, then you're going to get it on *my* lips.

F. MARCOS. I thought you liked my burning kisses.

DOVIE BEAMS. *(Laughing:)* Nooooo. Who's the rascal *now*—

    (IMELDA clicks the 'stop' button.)

    (The spotlight remains up on her for a few beats.)

(Her face is expressionless.)

(There is a long pause.)

(She half sings, in a monotone:)

IMELDA.

THERE'S BEEN A FLOOZY IN YOUR BED

PERFUME ON THE PILLOW AND A DENT IN THE SHAPE
OF HER HEAD

DON'T GIVE ME DIAMONDS

OR A DIVORCE

I'LL TAKE A MINISTRY

AND CARTE BLANCHE OF COURSE

(Lights fully out. A beat. Someone sings in the dark, half absentmindedly.)

AN ACTRESS (STRIAR).

A-OOOOOOOH, AAAAAAH, AOOOOOH

(LOOPY WITH LAUGHS AND LOOPY WITH LOVE.)

KAUFFMAN. *(Voiceover:)* Are you really not going to make a distinction between love and power?

WASHBURN. *(Voiceover:)* I guess I'm using 'love' as a term for…for love but also for, like, interdependence for for that thing where you, um, you know, where you at any point let someone else's existence kind of determine your own or your fate or your future or whatever. I mean I guess that's that's with these women that's what's like so fascinating and terrifying and aggravating to me. You know, that fantasy, I mean I totally know that fantasy that's totally my fantasy the one where you're with someone and you kind of through them you become this whole other thing. And this thing…which you become…is much more powerful.

KAUFFMAN. *(Voiceover:)* Well it wasn't just a fantasy. For them.

WASHBURN. *(Voiceover.)* Right. No.

(Lights up on JIANG QING and two other Ladies.)

(They are holding imaginary saucers and firmly gripping their imaginary teacups.)

(The Light of History:)

JIANG. "We must subject ourselves to rigorous self scrutiny and self criticism, we must transform ourselves, must rebel against ourselves, revolution" Revolution.

(They drop their imaginary teacups with a gesture.)

LADIES. Crash!

Revolution. Revolve.

(The women revolve.)

TITLE: OH MY GOD YOU'RE DEAD!

KAUFFMAN. Elena Ceausescu was in her sixties, yeah? When she died.

WASHBURN. Was she that young?

KAUFFMAN. Yeah, yeah I think they were.

WASHBURN. I guess those Eastern Bloc women…

KAUFFMAN. Do you know that I had a dream yeah they look a little bit old before their time.

ELENA. I'll have some more tea I think thank you.

LADY (STRIAR). Is there any left? I'll be happy to ring someone.

ELENA. Well there are dregs, yes, have them bring, why don't you have them bring more than one pot. At a time. Have them bring pots at a time. Five or six at a time. And line them up there, in a row.

LADY (NINA). Of course. They'll start boiling all of the water now.

ELENA. Yes, they should start boiling all of the water now. Water should boil at all times I like to keep water boiling at all times, a vat of it, I say 'it should boil always.'

KAUFFMAN. No but you have no idea!

WASHBURN. I mean she was like maybe we do too! We read

KAUFFMAN. How?

WASHBURN. The books! We read the books that's how we know!

ELENA. Look, just *thinking* about it makes me crazy look I'm trembling thinking about it my left leg that isn't a is that it's a normal kind of twitch. It's a completely normal kind of twitch. Our bodies aren't clockworks it's normal if it persists if it persists then I call in physicians. I wonder if the physicians like to see me naked. Half naked. I don't fill out a bra the way I used to but I wonder if my flesh excites them. I wonder if it excites them because it's still sexy or because they want to fuck the wife of a leader. How many men, statistically, would want to fuck—I mean I read something once, some survey, about Margaret Thatcher and the British Male Public which was pretty astonishing—you'd have to set up a…chart or a…one of those lines. With extreme and completely powerless beauty at one end and totally ugly total power at the other end. And you'd want to set up a—as you move through the chart—you'd have to have a room full of men with electronics strapped to their penises, but I wonder how you represent power like that since it's not like you're just flashing them porn, beauty is instant, power is only power is only power over time, power is something plus time, force X plus time is power. Beauty is instant sex is slightly less instant since it is a premonition of power which is over time but these are all microsecond distinctions. Oh…set up the experiment anyway. I'll enjoy walking into a room full of men with electronics on their penises and whacking a pointer on the blackboard.

Is the tea ready yet?

LADY (NINA). I think that the water—I think that it isn't boiling yet.

ELENA. I'll (just) nibble on these damp leaves.

LADY (STRIAR). Here I'll look at your leaves. I'll tell your fortune.

ACTRESS (NINA). This is the story of Elena Ceausescu…

ELENA. *(To the audience:)* Take a look at it from my perspective. I get a telegram "Country in turmoil, return at once."

ALL ACTRESSES. Gunshots!

ACTRESSES IN TURN. And now she's dead. And now she's dead. And now she's dead.

WASHBURN. I bet she was I bet Wang Guangmei was a bitch

KAUFFMAN. Um I'm sure well she sounded like she sounds like definitely a force to be reckoned with

WASHBURN. I mean I don't think she deserved what she got obviously.

> *(KAUFFMAN laughs.)*

KAUFFMAN. Yeah is that what you were saying?

WASHBURN. No, really. But but I begin to see like what category of aggravation Wang Guangmei must have been in

LADY (STRIAR). Here, won't you try on this dress?

LADY (QUINCY). Oh. No thank you.

LADY (STRIAR). Oh but really, really you must.

KAUFFMAN. Right

WASHBURN. If there are like if you had unlimited power where you would you just suddenly really want to take someone out?

LADY (QUINCY). *(Indicates her own costume:)* But this dress is a lovely dress. Just right for receiving guests.

LADY (STRIAR). Aha. But you aren't. Receiving guests. *(Leans forward and whispers:)* You are under attack.

KAUFFMAN. Right right.

WASHBURN. I mean I don't feel that I would cuz I'm not suffused with unlimited power and the complete arrogance that it gives you.

KAUFFMAN. Right

WASHBURN. Like there's no one in my life that I would actually want to parade around

KAUFFMAN. In ping pong

WASHBURN. In ping pong

KAUFFMAN. In a ping pong ball necklace.

WASHBURN. In ping pong balls with like their arms behind their back.

> *(Light of History.)*

WANG GUANGMEI. "I'm not going to put on that dress. It is not presentable."

RED GUARD (STRIAR). "Then why did you wear it in Indonesia."

WANG GUANGMEI. "It was summer at the time. I'm not going to put it on."

RED GUARD. "Let me repeat. You are under attack here today."

KAUFFMAN. Part of you know how when you're aggravated by someone even here I mean probably like 40 to 45 percent is them, but like probably the majority of the stuff is you being what envious of their career or envious of you know oh they always just get everything don't they

THE LADIES. "Fanaticism is the only force that God gave the heart to win its battles!"

WASHBURN. M-hm.

KAUFFMAN. You know what I mean, so it's really *(KAUFFMAN laughs.)* it's the envy it would

WASHBURN. You have someone in mind don't you.

KAUFFMAN. No actually I don't I actually don't have anyone in mind well I guess I I mean well yeah I could definitely come up with some people.

WANG GUANGMEI. "On no account can you encroach upon my personal freedom."

(Group Laughter.)

WASHBURN. I I don't know I think it's got to be what like 40%? 30% 40? of women (people/whatever) who would, in that position, like if you suddenly you're in a position where you have a lot of power, and you're not impeded I guess I can just see how, like, when you end up in Times Square by mistake or on 5th Avenue or Soho and you're just suddenly surrounded by Tourists and they're proceeding extremely slowly and it just it drives me nuts it's like, this is a working city, I am trying to get somewhere, for me it's them that are being incredibly rude and they are totally they are *in my way* and I have never—I don't think I have? No, of course I haven't I've never, actually, *shoved* a tourist but I know, you know, one day, I know I'm gonna, like it's bound to happen and for me it's that's the power I have I can shove somebody but it could easily like if I was if I had a nation kind of at my command I can see how that exact same impulse which is *annoyance* basically and *frustration* just sort of ends up becoming something very different.

RED GUARD. "You are a member of the reactionary bourgeoisie and a class dissident. You will not be given an iota of minimum democracy, let alone extensive democracy. Dictatorship is being exercised over you today, and you are not free."

(The Annes are looking at the book.)

KAUFFMAN. *(Reading from the book:)* So…the phone rings at Wang's residence in the leadership compound. The Red Guards of Qinghua University—

WASHBURN. Quinghua, or Chinghua?

KAUFFMAN. Oh. Um…

WASHBURN. I don't think we can, I don't think we can make assumptions that all Qs are Ch's can we?

KAUFFMAN. I'm sure we can't. We need an intern. Okay so the Red Guards take Wang into 'revolutionary custody' and from ten that night until the next morning her crimes as a capitalist-roader are read out like a catechism at a struggle meeting. And this transcript is very intense:

> *(WANG GUANGMEI is wearing a heavy coat, and a necklace made of ping pong balls painted to look like skulls.)*
>
> *(One RED GUARD holds her arms back, the other dangles an outfit in front of her.)*
>
> *(The sound of flash photography.)*
>
> *(JIANG QING is silently reading Anna Karenina.)*
>
> *(Time slows down.)*
>
> *(The Light of History has become terribly bright, and spills across their faces.)*

WANG GUANGMEI. "I will not put on that dress, come what may. If I have committed mistakes, I am open to criticism."

RED GUARD. "You are guilty. You are under attack today, and you will face further attacks in the future. Put on the dress you wore in Indochina."

WANG GUANGMEI. "That was for summer. There is winter clothing for winter, summer clothing for summer, and spring clothing for spring. I cannot put on summer dress now."

RED GUARD. "We know nothing about such bourgeois stuff as what is good for summer, winter, or spring or for receiving guests or for travel."

WANG GUANGMEI. "Chairman Mao has said that we must pay attention to climate and change our clothing accordingly."

> *(Group Laughter.)*

RED GUARD. "What Chairman Mao said refers to the political climate. And the way you stand in that respect, you will freeze to death even if you wear a fur coat."

WASHBURN. I'm sorry both your fish are on the ground is that cool.

KAUFFMAN. Yeah that's okay because they I just changed their water and

WASHBURN. Uh huh

RED GUARD. "Now, are you going to put on that dress."

WANG GUANGMEI. "No."

KAUFFMAN. When you first change their water they just kind of hang out at the bottom for a while.

WASHBURN. Why are they in trauma?

KAUFFMAN. I think they are a little bit tr—traumatized I mean I put stuff in the water so it doesn't but I saw them earlier like about a half hour

WASHBURN. M-hm.

KAUFFMAN. an hour ago swimming at the top and they sleep you know, fish.

WASHBURN. No.

KAUFFMAN. Yeah.

WASHBURN. Really?

KAUFFMAN. Oh yeah I've seen them.

WASHBURN. But not in a motionless way I thought fish slept on the wing or whatever.

KAUFFMAN. What?

WASHBURN. I thought fish slept you know flopping around.

KAUFFMAN. Really? I don't think so. Well not my fish.

WANG GUANGMEI. "If I were really opposed to Chairman Mao, I would deserve to freeze to death."

RED GUARD. "You are opposed to Chairman Mao."

WANG. "I am not against him now, and I will not oppose him in the future."

RED GUARD. "See what will happen at a quarter to seven. Try to defy us by not wearing that dress. We mean what we say."

>   (*Pause.*)

"There are seven minutes left."

>   (*Pause.*)

WANG GUANGMEI. "How about my just putting on the shoes?"

>   (*The* RED GUARD *glances over at* JIANG QING.)

>   (*Without looking up from her book,* JIANG QING *shakes her head, almost imperceptibly.*)

RED GUARD. "That isn't enough. You must wear everything."

JIANG QING. (*Reads from Anna Karenina:*) "Some supernatural force drew Kitty's eyes to Anna's face. She was fascinating in her simple black dress, fascinating were her round arms with their bracelets, fascinating was her firm neck with its thread of pearls, fascinating the straying curls of her loose hair, fascinating the graceful, light movements of her little feet and hands, fascinating was that lovely face in its eagerness, but there was something terrible and cruel in her fascination."

WASHBURN. Cuz otherwise the ocean would be full of like

KAUFFMAN. Well but

WASHBURN. sleeping fish

KAUFFMAN. Like there's

WASHBURN. at the bottom.

KAUFFMAN. no well not necessarily the bottom I mean there's also a current in the ocean that probably carries them around maybe it looks like they are I have no idea what I'm talking about but neither do you Anne okay?

WASHBURN. UNINTELLIGIBLE

(They laugh.)

EVA. Like Christ I harrowed Hell. Like Christ I stand before you to burst into flames. I am here to ignite you.

IMELDA. I think that there is an idea that people who are so very beautiful they are unmoved somehow by their own beauty but I assure you this isn't so. I look into a mirror and I take my own breath away. Vanity? Oh no. God made my face this way. He made it so that when people look at me they feel a catch in their chest, they are drawn to me. When I speak, they will listen to me; when I feel, they will feel with me.

Jesus said take this cup away from my lips. He said I don't want to drink from this anymore because the will of God—even Jesus felt this!—can be bitter. And there was a time, yes, early in my marriage when I said take this cup away from me. I don't want to drink any more. I would go into my bedroom and I would shut the door and I would climb onto my bed and I would kneel, on the coverlet, and I would hit my head, my beautiful beautiful head, that God gave me, I would hit it against the wall. *(She mimes driving her head forward.)* Over and over and over. I hit it into the wall, so many times, so hard, that I had dented the plaster, there was a kind of *(She raises her hand and pushes it forward against the air slightly to indicate.)* crater, in the plaster. And once I saw I had damaged the wall that was where I would aim my head. For that spot. And if I made another tiny crack, if I dented the plaster deeper, then I felt that I had accomplished something.

My husband took me to the States, to the NYU Medical Center and they did an examination and afterwards they took me aside. They said Imelda, you have me to make a decision. Do you understand? I looked up and my eyes were full of tears. I said tell me what this decision is. They said you have to understand that this is the life your husband has chosen. If you want to live, you will have to leave him. Or. You will have to change.

And so I began every morning to say affirmations. I said "My life is beautiful" "I love my life." The men in the living room, very early in the morning or late at night, the dirty feet, the cigars and loud voices and bags of money, I said "This is all part of a higher, idealistic purpose." When my husband said to me 'Stand this way, no, this way, sing, you have to dress like this and go here and say this, not like that, like this, wave your arm that way, sing, didn't anyone ever teach you to think?? Sing, that isn't how you cut a ribbon, my God' I put aside my laziness and I said I will listen to him, and I will understand. "I believe in this, I will become this, I am going to be this, my life is beautiful. I love this life. I love my life."

And one morning I wake up, I go to the mirror, I look into my beautiful beautiful face and I say 'I love myself' and I realize, suddenly, I realize…that it is *true*.

I am like a butterfly who has shaken herself finally from the chrysalis. I go to the window and I spread my wings to dry in the sun. The world is so beautiful, I am so beautiful, there is so much that I can accomplish! And there are tears streaming down my cheeks. They are tears of joy.

I think that we are all so scared to embrace ourselves. We are so afraid, of what we can become.

End of Act Three

ACT IV

Lights up on:

TITLE: IDEALISM IS POWERMONGERING
IT'S ALL POWERMONGERING.

KAUFFMAN. So power I don't know how do you talk about power? It's very like I don't know I feel like I have this whole relationship with them like

WASHBURN. M-hm

KAUFFMAN. I feel like I'm making discoveries about, what you know, well the whole power thing that you

WASHBURN. M-hm.

KAUFFMAN. Were so scared by, you know, when I said that I wanted power? And I it it it it it it occurs to me that the fact that I was l was like suddenly like 'I really want more power in my life'

WASHBURN. Uh-huh.

KAUFFMAN. and that these women are you know have become somehow a part of my psyche you

WASHBURN. Uh-huh.

KAUFFMAN. know? I—it seems significant to me that like this is you know this is something that I'm sort of yearning for. Didn't we already have this discussion?

WASHBURN. Well but not on tape.

KAUFFMAN. Oh we didn't? Okay. Cuz I feel okay right

WASHBURN. We were talking about you were saying you wanted power.

KAUFFMAN. I wanted power.

WASHBURN. And then we were talking about how I found that disturbing.

KAUFFMAN. Yeah.

WASHBURN. Then we were talking about your therapist taking your side even though she hadn't been part of the actual conversation, that I found that I found your will to power terrifying and she said well she's just not acknowledging

KAUFFMAN. M-hm.

WASHBURN. what it is about power and I was saying it wasn't that I had a problem with people desiring power it's that I was start—it's more that I was startled to have someone suddenly announce no I want more power.

KAUFFMAN. Because it's

WASHBURN. Right that's not

KAUFFMAN. just like

WASHBURN. done very often because people say like

KAUFFMAN. Right

WASHBURN. People say you know I'd really like to change the world or they say more

KAUFFMAN. Right right right.

WASHBURN. They say you know I'd really like to have a very specific effect on Bush's re-election campaign.

KAUFFMAN. Right right.

WASHBURN. They don't

KAUFFMAN. Right

WASHBURN. say I want power *(WASHBURN laughs.)* It's just that normally people sublimate that.

> *(A Lady glides onstage.)*
>
> *(Ladies glide onstage throughout the following discussion.)*

LADY. *(At* ANNE *and* ANNE:*)* I like your cute fish. They are really, really serene.

> *(She glides off again.)*
>
> *(*KAUFFMAN *almost registers this; manages to shake it off.)*

KAUFFMAN. It's really true and you know what now that I'm thinking about it it's not like if you were to ask me you know what is a community that you wanna impact or what it what is what is a cause that you wanna 'I don't know I just want the pow—I'll choose that after' *(*WASHBURN *laughs loudly.)* I feel like I do feel like I should be more important than I am now. And it's not like, you know, I should be featured in the New York Times on the front page every you know but I feel like I feel like I always imagined myself as being someone um who people who look to

WASHBURN. M-hm.

KAUFFMAN. at this point in my life.

WASHBURN. M-hm.

KAUFFMAN. You know really look towards and really just—I mean I don't know if I was thinking in terms of a a a a title or a it's not like a position specifically and I don't think also it's like

WASHBURN. Is it something where you're where you imagine—I mean I always I always imagine that the ladies that they imagined, that they had a picture of themselves being you know on a balcony like they had this idea of 'here I am and I'm waving to the populace' you know *before.*

KAUFFMAN. Oh yeah right.

WASHBURN. I mean do you have like an image you know an image

KAUFFMAN. I have this sort of

WASHBURN. 'Anne Kay in power.'

KAUFFMAN. Yeah I do actually I have this this is funny because I hadn't ever oh this is weird yeah

WASHBURN. What, what

KAUFFMAN. you know this really you're really going to—now you're going to be frightened.

WASHBURN. *What,* no.

KAUFFMAN. Okay because I'm in a—

WASHBURN. I'm completely pro-power I'm just startled by the

KAUFFMAN. Okay do you want to hear this?

WASHBURN. directness. Yes I do. Of your—yes. Tell me.

KAUFFMAN. And it's not this isn't something this isn't like a thing where I'm like 'this is what I want, someday' this is just the image.

WASHBURN. Okay

KAUFFMAN. It's just it's a kind of flash.

WASHBURN. Okay but a flash of what a flash of what.

KAUFFMAN. All right so I'm and this is just it's not at all extensive it's really just an image I think which I'm unpiecing which is that I'm in the not the green room I'm I guess it's like the you know makeup area of a TV studio I don't know like I'm really I'm really just but but it's pretty private but there's this intern there and I'm—and actually the lighting's very specific that's weird but uh so I'm going to go on in like 20 minutes and she's giving me a manicure.

WASHBURN. Are you an anchor woman?

KAUFFMAN. No no I'm there to do an interview show I'm going to give a

WASHBURN. Conan?

KAUFFMAN. No I think I feel like it's PBS.

WASHBURN. Oh so it's Charlie

KAUFFMAN. Yes or

WASHBURN. Rose.

KAUFFMAN. well it might be a new—it might be Charlie Rose.

(*A beat.*)

WASHBURN. So that's it?

KAUFFMAN. No because what I feel like I feel like what the image is about to me it's all about this assistant who is giving me—and it's not like I ever get manicures I mean God I mean what do I care about my nails

WASHBURN. Oh let me see

(KAUFFMAN *shows her nails.*)

KAUFFMAN. They're fine, I mean

WASHBURN. Yeah

KAUFFMAN. So yeah but it's all about well first of all it's all about I'm kind of bored, it's a boring moment for me like 'ho de hum' like I've done this often before and then what it's about is that the woman who is painting my nails she's like this young twenty-something you know

WASHBURN. Oh kind of

KAUFFMAN. Yeah very

WASHBURN. Kind of the hair

KAUFFMAN. Yeah

WASHBURN. Like a

KAUFFMAN. Yeah like a high power intern type and she's visibly I mean very very faintly but she's visibly but faintly but visibly I am not kidding Anne she is trembling.

WASHBURN. Oh because—just her hands or?

KAUFFMAN. Uh, no I think it's her entire body.

WASHBURN. Wow.

(*A beat.*)

WASHBURN. Is it because you're so scary or because you're so awesome

KAUFFMAN. Actually, I think it's a little of both.

(*A beat.*)

KAUFFMAN. (*Laughing:*) Now are you frightened?

(WASHBURN *opens her mouth to speak.*)

THE LADIES. INCOMPREHENSIBLE

KAUFFMAN. (*Laughing:*) Oh, I see

THE LADIES. OVERTALK OVERTALK OVERTALK.

WASHBURN. INCOMPREHENSIBLE sophisticated.

KAUFFMAN. Right right right.

WASHBURN. And very—

KAUFFMAN. Yeah.

WASHBURN. but I mean alright okay so because I know this is just an image but do you have…a…I mean is there a sense: okay: how do you feel about the fact that she's trembling.

KAUFFMAN. Oh I like it.

WASHBURN. You do.

KAUFFMAN. Yeah I think I really I *(Thinks for a moment.)* It's just how great is that, seriously, if that's what you are you know?

You are so—

WASHBURN. I am totally not frightened but you know what I think next time you go see your therapist I want to be there also so that I can make sure that my point of view is represented properly.

KAUFFMAN. I mean I feel like it's about making an impact. I just really want to be able to feel that I'm making a, like, enormous impact—like on these NYU kids that I'm teaching although I guess I wouldn't be teaching them anymore—I would teach, I would definitely teach, but I would for one thing be making a fuckload of more money and

WASHBURN. Wait wait wait but what. What would you be teaching that's my—

KAUFFMAN. I wouldn't be teaching in general but I'd definitely come in and do special seminars.

WASHBURN. Okay but what would they be on. That's my question.

KAUFFMAN. Well I'd want them to come from my own experiences I'd want to be really honest about that for one thing I mean I really don't believe in cultivating a mystique I mean it's so so so like if you could see these kids they are so like you know what it's like to be that age you know you are so cynical on the one hand I mean these kids my God and that's also that's New York for you but also l mean do you remember what that's like? You just really want to believe that there's someone that you really really want to be.

WASHBURN. M-hm

KAUFFMAN. And it just totally means so much to me to be able to be that to them. I mean actually when I really think about it and it's like Charlie Rose that's fine, or whatever, the New York Times Profile is great it's definitely of course it's a thrill I mean especially for my parents and honestly Anne I think that's what I think that's where I mean I don't think that's what I've been thinking about particularly but I think that's where my heart really is on this like the money is honestly not that important I mean it is but it isn't and the

whole being at a party and having people elbow their way over to me like it's
great but I think the thing that's going to mean the most to me…
What's going to mean the most to me is standing there,
in that classroom,
just with all these kids
and the room is dark it's a night seminar you know cause they've worked it
around my schedule and
the city
is glittering through the windows.
I'm in a pool of light
with all these little dim faces turned up at me
and there's a girl
there on the stage with me
she's I guess she's pretty you know she's
one of those gutsy alert girls you know,
maybe she's
—I don't know—
I don't know what this girl really is,
all I know is she's standing standing in front of me
and she's just overcome
because she's standing in front of me
and there's a tear streaming down her cheek and I reach over
and I wipe that tear away

> *(Rises, sings:)*
> LITTLE GIRL
> THERE'S SO MUCH INSIDE YOU THAT'S WAITING TO
>   UNFURL
> DARE TO BE BOLD
> AND WITH A TOUCH
> I WILL TURN YOU
> INTO
> GOLD
> *(A beat.)*

KAUFFMAN. I have so much love. That's what it comes down to. I just I
have so much love to give.

> *(A beat.)*

WASHBURN. *(Very dubious:)* H-hm.

KAUFFMAN. What, you're not really going to say that you don't care about
power or about being powerful.

WASHBURN. Um, no. I didn't say that at all.

> *(A Lady has a pink pastry box, tied up with a string. She holds it out.)*

LADY (IMELDA). *(To* ANNE *and* ANNE:*)* Won't you try this? It's made of delicacies, all chopped up.

A LADY (STRIAR). *(Trying to be polite:)* How much would that be in roubles?

A LADY (ELENA). We don't! Use! Roubles!

LADY (NINA). *(To* WASHBURN:*)* What do you think. Is this a mouth made for kissing? Or for biting?

WASHBURN. Um…

> *(There is a frenzy, which is increasing.)*

LADY (NINA). I think you should only use the color to contour your natural lip line. Never go outside of your natural lip line.

ALL THE LADIES. OVERTALK

LADY (ELENA). We don't! Employ! Robots!

LADY (IMELDA). *(Indicating her abdomen:)* It's from…well I'd have to pull up my dress to show you but it's from here…to here…

LADY (EVA). Classic red, pluck your eyebrows, and that's all! That's my advice!

LADY (JIANG QUING). Electricity? It's a hoax. The great cities are lit up by the burning of the past!

LADY (ELENA). I'll show you how a real woman of her people dies!

> *(*ELENA *strips off her Jackie O top to reveal a blouse spattered with gunshot wounds.)*

> *(Revolutionary Opera ensues. The actress who played Landlord* HUANG *takes the same stance for* TORVALD, IMELDA *takes* HUNG-HSI's *stance for* NORA. *As* JIANG QING *reads from the book* HUNG-HIS / NORA / ANNA *enacts the action like an opera, the other actresses provide percussion and backup line dancing. As the scene progresses the performative style shifts from revolutionary opera, to something else.)*

NORA. Our home has never been anything but a dolls house. I've been your doll-wife, playing with my own little dolls. That's all our marriage has been Torvald, a land of make-believe.

TORVALD. ruhr ruhr ruhr ruhr ruhr ruhr ruhr ruhr ruhr?

NORA. I can't help what people will say. I only know that I must do this.

TORVALD. ruhr ruhr ruhr ruhr ruhr ruhr ruhr.

NORA. Oh. Torvald. I must educate myself. And you can't help me with that. It's something I must do by myself. *(Dramatic beat.)* That's why I'm leaving you.

TORVALD. ruhr ruhr ruhr? ruhr ru—

NORA. I must stand on my own two feet if I am to find out the truth about myself and about life.

TORVALD. ruhr ruhr ruhr ruhr ruhr ruhr ruhr! ruhr ruhr ruhr ruhr ruhr! ruhr ruhr ruhr! ruhr! ruhr!

NORA. I know quite well Torvald that most people would think you are right, and that theories of that kind are to be found in books, but I can no longer content myself with what most people say, or with what is found in books.

ALL. Door slam!

(JIANG QUING snaps her copy of Anna Karenina open.)

NORA-ANNA AMALGAM. Yes I must go quickly!

JIANG QING. Anna said, not knowing yet where she was going. She longed to get away as quickly as possible from the feelings she had gone through in that awful house.

(JIANG QING skips ahead in the text.)

(Lightly, under her breath:)

Dad dah dah dah dah dah

NORA-ANNA AMALGAM. I must go to the railway station!

JIANG QING. She said to herself as soon as the carriage had started and swaying lightly, rumbled over the tiny cobbles of the paved road.

Dah dah dah dah dah dah

NORA-ANNA AMALGAM. "No, I won't let you make me miserable"

JIANG QING. *(She reads:)* She thought menacingly, addressing not him, not herself, but the power that made her suffer, and she walked along the train platform."

NORA-ANNA AMALGAM. 'My God! Where am I to go?'

JIANG QING. *(She reads:)* "She thought, wandering further and further along. At the end of the platform she stopped. A luggage train was coming in."

(JIANG QUING stands, continues reading:)

JIANG QING. The platform began to sway.

NORA-ANNA AMALGAM. All at once I know what I have to do.

JIANG QING. "With a rapid light step she went down the steps and stopped quite near the rails which were vibrating from the approaching train."

EVA. "She tried to fling herself below the wheels of the first carriage as it reached her;

ELENA. But the red bag which she tried to drop out of her hand delayed her and she was too late;

EVA. She missed the moment.

ELENA. She had to wait for the next carriage."

NORA-ANNA AMALGAM. I do not take my eyes from the wheels of the second carriage.

ELENA. And exactly at the moment when the space between the wheels came opposite her.

EVA. She dropped the red bag.

JIANG QING. *(Not reading:)* She drew her head back into her shoulders.

NORA-ANNA AMALGAM. I lean forward.

JIANG QING. And the light by which she had read the books filled with troubles, falsehoods, sorrow, and evil, flared up more brightly than ever before, lighted up for her all that had been in darkness

> *(There is an authorial frenzy in which* WASHBURN *tries to find a way to end the play; finding it, she hands a new page to* JIANG QING *who takes it and reads from it.)*

NORA-ANNA AMALGAM. And all at once…I step back.

JIANG QING. The passing train seemed to reverberate through her entire body before it slowed and stopped at the other end of the platform.

EVA and ELENA. She let that train pass on by!

JIANG QING. Passengers climbed off, and on. In one quick

> *(Checking the word.)*

motion?

> *(*WASHBURN *nods.)*

JIANG QING. she stooped and grabbed the red bag tightly by its wicker handle. She turned from the track and stepped briskly forward toward the street where passing carriages kicked up small plumes of dust and, I don't know, urchins wandered about or something—she strode forward and then started to run. A sweet bright breeze trickled against her face, the air was like gold, her lips parted in a joyous cry:

EVERYONE. Torvald! I'm coming back to you honey! I'm coming back! Nora's coming home!

WASHBURN. *(Exhilarated:)* You know I think what this project could really use is a guy director. One of those Michaels. Or I hear the Davids are good.

> *(*IMELDA *steps forward to sing. To the initial tune of 'Feelings,' morphing swiftly. The others—including the Annes—join in, later on in multipart harmony.)*
>
> *(Sound of dripping.)*

IMELDA.
> FEELINGS
>
> SO STRANGE TO FIND THAT
> FEELINGS

HAVE UNDONE ME AND REMADE ME
TIL I ALMOST

DO NOT KNOW ME
DREAMINGS
AND SILLY ROMANTICAL
SCHEMINGS
HAVE UNROLLED ME
AND RETOLD ME—

ALL JOIN IN. *(Ferocious:)*
AND THE STARS!
IN THE SKY!

WASHBURN.
"THEY TWINKLE AND TWANKLE"—OH, NO.

EVERYONE.
THEY ARE BITTERLY COLD! AND IMPOSSIBLY HIGH!

(DARLING) DREADFUL TO KNOW YOU
AND HORRIBLE TO CARE
LOOK AT THE WORLD OF OUR LOVE
AND THE CARNAGE THAT IS THERE

BURNT EMOTIONS EVERYWHERE

IMELDA.	**EVERYONE ELSE.**
THE WRECKAGE OF OUR SWEETNESS	SWEETLY SPEAKING ON LOVE
THE SPOILAGE OF OUR GRACE	DIVIINE LIQUOR OF LOVE
THE END OF ALL OUR KINDNESS	FATEFUL COSMIC SHOVE
THAT HARD COMPRESSION IN YOUR EYES	
IS THE EXPRESSION ON MY FACE	
LOVE WE HAVE TORN OUT OUR WIRES WE	FLOWERS, CHOCOLATES, AND BEES
HAVE SHAKEN OFF OUR SKINS WE	BIG EYES AND WOBBLY KNEES
ARE UNDELIGHTFULLY NAKED WE	LOVELY LIGHTHEARTED TEASE
ARE CLOTS OF ORGAN AND SINEW AND BLOODY RAW SHINS	BABY BABY OH PLEASE

(Weird Medley Part:)
THE LORD ABOVE LOVES US
    WE
KNOW THIS TO BE TRUE FOR
IF HE DID NOT LOVE US WE
WOULD LIVE AS WE WANT TO
    DO

THE LORD ABOVE LOVES US
    WE
KNOW THIS TO BE TRUE FOR
IF HE DID NOT LOVE US WE
WOULD LIVE AS WE WANT TO
    DO

SINGING THE WORDS OF OUR   THROBBING HEARTS AND
    LOVE   TREMBLING HANDS
THE WEIRD VOCABULARY OF   THE DEEP SEDUCTION OF
    LOVE   DEMANDS
THE WACKED   BRAIN CHEMISTRY AND
    PRONUNCIATION OF LOVE   GLOWING GLANDS

YOUR LOVE IS MY UNDOING
    BUT
IT IS RIGHT TO BE UNDONE
I REVOLUTIONIZE MY STORY
AND BLOSSOM INTO GLORY
UNDER YOUR BLAZING SUN

> *(The sound of dripping.* EVA *holds out a teacup. Dripping changes to plonking.)*
> *(A plonk, a plonk, a plonk and* EVA *quaffs the content of her teacup.)*
> *(The sizzling of a fire being extinguished.)*

End of Play

PARIS COMMUNE

by Steven Cosson
and Michael Friedman

INTRODUCTION

On a rainy day in 2001, I found myself leafing through books that I'd been assigned in college but had never read. One of these tomes contained an essay by Kristin Ross, a professor at NYU, about the culture of the Paris Commune of 1871. Ross described how near the end of the seventy-day revolt, the people who had driven the government out of the city threw an enormous concert in the Tuileries Palace, the former seat of Empire. At this concert, the great singer La Bordas sang her signature tune, *La Canaille,* the chorus of which goes "C'est La Canaille, et bien j'en suis," or "They are the lowest scum, and so am I." A few days later, the army from Versailles retook the city, and over the course of the infamous "Bloody Week" killed tens of thousands of people.

The image of this concert seemed like a show waiting to happen, though a crazy one, and the only person crazy enough to think it was a good idea, and, in the end, to push the project into fruition, was Steve Cosson. Steve and I began researching the Commune, and the more we read, an overabundance of material emerged. Two of the members of the Commune's government were songwriters—one of them, Jean-Baptiste Clément, wrote the Commune's anthem, *The Cherries of Spring,* as well as a series of astonishing songs chronicling the violence of the Commune's fall; the other, Eugène Pottier, wrote the words to *The Internationale,* a song that would have a healthy future in the twentieth century, during the Commune. We gained a couple heroines, the Anarchist virgin Louise Michel and the glamorous Communist Elisabeth Dmitrieff, a villain, Adolphe Thiers, and laughed at the underground rantings of Père Duchêne.

The piece has been through more revisions than I think we ever expected when we started working in 2002, and we have been lucky that so many institutions have given us their generous support along the way.

In the end, what has drawn us to this material is the way in which the Commune is a moment in which all sorts of forces—culture, class, politics, performance, violence, economics, journalism—meet in a single moment and are clarified. The opportunity to bring to life the forgotten people who tried to give themselves, as one puts it, the power to control their own lives, has been unforgettable. At the end, as the actors Can-Can into the future, the fragments of the history of revolution and labor go on and on. And the question—how much are people willing to take before they can't take it anymore—still lingers in our post-revolutionary society.

—Michael Friedman

CAST OF CHARACTERS

Men

MAN 1. Throughout: Baker and Actor/Baker. Also: Medical Student, Citizen 5.

MAN 2. Throughout: Père Duchêne and Actor/Père Duchêne. Also: Guardsman, Rossel, Worker Poster, Citizen 2, Dead Man 1.

MAN 3. Throughout: Thiers, Actor/Thiers, and Rigault. Also: French Soldier, Parisian Citizen 1, Minister, Club Leader, Courbet, Councilman 3, Citizen 1, Captain.

THE PIANIST

Women

WOMAN 1. Throughout: Seamstress and Actress/Seamstress. Also: Bertholde.

WOMAN 2. Throughout: Louise Michel and Actress/Louise Michel. Also: Parisian Citizen 2, Councilman 2, Citizen 3, Voice, Dead Woman 2.

WOMAN 3. Throughout: Elisabeth Dmitrieff and Actress/Elisabeth. Also: Parisian Citizen 3, General, Citizen 4, Councilman 4, Woman 1.

WOMAN 4. Throughout: La Bordas and The Dressmaker. Also: Councilman 1, Woman 3.

THE SOPRANO

SONGS

All songs translated and adapted by Michael Friedman.

Le Temps des Cerises (The Cherries of Spring): music and lyrics by Jean-Baptiste Clément

La Canaille: lyrics by Alexis Bouvier, music by Joseph Darcier

The Armistice: author unknown

Ah, Comme J'aime Les Militaires! (Oh, I Love Men in Uniform): lyrics by Henri Meilhac and Ludovic Halévy, music by Jacques Offenbach

Chanson de Mai (Song of May): music and lyrics by Jules Jouy

Les Canards Tyroliens (The Yodeling Ducks): lyrics by Cognard Frères, music by Thérésa

Leur Bon Dieu (God of the Bigots): lyrics by Eugène Pottier, music by Emile Bouillon

Galop Infernal: music by Jacques Offenbach

L'Internationale: lyrics by Eugène Pottier, music by Pierre Degeyter

Ah! Je Veux Vivre: lyrics by J. Barbier and M. Carré, music by Charles Gounod

Mon Homme (My Man): music and lyrics by Jean-Baptiste Clément

Le Capitain (The Captain): music and lyrics by Jean-Baptiste Clément

Tarantelle: music by Georges Bizet

La Semaine Sanglante (The Bloody Week): music and lyrics by Jean-Baptiste Clément

ACKNOWLEDGMENTS

This work-in-progress version of *Paris Commune* was presented as a workshop production as part of The Public Lab Series, The Public Theater, New York City, opening April 4, 2008. It was directed by Steven Cosson with the following cast:

LA BORDAS,
DRESSMAKER, and others .... Kate Buddeke
SEAMSTRESS, and others .... Ayşan Çelik
ELISABETH DMITRIEFF, and others .... Nina Hellman
THE SOPRANO .... IVA
LOUISE MICHEL, and others .... Jeanine Serralles
FRENCH ARMY SOLDIER,
ADOLPHE THIERS,
RAOUL RIGAULT, and others .... Brian Sgambati
BAKER, and others .... Jeremy Shamos
LE PÈRE DUCHÊNE,
PARIS GUARDSMAN,
GENERAL ROSSEL, and others .... Sam Breslin Wright

And the following production staff:

Choreography .... Tracy Bersley
Scenic Design .... Alexander Dodge
Costume Design .... Sarah Beers
Lighting Design .... Thomas Dunn
Sound Design .... Ken Travis
Musical Director / Pianist .... Dan Lipton
Assistant Director .... Jessica Chayes
Dramaturgs .... Jocelyn Clarke,
Abigail Katz
Production Stage Manager .... Emily Park Smith

Paris Commune was developed by The Civilians, (Steven Cosson, Artistic Director); a Page to Stage workshop production at La Jolla Playhouse, (Des MacAnuff, Artistic Director; Terence Dwyer, Managing Director); and a Public Lab workshop production at The Public Theater, (Oskar Eustis, Artistic Director; Mara Manus, Managing Director); and by residencies at the MacDowell Colony and New York Theatre Workshop.

Jeanine Serrales, Sam Breslin Wright, Ayşan Çelik,
Kate Buddeke, and Jeremy Shamos
in *Paris Commune*

The Public Theater, New York City, 2008
Photo by Carol Rosegg

PARIS COMMUNE

Scene One

An empty stage. We see musicians, they're playing "The Cherries of Spring." Two performers enter.

ACTOR who plays BAKER. Imagine. In this space. Right here. *(A gesture.)* A stage.

ACTRESS who plays SEAMSTRESS. A really BIG stage.

ACTOR/BAKER. Right. Palatial.

ACTRESS/SEAMSTRESS. Meaning that it is actually a palace. Imagine here we are on stage inside a palace. *(They both gesture.)* It's the Tuileries Palace in Paris in the center of Paris connected to, actually, part of the Louvre.

ACTOR/BAKER. And it's 1871. Because now, as in today—if you were to go to Paris today—this space, this Tuileries Palace we're imagining, is gone. Today it's just an empty space between the two sides of the Louvre. Gone.

ACTRESS/SEAMSTRESS. But in 1871 it's here.

ACTOR/BAKER. It's here. It's night. It's springtime.

ACTRESS/SEAMSTRESS. It's a concert.

ACTOR/BAKER. A very *unusual* concert.

(*Actress playing* LA BORDAS *evokes a little bit of the image of La Bordas singing at the Tuileries Palace.*)

LA BORDAS.
    WHEN WE SING AGAIN
    OF CHERRIES IN SPRING
    THE GAY NIGHTINGALE
    THE BLACKBIRD'S LONE CALL
    ALL ECHOING SWEET AND CLEAR
    THE PRETTY YOUNG GIRLS WITH MADNESS OF SPRING-
        TIME
    AND LOVERS WHO FEEL THE WARMTH OF ONE NEAR
    WHEN WE SING AGAIN
    OF CHERRIES IN SPRING
    THE BLACKBIRD'S LONE CALL
    IS ALL THAT WE'LL HEAR

ACTRESS/SEAMSTRESS. That might have been sung at the concert by Rosalie Bordas or "La Bordas" as she was known. Now, this singer would not otherwise be allowed inside the Palace, but she sang at the concert in the Tuileries Palace on this night—

ACTOR/BAKER. In springtime.

ACTRESS/SEAMSTRESS. And this song, "The Cherries of Spring."

ACTOR/BAKER. Or in French, "Le Temps des Cerises."

BOTH. "Le Temps des Cerises"

ACTRESS/SEAMSTRESS. This song from this moment forward would always mean "The Paris Commune."

ACTOR/BAKER. "The Commune." A time—a brief time—when the poor rose up and took Paris as their own.

ACTRESS/SEAMSTRESS. They took Paris and for a time, they imagined…well, simply…but, quite radically, they imagined that they controlled their own lives. And for this idea, let's call it *liberation* this idea demanded a new…city. A new world. I mean…BIG.

ACTOR/BAKER. BIG like this palace.

ACTRESS/SEAMSTRESS. Yes. And like this palace, now as in "today," The Paris Commune is gone.

ACTRESS/ELISABETH. But more. More than "gone." Erased. I would say, it was "erased."

ACTOR/BAKER. Ok. But the song, "Le Temps des Cerises," it survives. It was written by Jean Baptiste Clément who was, obviously, a songwriter but also—also he was a political player in the story of the Paris Commune and his song survives. In fact all the songs, here, in our show, by Clément and others, all of them have survived from 1871 until now. And as we have these songs, the Paris Commune survives.

(We see a bit more of LA BORDAS' performance.)

LA BORDAS.
BUT THEIR TIME IS SHORT
THE CHERRIES OF SPRING
WHEN WE WALK IN PAIRS
TO GATHER AND DREAM OF TOKENS FROM LOVERS
THESE CHERRIES OF LOVE
EACH DRESSED LIKE THE OTHERS
FALL DOWN FROM THE TREE LIKE BLOOD IN A STREAM

ACTOR/BAKER. And words. Words too survive. And so we can imagine the audience for the concert in the Palace because some of the audience, they wrote about it:

AUDIENCE MEMBER (played by ACTOR/THIERS). "I joined myself to a river of people from every rank of life. There were shopkeepers and their wives, workingmen, even washerwomen… Every class of Parisian was represented in the throng that swayed and hustled through the rooms." Of course, when one saw some of the poorest among them looking over the balconies of the Tuileries Palace one was inclined to ask, "Where do such creatures come from?"

ACTOR/BAKER. Yes, the common, working people of Paris were *inside* the Palace.

ACTRESS/SEAMSTRESS. La Canaille.

ACTOR/BAKER. "La Canaille." Would you say that translates better as "rabble," or as "scum"?

ACTRESS/ELISABETH. Scum? I mean, who says 'rabble' anymore?

ACTOR/BAKER. Fine then, scum. La Canaille, inside the Palace. We know, someone wrote about this, we know that "the vast staircase" some staircase in the Palace "…is littered with bedding. Shirts and stockings hang over the gilded railings. Names are scrawled on the walls in pencil and in ink and by the scratchings of a knife…" Right, because some of the Communard "scum" have been living here in the Palace. Washing out their socks, loading their guns…in the Palace!

ACTRESS/SEAMSTRESS. Right, loading their guns inside the Palace because…

ACTOR/BAKER. It's a revolution.

ACTRESS/SEAMSTRESS. See, it's a concert. In springtime. During a revolution.

ACTOR/BAKER. Listen:

AUDIENCE MEMBER (played by ACTOR/THIERS). The Palace is now completely full, and still another 2,000 people stand in a long line in the garden outside. In course of time the whole garden is full of people who look up at the lights streaming from the windows and sit about on chairs quietly smoking cigars and enjoying the lovely evening, listening to the occasional boom of a shell out beyond the gates of Paris.

ACTRESS/SEAMSTRESS. Right. Outside the gates of Paris, the opposing army—which is really the French Army that would very much like to take Paris back—they're skirmishing against the Commune's soldiers and they're firing shells that sometimes hit near the walls of Paris.

ACTOR/BAKER. While within the gates of Paris—the people gather for this concert inside the Palace, yes! Imagine! Thousands of people and an orchestra…actors reciting…political leaders and uh…there was something about an amateur violinist, yodeling ducks and some guy who made "obscene barnyard noises," I mean who knows? And then this song!

ACTRESS/SEAMSTRESS. This song thrown down like a gauntlet against the army outside.

ACTOR/BAKER. Someone there, someone wrote this down:

ANOTHER AUDIENCE MEMBER (played by ACTOR/PÈRE DUCHÊNE). La Canaille! They throw that name at us as the ultimate in-

sult. Fine then, that name will be our weapon. And La Bordas she's our war-
rior. She is a goddess of Liberty born from the slums of Paris. Let her sing.
Let her sing the song that has made her famous. La Canaille!

(Full fledged LA BORDAS *at the concert.)*

LA BORDAS.

LA CANAILLE

IN THE HEART OF PARIS' MIRE
THERE LIVES A RACE OF IRON BORN.
DEEP IN ITS SOUL A RAGING FIRE
THAT BURNS THE FLESH FROM BODY TORN.
ALL OF ITS CHILDREN BORN IN SLUMS

AND IF YOU SEE THEM I THINK YOU'LL KNOW WHY:
THEY ARE THE LOWEST SCUM!
BUT SO AM I!

NOT THE CRIMINALS FROM PRISON
THESE ARE THE HONEST WORKING MEN
WHO EVERY MORNING HAVE ARISEN
TO WORK WITH HAMMER OR WITH PEN.
THEY ARE THE FATHERS EARNING CRUMBS
SLAVING AWAY TIL THE DAY THAT THEY DIE.
THEY ARE THE LOWEST SCUM!
BUT SO AM I!

IT'S THE MAN WHOSE BODY IS THIN
WITH SUNKEN EYES AND DIRTY FACE,
WHOSE SHAKY HANDS AND HARDENED SKIN
COME FROM SOME DARK UNHEARD OF PLACE.
AND AS HE PASSES YOU HE HUMS
MOCKING YOUR SCORN WITH A LAUGH AND A SIGH:
HE IS THE LOWEST SCUM!
BUT SO AM I!

AND BY NOW THEIR ARMY IS COMING,
DRESSED ALL IN RAGS AND WOODEN SHOES.
THEIR MOTHER FRANCE CAN HEAR THEM DRUMMING
DRAPED IN HER FLAG TO WIN OR LOSE.
SOON YOU WILL SEE THEM WITH THEIR GUNS
AS TO THE ENEMY THEY CRY:
HERE ARE THE LOWEST SCUM!
AND HERE AM I!

Scene Two

ACTRESS/ELISABETH. The concert at the Tuileries Palace, May 21, 1871. We'll see more of that later. But now, let's break it down. La Bordas, a singer. La Canaille, a song. The stage? The overthrown Palace. And the audience: the people. As in "THE PEOPLE." And here's two who were there: a baker and his wife, a seamstress. These elements together are, yes, a concert, but more—it is an idea made *alive*. And this idea like she said: Liberation, the liberation of the poor to be specific, in this story, the story of the Paris Commune, this idea was *possible*. But where did it come from? And really—most important—how can it succeed? To answer that we have to go back to the beginning. Or a beginning. Eleven months before the concert. 1870. Before the Commune. Before everything changed. And now "A Day in the Life of the Baker and his Wife."

BAKER. I'm a baker. I work through the night for the bakery.

SEAMSTRESS. And I'm his wife. I work at a dressmaker's; I'm a seamstress. And sometimes, if necessary, I find other "work" at night.

BAKER. I'm also in the Paris Guard. A local volunteer group which pays a little extra money on top of my salary.

ACTRESS/ELISABETH. (Which is…a kind of amateur Army reserve, but nothing like the French Army. Ok?)

(Music plays.)

BAKER. The sun sets over Paris and I'm making my way through the cobbled streets to the bakery. Back home, she's putting the little ones to bed.

SEAMSTRESS. I send the little ones outside. I've taken in some sewing work and need to finish it soon.

BAKER. Ten hours of baking through the night and then in the morning I've got the deliveries.

SEAMSTRESS. A few stitches later and my visitor—a certain gentleman—comes by. Then he finally goes but now I can at least pay the butcher. I let the kids back in so we can all get a couple hours sleep.

BAKER. In the morning—

SEAMSTRESS. I send the little ones next door and the oldest girl—

BAKER. Our daughter

SEAMSTRESS. She's twelve. The girl's off to work. She sews buttons at a workshop.

BAKER. I'm finally home

SEAMSTRESS. I kiss him good morning

BAKER. Dead tired.

SEAMSTRESS. And off I go to the dressmakers to work all day.

BAKER. And off I go to sleep

ACTRESS/ELISABETH. With his face buried in pillows still damp with the sweat of some other guy. She's on her feet all day and on her back all night. While our guy here, he hasn't had any "intimate relations" for weeks.

BAKER. Months.

SEAMSTRESS. Weeks.

BOTH. A long time.

ACTRESS/ELISABETH. And they're poor. They are not the first people in human history to be poor. But in our story they are the ones who rose up. And this couple, powerless on their own—came together with others like them and they changed history. They are players in history. And this next part will lead us up—up to the uprising. And here's some foreshadowing: it involves cannons. Or "cannon" which is actually the plural of cannon. Keep an eye on the cannon. *(Gesture meaning plural.)*

ACTOR/BAKER. And so our couple, the Baker and the seamstress, they live in Montmartre. A neighborhood high up a hill. A workers' neighborhood—

ACTRESS/SEAMSTRESS. And this couple's daughter, our twelve-year-old, she might have been lucky and might have been one of the few to take some free classes at night after work. Maybe a class taught by a schoolteacher: Louise Michel.

ACTRESS/LOUISE. And this is from the memoir of that schoolteacher Louise Michel:

LOUISE. And so here she is. Here is Louise Michel.

ACTRESS/LOUISE. She writes about herself in the third person a lot, so don't be confused.

LOUISE. She is a menace to society, for she says that everyone should take part in the *banquet of life*. Louise Michel is a monster who maintains that men and women are not responsible for their own poverty. She claims it is instead stupidity which causes the evils around us. She claims that politics is a form of that stupidity and it is incapable of ennobling the human race. "Power monopolized is evil."

PÈRE DUCHÊNE. "The women of Paris are loyal buggers! Père Duchêne knows a bunch who'd even like to go to battle and fight for the people, like that brave citizen Louise Michel! She's a good patriotic fucker! But not everyone is as brave as Louise Michel! Some are scared of everything. Fuck!"

ACTRESS/ELISABETH. This is Le Père Duchêne. Which was a pamphlet, and we have no idea who wrote it because it was all in the voice of a character, a sort of King of the Scum. "Père Duchêne."

PÈRE DUCHÊNE. Fuck! Some women say to their men, "Keep your chin down and don't cause trouble with the bosses." Oh, god! If they're allowed to reason like that the people will be double fucked! Père Duchêne says well these women have not received a patriotic education! Send them off to a class with that schoolteacher in Montmartre.

ACTRESS/ELISABETH. OK. It's 1870. We've got our baker, his wife, and an anarchist in the schoolhouse on the hill of Montmartre. And now— The Emperor of France, Louis Napoleon, declares war against Prussia for reasons that mean a great deal to him but really mean nothing to our people. And while much of France supports this war—there are others, like Louise Michel who oppose it and everything that is this Empire. But these radicals or reds or whatever they are underground—their meetings in secret, their writings outlawed.

LOUISE. "Most of our meetings took place outside Paris. Often as we were returning home by little paths through fields, we talked excitedly. Other times we were silent, entranced by the idea of sweeping away twenty years of this shameful Empire. And when the Emperor was defeated at Sedan, we knew that the time had come."

ACTRESS/ELISABETH. Yes, Sedan. A town in eastern France. This is where the Emperor, with over 100,000 troops, is defeated. With that, so goes the Empire. It's over. A new shaky government takes its place and it…well it does very little. The Prussians march to Paris and encircle the city, cutting off food and supplies, for a long bitter winter, and this is "The Siege of Paris."

BAKER. The men of the Paris Guard, like the Baker, lead the effort to make more cannon—

ACTRESS/ELISABETH. Got that?

BAKER. —to defend the city. They're armed—barely—and, "We're ready to fight. We'll give our lives to save Paris."

ACTRESS/ELISABETH. But they're held back by this shaky new government.

SEAMSTRESS. And you can imagine, before there was hardly enough, and now… "How do we feed the children? There's nothing. Children in Montmartre—dying, while we wait, wait for what?"

ACTRESS/ELISABETH. Yes for what, keep waiting for this government that does nothing while people slowly starve to death? This is well, apocryphal at best, but during the Siege: A bourgeois couple haven't got a crumb to eat, but they do a have little dog that they love very much. They have no other choice but to cook and eat little Bijou. After dinner, Madame slowly places his little rib bones to the side of her plate and says, with a heavy sigh, "Oh poor little Bijou. What a treat he would have had."

ACTOR/BAKER. And we have a bourgeois character, mostly made up, some from letters. And we'll say this dressmaker, here, she owns a shop. Not in Montmartre, but down in the center of Paris.

SEAMSTRESS. And I work for her. (For very little money).

BAKER. And as with many women of her class, the dressmaker's husband fled Paris to avoid the draft into the French Army and wait out the war, leaving her to run the shop.

DRESSMAKER. Dearest, it's a small miracle that you left in time. Black flags hang from the houses, the streets are deserted the gaslights dark. Since you've left business has been terrible. For who will buy dresses at a time like this?

ACTRESS/ELISABETH. Good. Ok. The city—surrounded by Prussians. That cannon—sitting idle around the city, unused. The people—starving and eager to use said cannon against the Prussians—

ACTOR/BAKER. But they are prevented from doing so by this new government that says no, no, wait, wait let us work some diplomacy with the Prussians. Trust us. Do nothing. But instead, the people do something. Or at least *(Looking to* ACTRESS/ELISABETH:*)* they think something—an idea— and they print it and stick it up around the city.

ACTRESS/LOUISE. L'Affiche Rouge!

ACTRESS/ELISABETH. The Red Poster. And red means

ACTRESS/LOUISE. Drowned in the blood of revolutionaries.

ACTRESS/ELISABETH. So, it's on red paper.

ACTOR/BAKER. And the baker, for one, he'd see this red poster which reads:

ACTRESS/LOUISE. "Has the government fulfilled its mission? No! Their indecision and their apathy have led us to the brink of disaster. People are dying of cold and very nearly of starvation and the children are wasting away. The Government has shown what it is worth—it is massacring us. If the men of the government have any patriotism left their duty is to withdraw and to let the people of Paris organize their own liberation. They must let Paris secede from France, and make its own destiny. The Municipality or the Commune, whatever one chooses to call it, is the only salvation of the people.

ACTRESS/ELISABETH. This part is all in capital letters.

ACTRESS/LOUISE.
THE PEOPLE OF PARIS WILL NEVER ACCEPT SUCH SUFFERING
    AND SHAME.
MAKE WAY FOR THE PEOPLE! MAKE WAY FOR THE COMMUNE!

ACTRESS/ELISABETH. And you can imagine this would make the provisional government very nervous especially with all those cannon lying about. So the government, which now has an elected President, Adolphe Thiers, responds to this Red Poster.

THIERS. "The Prussian enemy is redoubling its efforts to intimidate us, and the citizens of Paris are being misled by dishonesty and calumny. Parisians: Courage, patience, and patriotism as your government does its job to protect you."

ACTRESS/ELISABETH. And then again a few weeks later:

THIERS. "Parisians: We did all that we could to defend you, but have been forced to grant a partial and very *temporary* occupation of Paris by the Prussians. If we did not agree to this, the Prussians would occupy Paris by force. You have been brave, now be dignified, and the cruel situation will be replaced by public prosperity."

ACTOR/BAKER. And the baker…

ACTRESS/SEAMSTRESS. And his wife. They must watch and do nothing as the Prussians occupy Paris.

ACTOR/BAKER. And the Parisians, hungry as they are, are even more enraged to see the hateful Prussian soldiers marching through their city as if they own it.

ACTRESS/LOUISE and ACTOR/PÈRE DUCHÊNE.
AS THE PRUSSIANS USE THEIR GUNS
TO STARVE PARISIANS JUST FOR FUN
AND OUR LEADERS ON THE RUN
SELL THEIR CITIZENS ONE BY ONE
THEY WANT ALL PARISIANS DEAD
AND SOON THEY'LL COME FOR YOU AND ME—
WELL FUCK THEIR DIPLOMACY
LET'S MAKE 'EM EAT LEAD!

ACTOR/BAKER. And the baker, remember he's in the Montmartre division of the Paris Guard, well this is what he would have heard at his next meeting. This is the response of the Paris Guard:

PARIS GUARD (ACTOR/BAKER). "We did not believe that our Government would betray us, even with the facts staring us in the face. But when our city was exploited; when a hideous peace settlement was rushed through; and finally when Paris suffered the humiliation of foreign occupation; then at last it dawned on us that we could count on no one but ourselves. Let them call us trouble-makers. Nothing could be farther from the truth. All we wish is the right to control our lives. No longer the exploiters who regard their fellow-men as property. We will be free men!"

ACTRESS/ELISABETH. So these are the ideas circulating in Paris. Ideas which, very soon, would lead to action. And action, yes that means cannon. Here's Louise:

LOUISE. Our so-called leaders decided they would disarm Paris. The cannon paid for with our taxes had been left out on some vacant land. Presumably so the Prussians would carry them away; the people would then be left unarmed and these reactionaries could then impose on us a new monarch.

Paris objected to that. And the idea was in the air that we should take back the cannon.

(ACTRESS/ELISABETH *checks in with the audience.*)

And so, men, women and children hauled the cannon by hand across the city.

SEAMSTRESS. I brought the oldest girl. It took us the whole night but by dawn our cannon were gathered together on the hill of Montmartre.

LOUISE. And then Montmartre, like Belleville and Batignolles, each of the worker's neighborhoods, each had a few hundred cannon.

DRESSMAKER. My darling, I fear we may be living on the side of a volcano. The peace conditions strike me as so oppressive, I am afraid we are on the brink of a civil war. And in Paris, everyone is saying that normalcy will never be restored until all the wretches in Montmartre are taken care of and their cannon taken away. But meanwhile, the hill of Montmartre has become a veritable camp. Three or four hundred of the Paris Guard stand watch there day and night. And this President Thiers does nothing!

ACTRESS/ELISABETH. So, President Thiers—who is, in fact, much beloved in the provinces—not so popular in Paris. Oh—and much, much less popular after a certain proclamation, demanding that all rents and debts incurred during the siege are now due. As one minister said:

ONE MINISTER (ACTOR/THIERS). "The Rothschilds have paid off their creditors, why shouldn't everyone else?"

ACTRESS/ELISABETH. The next day 150,000 Parisians go bankrupt.

PÈRE DUCHÊNE. "Regarding those poor patriot buggers who the landlords want to throw into the street, and regarding President Thiers' grand gesture to the money-merchants, Père Duchêne says: It is not enough to have starved us, to have covered us in blood, now he wants us to pay up. For six months we haven't made anything, we haven't sold anything; How are we supposed to pay up? Fucking hell! We won't pay!"

ACTRESS/ELISABETH. And all of that brings us to:

Scene Three

ACTRESS/ELISABETH. March 18, 1871. President Thiers orders the Army to sneak into the hill of Montmartre and reclaim the cannon, hopefully before dawn.

ACTRESS/LOUISE. And we have Louise's record of that day.

ACTRESS/ELISABETH. And we can imagine

ACTOR/BAKER. The baker

ACTRESS/SEAMSTRESS. The seamstress

ACTOR/GUARDSMAN (ACTOR/ PÈRE DUCHÊNE). A member of the Paris Guard, guarding the cannon

ACTOR/SOLDIER (ACTOR/THIERS). And a soldier in the French Army, sent to take them away

ACTRESS/DRESSMAKER. And the dressmaker at home in some other part of Paris.

ACTRESS/ELISABETH. And it's early. Very early.

LOUISE. As I wake, I see through my window that the night sky is just giving way to the first light. It's hours before classes but I'm restless so I dress and head outside.

ACTOR/BAKER. The baker would have finished his night of breadmaking, so, "I'm heading home to get my gun and then up to the hill." To take a shift guarding the cannon, even though he's been working all night.

ACTRESS/SEAMSTRESS. And I'm in bed, just woken up by the youngest.

(Child crying.)

LOUISE. It's quiet and still. With the streets of Montmartre closed there's only a few people about on foot. At the bottom of my street there's a barricade made from an overturned cart and some stones and in the night someone's added a red flag. Up on the hilltop about 200 cannon are guarded with vigilance by the Paris Guard.

GUARDSMAN. Me and my brothers of the Paris Guard, we're on the night shift to guard the cannon. And we're completely asleep.

SOLDIER. It's almost morning now and orders from the General are to remove the cannon before daybreak. We've about 100 soldiers of the French Army here on the hill of Montmartre but we haven't a single horse. It seems our General has forgotten to send them and we can't drag off the cannon by ourselves. And so we're waiting.

LOUISE. I decide to climb the hill. And here in Montmartre looking out in the first light of day, up here above the rooftops, all of Paris stretches out like a great dream and I feel that now—after so many months of sorrow—the vision of our new society might finally take hold.

BAKER. I've got my rifle and I'm climbing the hill.

SEAMSTRESS. I'm awake.

GUARDSMAN. I'm asleep.

SOLDIER. I'm still waiting.

LOUISE. I climb the hill.

ACTRESS/ELISABETH. And this is one of those strangely appropriate twists of history, because it was she, of all people, Louise Michel who first saw them—

LOUISE. Soldiers.

SOLDIER. Still waiting.

LOUISE. I run below and I scream, "WAKE UP! WAKE UP! THE CANNON!"

BAKER. Sound the alarm!

SEAMSTRESS. WAKE UP!

DRESSMAKER. It is never pleasant to be awakened early in the morning, but it is particularly unpleasant to be roused as I am today. To be awakened by such sounds—resounding from one end of the city to the other, first the drum and then the horn, calling I presume on all of the Paris Guard.

LOUISE. FOLLOW ME! Wake up! Wake up!

SEAMSTRESS. And I'm outside I'm running along with everyone else.

LOUISE. TO THE HILL! WAKE UP!

SEAMSTRESS. I see my husband leading a great crowd that's rushing up the hillside.

BAKER. I see my wife, "Up the hill" I'm shouting to her but she can't hear me.

SOLDIER. All of Montmartre is tearing up the hill. No reinforcements. No general and still no horses!

GUARDSMAN. And here we are face to face with the French Army.

BAKER. Here we are. Both sides armed.

SEAMSTRESS. Here we are...and nothing happens. We're looking at them, they're looking at us. And who knows what they're thinking, but I'm thinking, well, these soldiers...they're Frenchmen like us...and what's more, they're just...men. And they're probably hungry. So I walk up to one and I say, "Looks like you've been out here a while. You must be feeling the cold. Would you like some fresh bread?"

(Pause.)

SOLDIER. Thanks.

SEAMSTRESS. How about a little wine?

LOUISE. And the women, we spread the word.

BAKER. Now I'm running back up the hill with more men and more guns. And a sausage.

SEAMSTRESS. So now, here we are in a field full of cannon and everyone's having breakfast together.

LOUISE. I walk right up to one of the soldiers and I say to him "Well, if you've come to take back the cannon, what are you waiting for?"

(Pause.)

SOLDIER. Right then, the horses arrive!

GUARDSMAN. Get the rifles!

SOLDIER. Get out of the way!

LOUISE. The soldiers tie horses to the cannon-mounts with ropes and pre-
pare to drag the cannon away. And the people, without any thought of our
safety—

BAKER. We surge forward—

SEAMSTRESS. We throw ourselves onto the cannon.

LOUISE. Women and children even wrap themselves around the wheels—

SEAMSTRESS. Untie the horses! Will you let us be crushed?

SOLDIER. Back off!

BAKER. The ropes are stretched taut.

GUARDSMAN. Take the blades from the rifles!

SEAMSTRESS. And they give the blades to the women still wrapped
around the cannons.

BAKER. I shout to them to cut the ropes!

LOUISE. Cut the ropes! Cut the ropes!

GUARDSMAN. They're cut! Now everyone—drive off the horses!!

> *(Everyone screams at the horses.)*

ACTRESS/ELISABETH. But at that moment, the General arrives with
more troops.

SOLDIER. And the General, he commands us to raise our rifles.

GENERAL (ACTRESS/ELISABETH). Ready! Shoulder arms!

SEAMSTRESS. And the guns are pointing right at us.

BAKER. But instead of giving up the cannon…

LOUISE. Instead of fleeing…

SEAMSTRESS. We throw ourselves directly in front of the soldiers.

GUARDSMAN. Don't shoot!

SEAMSTRESS. Don't shoot!

BAKER. Hold your fire!

LOUISE. Will you kill your own people!

SOLDIER. The General orders us—

GENERAL. Make ready.
Fire.

> *(Silence.)*

Fire.

SOLDIER. He threatens any man who refuses to fire with death by hanging.

> *(Silence.)*

GENERAL. Fire! Fire!

LOUISE. We look right in the eyes of the soldiers.

SOLDIER. No one says a thing.

LOUISE. It's as though the shadow of death has suddenly flown away.

GENERAL. What, will you surrender to this scum?

SEAMSTRESS. And a soldier says,

SOLDIER. It's *you* who must surrender.

GENERAL. Fire! Defend me!

SOLDIER. I lower my rifle, and then I'm lifting the rifle butt in the air

SEAMSTRESS. Then another follows

GUARDSMAN. And another

BAKER. And another until all the soldiers are holding up their guns.

LOUISE. The soldiers are with us!

DRESSMAKER. Well, the girl hasn't shown up, so finally I go out and I find some breakfast at an open cafe. There are rumors of fighting in the streets. But in such times rumors fly about of the most contradictory kind.

SOLDIER. We drag the General off his horse and bind his arms—

GUARDSMAN. Death! Execute the bastard!

BAKER. No—let's put him on trial!

ACTRESS/ELISABETH. The General is weeping.

SOLDIER. He tells us he's a father and a grandfather.

BAKER. And then he's shot.

ACTRESS/ELISABETH. Eleven times.

(Gunshots.)

And with that, it's war.

ACTRESS/SEAMSTRESS. Do you imagine, in a moment like this, would you…think? I mean, would you be able to…or would you just…act?

ACTOR/BAKER. Montmartre is theirs. Really theirs. And Paris could be theirs. There's cannon gathered in other worker neighborhoods. So, in this moment, do you *think?*

ACTRESS/LOUISE. No you ACT.

SEAMSTRESS. And I'm running down the hillside.

BAKER. I'm running.

GUARDSMAN. We've blown up the arsenal. More arms and more cannon. From Belleville. From Batignolle.

SOLDIER. The other soldiers, they're running. They've sounded the retreat. But we're with the people and our numbers are growing.

ACTRESS/ELISABETH. And the revolt spreads. From the outer neighborhoods towards the center of Paris.

ACTOR/BAKER. Montmarte, St. Denis

ACTRESS/LOUISE. Batingolles, Belleville

ACTRESS/SEAMSTRESS. La Villette, the Latin Quarter, the Opera

ACTOR/BAKER. Until they take the center of the city.

ACTRESS/LOUISE. City Hall, Notre Dame, even the Tuileries Palace.

ACTRESS/SEAMSTRESS. Everywhere the people of Paris are *rushing*.

ACTOR/BAKER. And the government, surrounded. One by one they escape: jumping out of back windows, out through a secret tunnel. And President Thiers, snuck out of town, we don't know how, but he's gone! He gives up the city. The entire government gets out and escapes to—

ACTRESS/ELISABETH. To Versailles. About 12 miles outside of Paris.

ACTRESS/LOUISE. And suddenly—

ACTOR/BAKER. Yes, suddenly—

ACTRESS/SEAMSTRESS. There is no government in Paris. I mean IMAGINE! No government!

 (Music.)

PÈRE DUCHÊNE. Ah, Père Duchêne has good reason to be happy today, and, fuck! To the good patriots who chased all those fuckers out of the Capitol! So, O Patriots of Paris, do you know what we must do now? We must unite our forces and obtain a decisive advantage in the supreme combat which is coming between us patriots, who have killed ourselves for centuries working to feed those useless fuckers and the greedy capitalists. LONG LIVE THE COMMUNE!

 (An OPERA SINGER arrives with ADOLPHE THIERS.)

ACTRESS/ELISABETH. But yet…

Scene Four

An elegant SOPRANO takes the stage with THIERS.

SOPRANO.
  AH, I LOVE MEN IN UNIFORM
  I LOVE MEN IN UNIFORM
  I LOVE MEN IN UNIFORM
  THE WAY THEY DRESS IS SO REVEALING
  WHEN THEY MARCH I GET A FEELING
  AH, I LOVE MEN IN UNIFORM
  I LOVE MEN IN UNIFORM
  I LOVE MEN IN UNIFORM
  THE WAY THEY MARCH I JUST ADORE
  I UNDERSTAND WHAT WAR IS FOR

THIERS. Citizens of Paris, this insurrection within your walls would hand over Paris to pillage and send France to her grave. Your government orders the Paris Guard to rejoin with the Army of France to defend with one common accord their country and the Republic. These criminals, these Communards who affect to institute a government, must be delivered to justice, and the cannon taken away must be restored to the national arsenals.

SOPRANO.

> SO PROUD SO BRAVE
> I KNOW THEY'LL SAVE ME
> AND IN BATTLE
> THEY WILL NOT BE DEFEATED NO
> SO UNDEFEATED
> HOW I NEED IT
> HOW I NEED IT
> HOW I NEED IT
> HOW I NEED IT
> OH, I DO NOT KNOW
> WHAT I WOULD GIVE
> I DO NOT KNOW WHAT I WOULD GIVE
> AH...

THIERS. The Government counts upon your assistance, and let good citizens separate from the bad. Parisians!! We speak to you thus because we esteem your good sense, wisdom and patriotism, but if you fail to heed this warning, we shall have no other recourse but to employ force because there must be peace at all costs without a day's delay so that order may return. Order—complete, immediate, and unalterable.

SINGER.

> OH I JUST LOVE THE MILITARY
> FROM THE FRONT OR FROM THE SIDE OR FROM THE
>   BACK
> OH I JUST LOVE THE MILITARY
> FROM THE FRONT OR FROM THE SIDE OR FROM THE
>   BACK
> OH I JUST LOVE THE MILITARY
> OH I JUST LOVE THE MILITARY
> AH, I LOVE THE MILITARY MEN!

(The BAKER *puts a poster over the* SINGER's *mouth.)*

Scene Five

BAKER. And now the Baker, he's putting up these posters from the Paris Guard: "Citizens: We have defended Paris. Aided by your generous courage, the Paris Guard expelled the government which was betraying us. But our mandate has expired, and we do not pretend to take the place of the old government. This is not a military coup, but a legitimate change of power. Hold communal elections, and we will step down. And let Paris write a fresh page in the book of history!"

ACTRESS/ELISABETH. Aha—history! Let's take a look, shall we, at a brief history of revolution in France.

ACTRESS/SEAMSTRESS. Along with a history of the Can-Can. To make it more entertaining!

(Can Can music and dancing begin.)

ACTOR/PÈRE DUCHÊNE. 1789: The French Revolution. The bourgeoisie declares an oath against the monarchy on a tennis court, as the workers pull down the Bastille and march on Versailles.

ACTOR/BAKER. The exact origins of the Can-Can are unknown. Some believe it was imported from Algeria,

ACTOR/THIERS. 1792: In the September Massacre, revolutionaries execute 1,200 aristocrats.

ACTRESS/SEAMSTRESS. Or it may have originated in Egypt, where certain hieroglyphics show women kicking their legs in the air.

ACTOR/BAKER. Others believe it to be a hybrid born of the Polka and the Quadrille—

ACTOR/PÈRE DUCHÊNE. 1793: Thousands of anti-revolutionaries are executed in Robespierre's Terror.

ACTRESS/SEAMSTRESS. Or perhaps it originated with the women of Brittany, who used to lift up their skirts and kick their legs up to the ceiling.

ACTOR/THIERS. 1794: Terror Ends. Robespierre is assassinated.

ACTOR/BAKER. In any case, the dance first appeared in the working class dance halls of Paris around the turn of the 18th century.

ACTRESS/SEAMSTRESS. It was a dance for couples, who would engage in scandalous, even lewd high kicks and explicit gestures.

ACTOR/PÈRE DUCHÊNE. 1799: Napoleon Bonaparte seizes power.

ACTOR/BAKER. Kicking

ACTOR/THIERS. 1804: Napoleon declares himself Emperor.

ACTRESS/SEAMSTRESS. And thrusting

ACTOR/PÈRE DUCHÊNE. 1814: Napoleon is exiled

ACTOR/BAKER. And shaking!

ACTOR/THIERS. a new monarchy is proclaimed.

ACTOR/PÈRE DUCHÊNE. 1830: In a Revolution against the next monarchy, 2,000 killed.

ACTRESS/SEAMSTRESS. The dance was first known as the chahut, or "uproar." Later as the "Can-Can" or "scandal."

ACTOR/THIERS. 1848: In another revolution against another monarchy. 3,000 killed.

ACTRESS/SEAMSTRESS. Soon the Can-Can is the sensation of Paris!

ACTOR/BAKER. But then it is outlawed! Order prevails and the indecent Can-Can, this filthy dance of the canaille—it's GONE.

ACTRESS/SEAMSTRESS. But really, the Can-Can, and the energies it represents, simply moves *underground*.

ACTOR/THIERS and ACTOR/PÈRE DUCHÊNE. 1871. The Paris Commune!

ACTRESS/SEAMSTRESS. And then…

(*Music stops.*)

Scene Six

ACTRESS/ELISABETH. Indeed "And then…" because, as we have just seen, for every revolution, there is always "and then…" Yes? So, the people of Paris have their city. An idea into ACTION. Hurrah. But with ACTION: *REACTION*. President Thiers and the class he represents will have some sort of response, don't you think? If we look at history, people in power generally don't typically hand over the power with grace and kindness and like, a little note with you know, "Here, people, here's a few tips to help things go smoothly in your new government. Good luck with your new egalitarian society." No. I would argue, at this point in the story the time is now for Paris to attack them *before* they attack Paris. Because what did Thiers say?

ACTOR/THIERS. "We shall have no other recourse but to employ force."

ACTRESS/ELISABETH. So to defeat its enemies and bring this world into being, Paris needs to act with force, leadership and authority.

ACTRESS/LOUISE. Hold on, "authority?"

ACTRESS/ELISABETH. Yeah?

ACTRESS/LOUISE. Isn't the whole point of the Commune that it's—that it will be *different?* I think, sure, Louise Michel says too that the Commune will have to—it should be ready to fight to *defend* itself. And Louise, yeah, she's prepared to fight and die even—but for *liberation*. Which I think is by definition the opposite of "authority," right?

ACTRESS/ELISABETH. Well no. I mean, not necessarily. Not if the authority serves the people. If you're going to take over a city you're going to need some sort of effective and decisive leadership, right?

RIGAULT. Paris, we are making a revolution!

ACTRESS/ELISABETH. Exactly.

ACTOR/BAKER. New character. This is a…somewhat flamboyant Communard: Raoul Rigault.

RIGAULT. The strongest will shoot the others!

ACTRESS/ELISABETH. That's not the point I was trying to make.

RIGAULT. Bourgeois society accepts war, but TERROR—the systematic destruction of one's definite enemies—it regards with horror. Why? Because the bourgeoisie are afraid of human nature. When they murder, they murder in the dark. I wish to murder in broad daylight.

ACTRESS/ELISABETH. Look I'm saying, yes, take power with force and authority. I'm not saying take power *insanely.*

ACTRESS/LOUISE. Yes, but Louise Michel I think would argue that the combination of force with authority will potentially or maybe definitely, ultimately will lead us to Terror. State Terror. Or crazy person Terror.

(ACTRESS/ELISABETH *gestures for* RIGAULT *to leave.*)

The idea of the Commune is *liberation* from that, precisely that abuse of power. And that it's *possible* for the Commune to succeed you know, without it. Consider this: right now, at this point in the story, the Commune has a window of opportunity. Establish this new egalitarian Paris as *legitimate.* And Thiers will be forced to recognize its rightful existence.

ACTOR/BAKER. (*To* ACTRESS/LOUISE:) Right right right. Like the Baker said, from the Paris Guard poster: "This is not a military coup, but a legitimate change of power. Hold elections!"

ACTRESS/ELISABETH. But—

ACTOR/BAKER. (*To the audience:*) So, next, the Commune holds elections.

(*Music plays.*)

LA BORDAS.

SONG OF MAY

AS FLAGS FLY AROUND THROUGH THE AIR
TRAILING FIRE AS THEY COME RAINING DOWN
THE SHOUTS RING ABOUT EVERYWHERE
RAINING DOWN ON THE WALLS OF THIS TOWN

SEAMSTRESS. The streets are FILLED with posters:

WORKER POSTER (ACTOR/PÈRE DUCHÊNE). Fellow-workers, elect the Commune! Put an end to class conflict and bring forth a new era of social equality. What do we demand?

BAKER. The co-operative organization of production and the right of every worker to receive the full value of his labor.

LOUISE. Free and secular education.

BAKER. The right to assemble.

LOUISE. Freedom of thought. Freedom of speech. All forms of expression and free elections!

LA BORDAS.

NO SONG COULD BE HALF AS PRETTY
AS THE SOUNDS THAT FILL THE CITY

DRIVING OUT THE WINTER AND HER ICY COLD
ASKING WHAT WILL THE FUTURE HOLD?

THIERS. Citizens of France: I speak to you now with a heavy heart. At this moment, our state is no doubt most painful, but, we can see foreshadowed a not too distant termination of the crisis. Whatever may be the means employed, they will be painful; and if we must fire on that Paris which is always so dear to France, our heart will bleed. But we appeal to the judgment of the country: Are we at fault?

(Applause. Shouts of "NO!")

Each day the word conciliation is addressed to me. Ah! if it only depended on me, what sacrifices would I not make to put an end to this terrible war! France, we are in the presence of a new barbarian invasion; they are not at our gates, but among us, in our cities. And we must now heal our society at whatever cost.

LA BORDAS.

BUT TODAY THE SUN SHINES DOWN LIKE GOLD
THE GRASS IS GREEN, THE GARDENS BLOOMING
WHITE
AND IN THIS ROOM, A STORY WILL BE TOLD
HOW WILL IT UNFOLD?

ACTOR/BAKER. "Workers of Paris! If you are tired of vegetating in ignorance and coughing in misery, if you want your sons to be men and not animals reared for the factory and the battlefield, if you no longer want your daughters to be the instruments of pleasure in the hands of the wealthy! Paris, elect the Commune, and France will have no choice but to recognize us!"

ALL.

SOON THE LEADERS ALL WILL TREMBLE
AS THEY SEE THE WORLD ASSEMBLE
COMING LIKE A WAVE UPON THEIR SANDY SHORE

LA BORDAS.

WHO IS RICH NOW? AND WHO IS POOR?

ALL.

LISTEN UP, YOU CRINGING BOURGEOISIE
YOU CANNOT CRY AND TRY TO SAVE YOUR HEAD
AND IF YOU TRY TO SIP YOUR TEA
WE'LL MAKE YOU WISH THAT YOU WERE DEAD!

ACTRESS/SEAMSTRESS. Drumroll, please.

(Drumroll.)

The voting polls are open, and as one citizen writes, "the voting paper, has replaced the rifle." And imagine 200,000 people waiting outside of City Hall. Murmuring. Ok audience participation time, all of you on this side repeat after me: rutabaga, rutabaga! Very good. And on this side: rhubarb, rhubarb! A little louder. Ok that's too loud… Good. Perfect. NOW! Thousands of Parisians, as red flags stream overhead, waiting to see what the outcome will be. And from City Hall, the announcement—

ACTOR/BAKER. The Commune is elected!

PÈRE DUCHÊNE. Fuck!

CHORUS.

>BUT TODAY, THE SUN SHINES DOWN LIKE GOLD
>THE GRASS IS GREEN, THE FLOWERS ALL ARE WHITE
>AND IN THIS ROOM, A STORY WILL BE TOLD
>WHO CAN SAY WHAT THE FUTURE HOLDS?

(The Marseillaise plays.)

ACTRESS/SEAMSTRESS. Who were these unknown men—

ACTRESS/LOUISE. 63 of them in total.

ACTRESS/SEAMSTRESS. —who were elected as the Council of the Commune?

ACTOR/BAKER. Nineteen of them came from the Paris Guard—

ACTRESS/LOUISE. Thirty-three were under the age of thirty-three

ACTOR/BAKER. Thirty-three were craftsmen

ACTRESS/LOUISE. Three doctors, three lawyers

ACTRESS/SEAMSTRESS. Two songwriters, Jean-Baptiste Clément and Eugène Pottier

ACTRESS/LOUISE. The famous painter Gustave Courbet!

ACTRESS/SEAMSTRESS. Two were mystics, one known for his belief in magnetism—

ACTOR/BAKER. One was both a veterinarian and a wine merchant.

ALL.

>BUT TODAY, THE SUN SHINES DOWN LIKE GOLD
>THE GRASS IS GREEN, THE FLOWERS ALL ARE WHITE
>AND IN THIS ROOM, A STORY WILL BE TOLD
>WHO CAN SAY WHAT THE FUTURE, WHAT THE FUTURE
>   HOLDS?

Scene Seven

ACTOR/BAKER. And after a simply extraordinary day—thousands of people in the center of Paris, singing, throwing hats, waving rifles, the Baker, he goes to work. It is after all nighttime again.

SEAMSTRESS. And the seamstress she's got one child asleep on her shoulder, and the older girl she's…god knows where. So off she goes back to Montmartre.

ACTRESS/ELISABETH. And finally my character arrives in our play! She's a young Russian Woman, Elisabeth Dmitrieff, not her real name, but, well, an alias is necessary for a revolutionary. She had landed somehow in Geneva among Karl Marx's small but growing International Workingmen's Association, and then through Marx—we're not sure why—she finds herself here in the heart of Paris. And when I say young, I mean…twenty.

ELISABETH. Dear Sir, I do not know if you have written back to me for it is impossible to receive the post here in Paris. I am sure you have learned already, some members of the International have been elected to the Council of The Commune. I have spoken to these Parisians and they welcome the support of the other European branches. And yes, in general the International here is not so strong, but they have, for many years, believed in the workers cooperative. They believe, in their way, in taking control of production.

(ACTRESS/LOUISE *interrupts:*)

ACTRESS/LOUISE. Excuse me. Do you mind?

(ACTRESS/ELISABETH *signifies ok.*)

ACTRESS/LOUISE. I just want to—that "workers cooperative" that's important. And like she said it's not just Marx's idea but it's also French—this idea that to liberate the worker you have to get rid of private ownership all together. So the factories, the shops—dressmakers, bakeries, etc.—would be *shared* collectively. Is that [*implied:* clear]? *(To* ACTRESS/ELISABETH:*)* Ok.

ACTRESS/ELISABETH. And I know, we did not expect it to happen here but I tell you as I walk in these streets that this is it. This is the socialist revolution!

ACTRESS/LOUISE. Exactly!

ACTRESS/ELISABETH. It is here for you to embrace. But there is no knowing how much time we have. The French army surely, they are planning their attack. So we must grab this moment and help these Parisians secure a decisive victory. You and the International can make it so with your leadership. In Paris, it is not the same spirit of organization as it is in London, or Germany. It is something quite different. But this is the city that rose up first. And if we can succeed here, I am sure, Paris will lead Europe into the future.

ACTRESS/LOUISE. Sorry, whose leadership?

ACTRESS/ELISABETH. The International. And the Parisians too, of course. *(To the audience:)* An example: Elisabeth Dmitrieff and Louise Michel along with other Parisian women, they found the Union of Women.

ACTRESS/LOUISE. Louise belongs to its central committee.

ACTRESS/ELISABETH. The Union of Women is *federated*, meaning lots of small groups, local groups all very *horizontal* meaning…"self directed." *(She looks at* ACTRESS/LOUISE *who looks back approvingly.)* But the Union leadership gives this federation a good vertical backbone with a solid and accountable leadership structure. It is NOT *(She looks at* LOUISE*)* anarchy. And the Union of Women has a plan for women's work, a plan that will soon mean something for the bosses, and the shop owners, and indeed, the dress-makers…

DRESSMAKER. Dearest, whatever you read in the newspapers do not worry for my sake. I am well. Though one hears such talk. The girls at our shop are fine, but it seems that some of these "Communards" believe the workers should take over the shops for themselves. As if they had the right! But I am resolved to endure this absurd insurrection. I trust it will not be long. This "Commune" surely will not last.

ACTRESS/ELISABETH. So you can imagine, this dressmaker isn't going to give up her shop voluntarily. Someone is going to have to take it by force if necessary.

RIGAULT. The guillotine is respectable, but it is much too slow, and it's old hat. I have conceived of plans for a new means of execution! It's electric. You strap the prisoner to a chair wired to current, pull a switch and voila!

ACTRESS/ELISABETH. Yes, but Rigualt never actually built his "electric chair." And he is the exception.

ACTOR/RIGAULT. Yeah, but then the Commune appoints Rigault as prefect of Police.

ACTRESS/LOUISE. Yes, that's true.

*(*ACTRESS/ELISABETH *shoos him away.)*

ACTOR/RIGAULT. Okay.

*(*ROSSEL *enters.)*

ACTRESS/ELISABETH. Ah! Here's a leader. This is promising—some officers from the French Army actually switch sides and join The Commune. This is General Rossel:

ROSSEL. To Versailles, I have the honor to inform you that I am going to Paris to put myself at the disposal of the government forces that can be made there. Knowing that there are two sides in this battle, I am placing my-self without hesitation on the side of that which does not include in its num-ber the Generals capable of capitulation to the Prussians.

ACTRESS/ELISABETH. So right now, the Commune Army has its Gen-eral, our soldiers are strong and ready—the French Army is in shambles. So the time is now to mobilize, organize and get serious!

Scene Eight

ACTRESS/SEAMSTRESS *and* ACTOR/BAKER *enter in duck suits.*

YODELING DUCKS.
WHEN LITTLE DUCKS WALK TWO BY TWO
THERE IS A REASON THAT THEY DO

AND WHEN THEY MEET IN GROUPS OF THREE
THEY'RE HAPPY FOR THE COMPANY
THEY SIT AND CHATTER HAPPILY
QUACK QUACK QUACK QUACK QUACK!
BUT IF THE DUCKS WORK COMMUNE-ALLY

(They sing:)
YO-DE-LAY-HI-HOO
YO-DE-LAY-HI-HOO
YO-DE-LAY-HI-HOO

BUT WHEN A DUCK IS LEFT ALONE
HE MAKES A SAD AND PLAINTIVE TONE
HE WORKS ALL NIGHT, AND ROTS HIS BRAIN
HIS LIFE IS MEANINGLESS AND VAIN
AND YOU CAN HEAR HIS SAD REFRAIN
QUACK QUACK QUACK QUACK QUACK!
ONLY THE COMMUNE CAN SOOTHE HIS PAIN,

(Singing:)
YO-DE-LAY-HI-HOO
YO-DE-LAY-HI-HOO
YO-DE-LAY-HI-HOO

YO-DE-LAY-HI-HOO
YO-DE-LAY-HI-HOO
YO-DE-LAY-HI-HOO

ACTRESS/SEAMSTRESS. Paris, yodel with me!

YO-DE-LAY-HI-HOO
YO-DE-LAY-HI-HOO
YO-DE-LAY-HI-HOO

(They take off their duck heads.)

ACTRESS/SEAMSTRESS. Well.

ACTOR/BAKER. Yes. Here we are.

ACTRESS/SEAMSTRESS. Yes. So…we have a *government.*

ACTOR/BAKER. The Council of the Commune, And think, in Paris, months before this—an Empire. And now, a Commune. So how does it work?

ACTRESS/SEAMSTRESS. Well, each councilman represents a district.

ACTOR/BAKER. If a councilman fails to serve the needs of his district—

ACTRESS/SEAMSTRESS. And we would know, because in each district: public meetings, public clubs, newspapers…

ACTOR/BAKER. And all business in the Commune: transparent, public. So, if he fails, he's recalled and replaced.

ACTRESS/SEAMSTRESS. Accountable…

ACTOR/BAKER. To US.

ACTRESS/SEAMSTRESS. So what do we need?

ACTOR/BAKER. Well, we got our rents forgiven, we got our tools back from the pawnshops, and we can vote—I can vote.

ACTRESS/SEAMSTRESS. Yes, but the seamstress, now that there's this idea of the future, she's thinking, maybe for the first time, "So then, what? What is this new society going to do for me to actually make my life better?"

ACTRESS/ELISABETH. I got this! Hold on. This is from the Union of Women which has an *Organizational Plan.*

ELISABETH. Item number five: "Dresses and underwear. Workers will work for shared wages set by the worker-owned and—controlled cooperatives. These will secure a consistent and reliable income and free workers from dependence on the bourgeois fashion cycle. While the demand for luxury goods will surely decline in the new egalitarian society, shared ownership will give us a decisive advantage against the capitalist markets." There.

ACTOR/BAKER. Well what about bakers? We're still working fourteen hours through the night.

ACTRESS/LOUISE. Well, call a meeting.

Scene Nine

BAKER. All bakery workers of Paris will meet to discuss our syndicate next Thursday.

CLUB LEADER (ACTOR/THIERS). People! We've got just one means to succeed and that's ourselves! Believe in the Commune. Hope for the Commune.

MECHANICS MEETING (ACTOR/PÈRE DUCHÊNE). The Syndicate of Mechanics will meet on Monday. Order of the day—social emancipation.

CLUB LEADER. But people—stay vigilant! Your liberation rests in your own two hands. So use your press. Use these public meetings. And put pressure on those that represent you!

ACTRESS/LOUISE. The Union of Women for the Defense of Paris and the Healing of the Wounded invites its members to a meeting on Sunday.

CLUB LEADER. We've been told before we had representatives. And what were they? Just a choice between different masters. And none of them willing to get in the way of money.

ACTRESS/LA BORDAS. Artists and free-thinkers are invited to meet today at the school of Medicine.

CLUB LEADER. Every government out there says it represents the people. But every government gets used to the money. And then so much for the people.

ACTOR/ELISABETH. The International Workers Association invites its members to send delegates to the Commune tomorrow 8pm.

CLUB LEADER. Elections mean crap unless we get in there and get involved.

ACTOR/BAKER. An urgent meeting of all artillery of the Paris Guard, today at the communal school.

CLUB LEADER. Use every means we have to speak up. And speak loud.

ACTRESS/SEAMSTRESS. There will be a course in Arabic on Wednesday and Friday at the College De France.

PÈRE DUCHÊNE. It's a beautiful day, this Easter day, because, for us, it isn't that sans-culotte Jesus who is being resuscitated, but the Revolution, Fuck! Père Duchêne has baptized his new daughter in the name of the Revolution! And he's proud as a fucking peacock. And Père Duchêne is sure of one thing: this girl's not gonna get taught by some blasted nun who'll tell her to just accept her lousy lot in life. She's going to get a good fucking education cause an educated girl'll grow up to be a good patriot mother. She won't let her kids betray the people. Good god, no! She'd rather jump in the fucking river! Fucking hell! No Lie! Christ!

ACTOR/THIERS.

GOD OF THE BIGOTS

JEALOUS GOD CAN YOU HEAR ME?
YOU ARE NOTHING MORE THAN A LIE
IT IS TIME, YOU FICTIONAL RULER
THAT WE TEAR YOU DOWN FROM THE SKY
YOUR HEAVEN AND HELL
NO MORE THAN JOKES
WHICH MAKE FREETHINKERS ALL WANT TO LAUGH!

PÈRE DUCHÊNE. I'm going to say something and then I'll prove I'm right. GOD DOES NOT EXIST! *(He waits.)* See, nothing happened. I'll do it again *(Up to the heavens:)* GOD DOES NOT EXIST! Well, either he's not there or he's a coward.

GOOD GOD OF THE BIGOTS
WE'RE FREE OF ALL YOUR CRAP!
GOD OF ALL THE BIGOTS
YOU WERE FULL OF CRAP!

SEAMSTRESS. I've got something to say about nuns—

PÈRE DUCHÊNE. I've got something to say about priests. They say we need building materials to make barricades? Well shoot the priests. Bag up the corpses. And make the barricades out of them!

SEAMSTRESS. No this is serious. Our hospitals are still run by nuns and I think our wounded should be cared for by female citizens and not those nuns. They'll poison the water those bitches.

ALL MEN.
> GOOD GOD OF THE BIGOTS
> WE'RE FREE OF ALL YOUR CRAP!
> GOD OF ALL THE BIGOTS
> YOU WERE FULL OF CRAP!

LOUISE. Paris will not give in, for it bears the flag of the future. The women of Paris will prove to France and to the world that at the hour of greatest danger we are as capable as our brothers of giving up our lives to the cause. For who was it who threw themselves in front of the cannons that fateful day? The women!

WOMEN.
> IF WE FREE OURSELVES OF THE CHURCH
> WE CAN FREE OURSELVES OF THE STATE
> WHEN WE LEAVE THE STATE IN THE LURCH
> SOON THE OWNERS WILL MEET THE SAME FATE

LA BORDAS.
> AND SOON THEY'LL SEE THAT ALL THE SCUM
> HAS RISEN AT LAST TO THE TOP!

WOMEN.
> GOOD GOD OF THE OWNERS!
> YOU BETTER GIVE IT UP!
> GOD OF ALL THE OWNERS!
> WE ARE FREE AT LAST!

LA BORDAS. Marriage, my sisters, is the greatest human error. To be married is to be a slave. And will you be a slave? All for the free women! None for the slaves!

ALL.   AND GOD OF THE BIGOTS!
> WE WON'T LET YOU RULE US NOW!
> GOD OF ALL THE BIGOTS!
> YOU CAN'T RULE US NOW!

ACTRESS/ELISABETH. And the idea of shared ownership it spreads throughout Paris. Workers associations spring up everywhere, among the medical students—

MEDICAL STUDENT (ACTOR/BAKER). The goal—to share our resources and create the means for mutual security!

ACTRESS/SEAMSTRESS. Among artists, led by the master painter Gustave Courbet—

COURBET (ACTOR/THIERS). Art should be run by Artists, free of commercial considerations and the successful artists should share their profits with the less successful.

ACTRESS/ELISABETH. Among actors, musicians, and singers:

LA BORDAS. Some performers earn an enormous amount, while others earn very little. It's high time that every working artist has a chance to live with basic human dignity!

ACTRESS/ELISABETH. The idea of liberation—somehow it spreads by balloons or god knows what to the other cities in France—

ACTOR/BAKER. To Lyon

ACTRESS/SEAMSTRESS. Marseille

ACTRESS/LOUISE. Toulouse

ACTRESS/ELISABETH. This idea is indeed infectious! Foreigners arrive from Russia, Austria, England, all over!

LOUISE. Citizens! Power shared is true freedom. It is time that fraternity replaces charity, and federation replaces hierarchy! If I were the only person saying all this, people could say that I was a pathological case. But there are thousands of us now, millions, none of whom gives a damn about authority. You see? Do you see?! It's a simple thing. DON'T BEG FOR YOUR PLACE IN THE WORLD, TAKE IT!

ALL.   AND GOD OF THE BIGOTS
WE'RE FREE WE'RE FREE WE'RE FREE
GOD OF ALL THE BIGOTS (AND THE LANDLORDS!)
WE ARE FREE FREE FREE
(AND GOD OF THE DEPARTMENT STORES! AND THE
    ARMY! YES, THE ARMY!)
GOD OF THE ARMY (AND THE FUCKING BUREAU-
    CRATS!)
WE'RE FREE WE'RE FREE WE'RE FREE (SO TAKE THAT,
    ALL OF YOU!)
GOD OF THE BIGOTS AND THE ARMY AND THE LAND-
    LORDS WE'RE FREE FREE FREE!

BAKER. And night baking must be abolished!

ACTRESS/ELISABETH. And it is, by decree of the Commune.

Scene Ten

Music.

PÈRE DUCHÊNE. Yes, my dear bakers, won't it be nice to spend an evening at home? And then go to work in the morning like everybody else? Now there are still assholes out there who say: "Now we won't have warm rolls to dip in your sacred café au lait! Well, Père Duchêne has never drunk anything like that in his whole stinking life! A good pint and a crust of bread, that's what this stomach gets in the morning—

ACTRESS/ELISABETH. *(To* PÈRE DUCHÊNE:*)* Thank you. *(To audience:)* A small thing you would think for a government to make a decree and end night baking. But indeed this is Paris after all and it is no small thing to say to an entire city now your bread will be not so fresh. The bakers may be happier but the customers, less so. And as with the customers, so go the bakery owners. And with that, may I introduce "The Council of the Commune debates following their decree to end night baking."

COUNCILMAN 1 (ACTRESS/LA BORDAS). Yesterday the bakery owners held a meeting and they are now asking that night-work continue for just a while longer. However, in retaliation for this the workers threatened to smash the windows of all the bakeries.

COUNCILMAN 2 (ACTRESS/LOUISE). I have to say, I think our decree was voted on rather impulsively—

COUNCILMAN 1 (ACTRESS/LA BORDAS). Councilmen, it is not our place to intervene in matters between employers and workers.

COUNCILMAN 4 (ACTRESS/ELISABETH). On the contrary, we are here to make social reforms and this decree is the only truly socialist reform to make it out of this Council.

COUNCILMAN 3 (ACTOR/THIERS). Indeed, you do not realize how long the bakers have been asking for this decree. This work is immoral; we cannot divide society into two classes and force these workers to labor only at night and never see the light of day. If we change our decision now the bakery owners will have all the advantage on their side!

COUNCILMAN 4 (ACTRESS/ELISABETH). And the workers themselves cannot stand up for their rights without fear of losing their jobs. And furthermore, every day we are told that the workers should educate themselves, but how can you educate yourself when you work at night?

COUNCILMAN 3 (ACTOR/THIERS). Let us say to the owners: here are the complaints made by the workers; and if you do not wish to yield to them, if you threaten us with closing down your shops, then we will resort to requisition. We will take over your businesses and employ the workers ourselves.

COUNCILMAN 2 (ACTRESS/LOUISE). I could not for the life of me care whether we have freshly baked bread or not; what concerns me—

PÈRE DUCHÊNE. Fuck! Fuck! Fuck! Commune! Père Duchêne is losing the tenderness he felt for you in the first days, for it seems that you are scared! The people are hungry for change and what do you do? You debate! All we see are the same old procedures but no revolutionary measures. I tell you, if you don't take things from the owners through sweeping legislation then we will we have to take everything when and how we decide. And your posters, "Death for Looting," "Death for Stealing," won't make a difference.

THIERS. PARISIANS: Judge the Commune by its works. It violates the rights of property, it converts your shops and streets into deserts and puts a stop to all work in Paris. If you do not act to end this regime yourselves, we will be forced to act with more energetic means. Think upon these things. In a very few days our army shall be in Paris.

ROSSEL. "Members of the Commune, you entrusted me with the post of war delegate, but I no longer feel able to accept this position of authority when the men under me do nothing but hold discussions and refuse to obey orders. I am not a man to hesitate in taking punitive action. But I do not want to initiate tough measures and find myself alone in bearing the blame for the executions that are necessary to turn this chaos into organization, obedience and victory. In the meantime, the enemy has mounted several attacks for which I would make them pay if I had the smallest military force at my command. I am therefore resigning and request a cell in Mazas Prison."

ACTRESS/ELISABETH. And here's a letter from Karl Marx, "The Parisians are succumbing. It's their *own fault*. They've simply got too much decency. After March 18th they wasted time scrupulously establishing their legality with elections giving that mischievous abortion Thiers," Wow. "That mischievous abortion Thiers time to concentrate hostile forces. They have failed to take over the National Treasury. And they have failed to organize an effective military. I'm afraid there's now little likelihood of establishing the dictatorship of the proletariat in Paris."

ACTRESS/LOUISE. Wait. Karl Marx can fault the Commune for "scrupulously establishing their legality," but that's the whole point! Liberation is not the "dictatorship" of anybody. Liberation demands that power be *shared* by the people. Equally. So the people had to have the chance to elect the Commune. Or that "decency"…that "too much decency" that Marx is criticizing… I mean, what is "too much decency?"

ACTOR/BAKER. It's a good point.

ACTRESS/ELISABETH. Look, I'm not arguing against decency. But remember we are talking about poor people like you two who have nothing. If you're going to have something you have to take it away from other people and once you get it you need authoritative power to keep it. That's "the dictatorship of the proletariat." Right?

ACTOR/BAKER. Yes.   **ACTRESS/SEAMSTRESS.** No.

ACTOR/BAKER. I mean…

ACTOR/BAKER. No.   **ACTRESS/SEAMSTRESS.** Yes.

ACTRESS/LOUISE. But what I'm saying, at least how I understand Louise Michel, she's saying that in order for workers or anyone else—in order to control your own lives you have to fight and keep fighting against anyone who tries to take power over you whatever words they use to describe it. Look, I think Elisabeth and Louise both want the same thing for these two but what does Karl Marx in his letter what does he have to offer them?

ACTRESS/ELISABETH. A chance to win.

ACTRESS/LOUISE. But at what price? I mean, look at the history.

ACTRESS/ELISABETH. The history is complicated.

Scene Eleven

ACTRESS/LOUISE. Well then, let's take a look—"A Brief History of LABOR."

ACTRESS/SEAMSTRESS. And The History of the Can-Can. Part 2.

(Dancing begins.)

ACTRESS/ELISABETH. 12th Century B.C.: Workers in Egypt organize the first known strike in history.

ACTRESS/SEAMSTRESS. Despite being suppressed, the Can-Can continues to be danced in private dance halls,

ACTOR/BAKER. Where it develops certain characteristic moves.

ACTRESS/LOUISE. 1799: England outlaws trade unions.

ACTOR/BAKER. Circling the legs…

ACTRESS/ELISABETH. 1833: England passes the first child labor laws. The workday of children under the age of 18 is limited to *twelve hours*.

ACTOR/BAKER. The pigeon wing…

ACTRESS/LOUISE. 1842: A general strike cripples England.

ACTOR/BAKER. And the high kick! By 1844 the Can-Can's popularity is soaring again.

ACTRESS/ELISABETH. 1864: Karl Marx's International Working Men's Association is founded in London.

ACTOR/BAKER. In fact, underground it becomes even more popular than ever.

ACTRESS/LOUISE. 1866: The first National Labor Union formed in America.

ACTRESS/SEAMSTRESS. Some women dance without any underwear and with each kick you get a straight shot of her naked—

ACTRESS/ELISABETH. 1871: Cities across America react to the Paris Commune by passing sweeping anti-labor legislation.

ACTRESS/SEAMSTRESS. Many disapprove of the dance because it leaves women hopelessly out of breath.

ACTOR/BAKER. And allows them to dance completely out of control.

ACTRESS/LOUISE. 1884: Hundreds of thousands of workers strike in Chicago. Some are killed by police

ACTOR/SEAMSTRESS. It's a dance of freedom, without imposed order, or even apparent organization.

ACTRESS/ELISABETH. 1917: The Russian Revolution.

ACTRESS/LOUISE. 1936: The Spanish revolution.

ACTRESS/ELISABETH. 1937: United Auto Workers win a major stand-off against General Motors.

ACTRESS/SEAMSTRESS. In fact, it is the first popular dance in history in which individuals dance entirely as individuals.

ACTRESS/LOUISE. 1959: The Cuban Revolution.

ACTRESS/ELISABETH. 1984: Margaret Thatcher crushes striking coal miners.

ACTRESS/LOUISE. 1988: Less than 17 percent of the American workforce is unionized.

ACTRESS/ELISABETH. 1999: Massive protests against the World Trade Organization in Seattle.

ACTRESS/SEAMSTRESS. Today a DVD of the film *Can-Can* starring Shirley MacLaine sells on Amazon.com for $14.99.

ACTOR/BAKER. For packaging this DVD, a worker in China makes 37 cents a day.

ACTRESS/SEAMSTRESS. So this idea of liberation…

ACTRESS/ELISABETH. Yeah?

ACTRESS/SEAMSTRESS. It seems impossible.

ACTRESS/LOUISE. Not impossible. Ongoing, maybe.

   (Dancing stops.)

ACTOR/BAKER. But, "today" *(Referring to the DVD spot on the timeline:)* the jobs just go to wherever has the cheapest labor so the workers—like us—always lose, somewhere.

ACTRESS/ELISABETH. Well, I think what Elisabeth would say is that the struggle is international and workers need to unite across national boundaries.

ACTOR/BAKER. And that sounds—like she said *(Referring to the* SEAMSTRESS*)* impossible.

ACTRESS/LOUISE. If we can just hold here for one moment and figure this out…

THIERS. Parisians: It is the Commune that oppresses you!

ACTRESS/ELISABETH. But we can't because next in the story Thiers sends his last message to Paris.

ACTRESS/SEAMSTRESS. Well, then: The Grand Finale of the Can-Can! Typically, the Grand Finale keeps going and going and going!

(Can-Can finale simultaneous with THIERS' *last message.)*

THIERS. Parisians: We would have preferred that you should liberate your-selves from these tyrants; but since you cannot do so, we have collected an army, which comes not to conquer, but to deliver you. Unite then: open your gates, which the Commune has closed against law, order, prosperity, and the safety of France. Parisians! France desires to put an end to this Civil War. She is marching to deliver you. Soon we will be at your gates.

Scene Twelve

ACTOR/BAKER. And now, we're back at the concert at the Tuileries Pal-ace. It's May 21, 1871. *(They both do The Palace gesture.)*

ACTRESS/SEAMSTRESS. Elisabeth Dmitrieff takes the stage.

ACTOR/BAKER. And she speaks to the audience of thousands. *(Gesture.)*

ELISABETH. People of Paris, look around you. Look at yourselves. Here you are on this night of celebration and you see, you see what you have won, so far. You see this Palace and it is yours. All of Paris. It is yours. And here in Paris you will live. Liberated. But only if you can win for good. My friends, I do not need to remind you that outside this city there is an army waiting, maybe coming. And maybe soon, there is fighting I don't know. But I know, whatever happens you will fight for the future. With your strength now you will join with workers everywhere. Not just France. But Germany. England. Everywhere. Paris, your enemies they are united. But the people. All the people. We are many more. And when we are united nothing can stop us. And so we win. Now, I am no brilliant singer, but I hold here a new song written by your own Eugène Pottier. He is a member of your Council. He is a member of the International Workers Association.

This song. He writes it for you and what you will do. YOUR song. And now you must sing for workers everywhere. You learn it now with me.

*(*ELISABETH *sings.)*

THE INTERNATIONALE

ARISE YOU PRISONERS OF STARVATION
ARISE YOU WRETCHED OF THE EARTH
FOR JUSTICE THUNDERS CONDEMNATION
A BETTER WORLD'S IN BIRTH

NO MORE THE CHAINS OF RULING NATIONS
SO ALL YOU SLAVES, STAND FIRM AND TALL
THE WORLD SHALL RISE ON NEW FOUNDATIONS
WE WHO WERE NOTHING SHALL BE ALL.

IT'S THE LAST HOUR OF COMBAT
LET EACH STAND IN HIS PLACE
THE INTERNATIONALE
SHALL FREE THE HUMAN RACE.
IT'S THE LAST HOUR OF COMBAT
LET EACH STAND IN HIS PLACE
THE INTERNATIONALE
SHALL FREE THE HUMAN RACE.

(Applause that changes and erases the concert.)

Scene Thirteen

ACTRESS/SEAMSTRESS. It's three o'clock in the morning. The concert at the Tuileries Palace has been over for hours and most of Paris lies asleep. Come, through the silent night—west from the Tuileries Palace along the Champs Elysées with its expensive boutiques—at the far side of Paris, over the dark waters of the Seine, at the Gates at St. Cloud not a guardsman in sight.

ACTOR/BAKER. A solitary man passes by he sees the Versailles troops outside and knowing the coast is clear the traitor waves them in. And under cover of night, the army sneaks in one by one.

ACTRESS/SEAMSTRESS. And the killing has already started.

(Explosion.)

(Song: The SOPRANO *sings "Ah! Je Veux Vivre" from Gounod's "Romeo and Juliette." Explosions. A shell hits. Sounds of warfare. Various* CITIZENS *appear.* SOPRANO *continues while the Communards build barricades.)*

CITIZEN 1 (ACTOR/THIERS). The hour of revolutionary war has struck! This is the struggle of the future against the past! Paris! Take arms and defend your city!

(A shell hits outside. The people build a barricade.)

Enough of military officers! Enough of gold-embroidered uniforms! Make way for the people! *(Begin* CITIZEN 2.*)* If you are determined that the generous blood that has flowed like water these past six weeks should not have been shed in vain, if you wish to live in a free and egalitarian France, if you wish to spare your children the suffering and misery you have endured, then you must rise as one man. The Commune counts on you, count on the Commune!

CITIZEN 2 (ACTOR/PÈRE DUCHÊNE). A desperate man fighting for his children is worth ten soldiers fighting for their officer's pay.

CITIZEN 3 (ACTRESS/LOUISE). The Versailles Army has occupied part of Paris but do not be disheartened!

CITIZEN 4 (ACTRESS/ELISABETH). We requisition all objects necessary for the construction of barricades. Any citizen who refuses to aid the cause shall be immediately shot.

CITIZEN 5 (ACTOR/BAKER). Citizens, we must destroy what we cannot defend, even if it be an entire city. All sentimentality is treason! Once these people are faced with their own ruin and death they will submit to us unconditionally!

ALL. To arms! To arms!

CITIZEN 1. Let Paris bristle with barricades, *(Begin* CITIZEN 2.*)* When the people have a rifle in their hands and cobble-stones under their feet they have no fear! To arms! *(Begin* CITIZEN 3.*)* Citizens, to arms! And from behind our improvised ramparts *(Begin* CITIZEN 4.*)* let our war-cry ring out against the enemy, our cry of pride, our cry of defiance, and our cry of victory—for thanks to its barricades—

CITIZEN 2. Turn over carriages, take the doors off their hinges, throw the furniture out the windows!

CITIZEN 3. Cover the street with broken bottles and planks with nails—

CITIZEN 4. Pelt them with furniture and anything else!

ALL. *(After* CITIZEN 1 *is finished:)* Paris is impregnable!

    (Gunshot, the BAKER *is killed. The* SOPRANO *finishes.)*

Scene Fourteen

    LOUISE *on the battlefield.*

LOUISE. When this battle is over. People might say that I'm brave. Not really. People are simply entranced by events. It isn't bravery now. It is beautiful, that's all. Barbarian that I am, I love cannon, the smell of powder, and the sound of machine-gun bullets in the air.

    *(*ELISABETH *at a train station.)*

ELISABETH. Dear Sir, I promised the people that the world would come to their aid. The people of Paris are fighting heroically, but we never expected to be abandoned in this way. I am a pessimist, you know; I have no illusions and I expect to die one of these days on a barricade. But it will not be in Paris—I believe too much in this cause to die here, now. And if the people find the chance to rise again I hope I may be alive to see it and hope that you and the world will not sit idly by and watch them get slaughtered.

    (The DRESSMAKER *at home.)*

DRESSMAKER. The raking sound of the machine guns, the cannon fire shakes the house, the racket of the paving stones, the yells of the combatants, the horrible, horrible, sound of bodies falling. I can scarcely bear it. This morning, soldiers come by the house of our neighbor. Are they going to shoot him here in front of his wife? Thank goodness no. The soldiers carry him into the street, they're going to march away, when the prisoner lifts his arms—

VOICE (ACTOR/BAKER). Long live the Commune!

DRESSMAKER. And right then the window above opens and a grey-haired woman leans out—

VOICE (ACTRESS/LOUISE). Die in peace my beloved I will avenge you!

DRESSMAKER. The soldiers go back into the house. I fall back into a chair; I shut my eyes not to see, and I press my hands on my ears, not to hear, but the horrible noise is triumphant and I hear it all the same.

(Musket shots.)

ACTRESS/SEAMSTRESS.

MON HOMME

I SEARCH IN VAIN WHEN HOPE IS DEAD
BELOW THESE STREETS THIS RUINED LAND
AND STILL THIS BLOOD RUNS BLACK AND RED
AH, YES, YOU UNDERSTAND.
A GALLANT MAN AND ONE, THEY SAY,
WHO NEVER FLED FROM DANGER'S WAY.
AND HIS NAME IS MARTIN.
SOLDIER, HAVE YOU SEEN HIM?
HE'S MY MAN.

IS THERE SOME MORAL HERE AT LEAST?
AND FOR WHAT COMFORT CAN I SEEK?
THEY WORKED HIM LIKE SOME NAMELESS BEAST.
SIX DAYS IN EVERY WEEK.
HIS HEART IS PLANTED FIRM AND TRUE
AND OH, HIS SHOULDERS CLOSE TO YOU.
AND HIS NAME IS MARTIN.
SOLDIER, HAVE YOU SEEN HIM?
HE'S MY MAN.

FOR TWELVE YEARS NOW THIS MAN I'VE KNOWN
HE HASN'T CHANGED NOT TO THIS DAY.
SIX HEALTHY CHILDREN IN OUR HOME
WITH ONE MORE ON THE WAY.
SO WHAT AM I TO SAY TO THEM
IF HE DOES NOT COME HOME AGAIN?
AND HIS NAME IS MARTIN.

SOLDIER, HAVE YOU SEEN HIM?
HE'S MY MAN.

(A hail of bullets. She runs off.)

FRENCH ARMY OFFICER. *(From off stage:)*
Loyal French Soldiers:
In tearing the city back from the hands of the wretches
you will preserve it from complete ruin;
you will give Paris back to France!

Scene Fifteen

THE CAPTAIN

CAPTAIN (ACTOR/THIERS).
TO THE WALL, THE CAPTAIN SAID.
HIS MOUTH WAS CRUEL, HIS FACE WAS RED.
TO THE WALL.
WHAT HAVE YOU DONE?

DEAD MAN 1 (ACTOR/PÈRE DUCHÊNE).
OH YOU ARE BRAVE
IF YOU ARE HUNGRY THEN YOU EAT,
YOU DO NOT WISH TO BE A SLAVE
NOR TO BE PULLED DOWN BY DEFEAT.
ALL THIS IS RIGHT AND MANLY TOO
BUT IF YOU KILL ME, OH MY FRIEND,
YOU'LL BE A BEAST CAGED IN A ZOO,
DO YOU WANT TO BE LIKE THEM?
DO YOU UNDERSTAND MY LOGIC?
WELL LONG LIVE THE REPUBLIC!

(Gunshots.)

ACTRESS/SEAMSTRESS. A young woman dressed in silk runs into the street, fires into the air with a revolver, and says—

WOMAN 1 (ACTRESS/ELISABETH). Shoot me at once!

ACTRESS/SEAMSTRESS. She's about to be bound and taken to Versailles but—

WOMAN 1. Save me the trouble of the journey!

(She opens her arms and is shot.)

CAPTAIN.
WHAT HAVE YOU DONE.

WOMAN 2 (ACTRESS/LA BORDAS).
OH SHOOT ME DEAD,
A SOLDIER DRUNK AND BADLY KEPT,

HE SHOT MY FATHER IN THE HEAD,
AND MY CRIME IS THAT I WEPT.

(Gunshots.)

ACTRESS/SEAMSTRESS. Two soldiers apprehend an old woman and she screams "I had two sons they were killed at the front. I had two more sons they were killed at the gates. And my husband died at this barricade—so do what you want with me!"

(Gunshots.)

CAPTAIN.

WHAT HAVE YOU DONE?

WOMAN 3 (ACTRESS/LOUISE).

I WAS A NURSE,
I NEVER FOUGHT BUT MADE MY WAY,
AND HEALED FOR BETTER AND FOR WORSE,
COMMUNARDS AND VERSAILLAIS,

BERTHOLDE (ACTRESS/SEAMSTRESS).

I AM CALLED BERTHOLDE.
AND I AM TWELVE YEARS OLD.

(Gunshots.)

CAPTAIN. The General orders that you are to be shot on your knees. As you die, you will say, Long live the Army of Versailles!

COMMUNARD (ACTOR/BAKER).

YOU DIRTY SLOB!
QUICK ORDER ME TO BE UNDONE
ALREADY I HAVE DONE THE JOB
WITH MY LITTLE GUN.
WITH ONE SHOT YOU SEE THE MOON
AND WITH TWO, LONG LIVE THE COMMUNE!

(Everyone reprises their verse in a round. Gunshots after gunshots. The people line up and are killed, over and over, ending with a sequence of single gunshots. SOPRANO enters and singers Bizet's "Tarantella." She crosses through the killings and her final note cues the final shots.)

Scene Sixteen

LOUISE. We've been pushed out to the cemetery of Père Lachaise in the Northeast corner of the city. We're trying to defend the cemetery, but we've few fighters left. Shells tear the air, marking time like a clock. It looks magnificent in the clear night, and the marble statues on the tombs seem to be alive. I send myself out on reconnaissance and I enjoy walking alone in the empty zone of the shelling. Luckily the shells hit either just before me or just after. One shell strikes an enormous cherry tree full of flowered branches—and right then the General of the Commune passes by—and the blossoms of the cherry tree fall silently all around us, each one lit up by the glow of the shelling. The General holds out both his hands to me and tells me "It's all over."

LA BORDAS.

THE BLOODY WEEK

NO ONE IS HERE BUT SOLDIERS AND THIEVES
STREETS ARE EMPTY, DARK, AND BLEAK
ONE SAD OLD WOMAN WEEPS AND GRIEVES
WIDOWS AND ORPHANS BARELY SPEAK
MISERY POURS FROM EVERY DOOR
TURNING THE HAPPY STREETS TO MUD
ALL OF THE FASHION TURNED TO WAR
AND THE STREETS ARE PAVED WITH BLOOD

AND YET…
SHAKE OFF THAT BITTER TUNE
THESE DREADFUL DAYS WILL HAVE AN END
REVENGE IS COMING SOON
WHEN ALL THE POOR WILL RISE AGAIN, AGAIN
WHEN ALL THE POOR WILL RISE AGAIN

THEY HUNT THEY CAPTURE AND THEY KILL
ANYONE WHO BLOCKS THEIR WAY
MOTHERS AND DAUGHTERS STANDING STILL
OLD MEN AND CHILDREN WITH NOTHING TO SAY
(Start THIERS. *Sounds of Paris burning.)*
MEN FROM THE BANK AND MEN FROM THE STREET
LOVERS AND GIRLS AND MEN WITH GUNS
SEE THEM LIKE FLIES TO ROTTEN MEAT
ON THE BODIES OF THE FALLEN ONES

THIERS. Paris is burning! The last acts of the insurgents are abominable. Last evening we succeeded in occupying the area around the Opera House. Early this morning we took the Place de la Concorde, and The Place Vendôme. At the present moment City Hall is on fire. The flames were prevented from reaching the Louvre, but the Tuileries Palace—

(Fire sounds end.)

ACTRESS/SEAMSTRESS. And now imagine, all of you were at the Tuileries Palace for the concert just days ago. Only now in this section everyone's been lined up and shot. And that section there, all of them were dragged out of their homes and shot. And everyone in the back and outside in the gardens all the people who couldn't squeeze inside The Palace well all of them too. And now imagine 15, 20, 25,000? In just one week—gone. And is there some way to ask them did they expect it? Was it worth it? Well no there isn't because They're DEAD. And the Tuileries Palace…it's—on—fire.

(Explosion, blinding light, fireball.)

AND YET…

SHAKE OFF THAT BITTER TUNE

THESE DREADFUL DAYS WILL HAVE AN END

REVENGE IS COMING SOON

WHEN ALL THE POOR WILL RISE AGAIN, AGAIN

WHEN ALL THE POOR WILL RISE AGAIN.

Scene Seventeen

VOICE OFFSTAGE. Inhabitants of Paris: The army of France comes to save you! Paris is delivered.

LOUISE. In May 1871 the streets of Paris were dappled white as if by apple blossoms in the spring. But no trees had cast down that mantle of white; it was chlorine that covered the corpses.

VOICE OFFSTAGE. Today the struggle is finished. Order, production, and security will now resume.

LOUISE. Six months after the hot-blooded butchery of Paris, the trials began. By June 1872 the Versailles "justice" had delivered 32,905 verdicts.

PROSECUTOR (ACTOR/PÈRE DUCHÊNE). December 16, 1871. The Case against Louise Michel. She is a she-wolf hungry for blood. She and her hellish plots are responsible for the death of hostages and the misery of many. What do you have to say in your defense?

LOUISE. I don't want to defend myself, nor do I want to be defended. I have only this to say. We never wanted anything but the triumph of the great principles of Revolution. I swear it by our martyrs who some day will find their avenger. Since it seems that any heart that beats for liberty has the right only to a small lump of lead, I demand mine. But if you let me live, I will not stop crying for vengeance—

PROSECUTOR. I cannot allow you to continue speaking—

LOUISE MICHEL. I have finished. If you are not cowards, kill me.

PROSECUTOR. Louise Michel you are sentenced to deportation to New Caledonia with the other prisoners of the Commune

LOUISE. I would have preferred death.

"Memory crowds in on me and I keep forgetting that I am writing my memoirs. In my mind it is a spring night, now it is May 1871, and I see the red reflection of flames. It is Paris afire, and I see it still as I sit here writing. I see in my deepest thoughts a series of tableaux where, century after century, an ensemble of millions of human existences disappears into nothing. They are part of history now, but who can say what part? For who will tell their story?

Who will record the crimes that power commits, and the monstrous manner in which power transforms men? And who will listen?"

Scene Eighteen

ACTRESS/LA BORDAS.
> I ALWAYS WILL LOVE, THE CHERRIES OF SPRING,
> THE SEASON WHICH LEAVES A HOLE IN MY HEART,
> A WOUND THAT IS NEVER HEALED.
> AND ALL THAT MAY BE BY FORTUNE REVEALED
> IT NEVER WILL SOOTHE THE GRIEF IN MY SOUL.
> I ALWAYS WILL LOVE THE CHERRIES OF SPRING,
> AND THINK OF THE HOLE I GUARD IN MY HEART.

ACTRESS/SEAMSTRESS. 1872: The inventor of haute couture, Charles Frederick Worth, buys pieces from the ruins of the Tuileries Palace at an auction to decorate his country home.

ACTOR/BAKER. By 1875, the Can-Can is danced at the Moulin Rouge for tourists and visitors.

ACTRESS/SEAMSTRESS. Nearby, on the site where Louise Michel defended the cannon, Thiers constructs the enormous Sacre Coeur Basilica, the basilica is now a favorite site for photographs of the city.

ACTOR/BAKER. 1880: Louise Michel returns to Paris from exile and takes up the black flag of Anarchism.

ACTRESS/LOUISE. She writes an angry letter to the President of the Republic on the anniversary of the fall of the Commune each and every year until she dies.

ACTRESS/SEAMSTRESS. 1917: The Russian Revolution adopts The Internationale as the national anthem.

ACTOR/BAKER. 1942: During the German occupation of Paris in World War II, Charles Trenet records a popular version of "Le Temps des Cerises" by communard Jean-Baptiste Clément.

ACTRESS/SEAMSTRESS. 1959: The Soviets launch the first rocket to the moon which carries the red flag of the Paris Commune.

ACTOR/BAKER. May 1968 in Paris: The massive student and worker uprisings are called "Le Temps de Cerises" after the song.

ACTRESS/ELISABETH. 1971: East Germany issues a commemorative stamp for the centenary of the Paris commune

ACTOR/PÈRE DUCHÊNE. Today, a copy of that stamp sells on eBay for $1.95 (Australian Dollars)

ACTOR/THIERS. 1989: In Tiananmen Square students and workers sing The Internationale moments before the shooting.

OPERA SINGER. 1996: An opera singer performs "Le Temps de Cerises" at the funeral of French President François Mitterand.

RECORDING (Charles Trenet)

J'aimerai toujours le temps des cerises
C'est de ce temps-là que je garde au Coeur
Une plaie ouverte
Et dame fortune, en m'étant offerte
Ne pourra jamais fermer ma douleur
J'aimerai toujours le temps des cerises
Et le souvenir que je garde au Coeur.
Et le souvenir que je garde au Coeur.
Et le souvenir que je garde au Coeur.
Et le souvenir que je garde au Coeur.

ACTRESS/SEAMSTRESS. And today if you go to the empty space where the Tuileries Palace used to be you'll see a plaque that reads: "In 1871 the Tuileries Palace was destroyed in a fire."

End of Play

SHADOW OF HIMSELF

by Neal Bell

INTRODUCTION

In working as a guest writer with The Civilians, I had to overcome one big stumbling block: how fascinating I found the raw, unmediated interview material The Civilians actors gathered, during the summer we collaborated together. Steve Cosson had asked me, as an experiment, to come up with a way of turning this particular group of interviews—about 'protectors, defenders and masculinity'—into some kind of a "fiction." And when I heard the actors presenting their interview material to the group—speaking without notes, in the voices of the people they'd talked to—I was mesmerized: both by the astounding way in which The Civilians actors seemed to BECOME the people they'd interviewed, as they presented to the company…and by the powerful reality of the words these real-life characters were speaking. Steve did his own version of cutting-and-pasting these interviews together, for a public presentation of the raw material—and my challenge was to do…something *else*. But what that 'something else' might be wasn't clear at all—until I happened to think about the legend of Gilgamesh…and realized that 'Gilgamesh' wasn't just a random "where did THAT come from?" thought. That epic—which has haunted me for decades—addresses a number of the issues and concerns that the "masculinity project" had brought up—and I thought it might work, as a meditation on the interview material, if I retold the tale of Gilgamesh, moving backwards and forwards in time, reframing the words of the men and women who'd spoken so eloquently in The Civilians interviews. I've always been a lover of story—and *Gilgamesh* gave me a solid structure to work with and depart from. I've been fortunate to have several opportunities to develop and refine the script—beginning with The Civilians themselves, when they were guest artists of the Orchard Project. I'd also like to thank the New York State Arts Council, for the grant that made it possible for me to do this work with the Civilians. Long ago I'd done a version of collaborative documentary theatre—for a project about the Chicago Conspiracy Trial. I've wanted a shot at that group experience ever since—and *Shadow of Himself* was, for me, a great opportunity—decades later —to try that kind of experiment again.

—Neal Bell

CAST OF CHARACTERS

GIL, a king

NK, an opponent, then a friend

GIL'S MOTHER / A YOUNG WIFE / A TEMPLE WHORE / A BODY / HUMBABA / FARAWAY, an immortal

YOUNG MAN 1 / SOLDIER 1 / HUMBABA / SCORPION 1

YOUNG MAN 2 / SOLDIER 2 / HUMBABA / SCORPION 2

The play is written to be performed by four men and one woman—any doubling possible.

3 actors play the monster Humbaba.

Any combination of actors plays the Chorus.

SETTING

The very distant past, and the present.

Near the Euphrates River.

ACKNOWLEDGMENTS

Shadow of Himself was commissioned and developed by The Civilians. The play takes inspiration from a workshop that involved the following participants:

Actors .... Emily Ackerman, Maria Dizzia, Michael Esper, Matt Maher, Brian Sgambati

Director .... Steven Cosson

Assistant Director .... Jordan Young

Research Coordinator .... Bixby Eliot

Research Assistants .... Sarah Bishop-Stone, Adam Bradley, Katie Honaker, Sarah Marcus

Acting Apprentices .... Soneela Nankani, Eric Piatkowski, Nate Wheeler, Samantha Sklaar

Developed with the support of The Public Theater and The Orchard Project.

SHADOW OF HIMSELF

(1)

In a palace, long ago.
GIL, the King, arm-wrestles a SOLDIER.
The CHORUS *watches him.*

CHORUS. Look at these towering walls—he made them.
Climb to the top and see how broad—
walk along them, looking down at the city he built,
in his image:
bright sheen of his muscles: floating oil on water, on fire—
the movement of his thought, like a blade—
the beauty of his fury in battle,
brave to the point of stupidity—
these made him a god—

> *(GIL pins the* SOLDIER's *arm, with a thud.)*

—in his own eyes.

> *(The* SOLDIER *slouches away.)*

GIL. Another!
Bring me an *equal!*

> *(SOLDIER 2 approaches—GIL launches into pinning him.)*

CHORUS. As a god, he demanded tribute:
their daughters and their wives,
virgins, whores, mothers and children—
ones who were tight, in their youth,
ones who were looser, in their age—
he was a stake at the bottom of the gaping pit
into which they fell—
those who weeded the crops,
baked the bread, or wrote romance novels,
tended to the loom, or the Pilates class,
or the orgies—
they fell into his maw, and when he was sated—
he spat them out.

He took their men to war
and did not return them.
No deposit.

> *(GIL pins the* SECOND SOLDIER's *arm, looks around for other challenges.)*

GIL. A *worthy* opponent, I said! An equal!
Who is left? *(Pause.)* No one?

(Pause.)

I am the strongest man alive—
the bravest, and the most beautiful.
Only Death could defeat me—and even He
would tremble before me, drizzle of shit
running down his bony legs, before I was undone.

(Pause.)

Now bring me women!

(A WOMAN *approaches.)*

CHORUS. One future he will never see:

GIL. *(To a* WOMAN *in a singles bar:)* Did it hurt?

WOMAN. What?

GIL. When you fell from the sky.

(She looks at him, uncomprehending. He has to explain:)

Because—you know—…

WOMAN. I didn't fall from the sky.

GIL. No, I know—but—…
I mean, like—if you were an angel…

WOMAN. But I'm not.

GIL. But if you were.

(Pause.)

WOMAN. Does this ever work?

GIL. *(Shaking his head:)* Do you want to fuck?

WOMAN. Fuck yourself, you're closer.

(She moves away.)

CHORUS 1. One future disappearing…

CHORUS 2. Why will he never see it?

CHORUS 1. Because—when he believed that he was a god—
he was mistaken.

(Pause.)

He won't see enough of Forever to participate in Speed Dating.

CHORUS. Then how will he learn humility?

GIL. Bring me women! *Now!*

(Another WOMAN *approaches.)*

Lie down.

WOMAN. My man would kill you.

GIL. Then where is he?

>   *(She doesn't answer.)*

Lie down on your back. Spread your legs.

WOMAN. You saw him die.

GIL. When?

WOMAN. In the night—in the valley—when the enemy fell upon you.

GIL. Was it my brave lieutenant with the spear jammed into the socket
of his eye? Or ripping away his jaw—
that brave lieutenant?

>   *(Pause.)*

Men die in battle so that you can live.

WOMAN. —to be raped by you.

GIL. Should we stop fighting?
Lose what we had paid with our blood to win?

>   *(Quoting Dubya:)*

"Best to honor the sacrifice of our fallen troops—"

WOMAN. —to be raped by you.

>   *(Pause.)*

GIL. Lie down on your back. Spread your legs.
Open yourself with your fingers.
I can reach inside of you, where you bleed—

WOMAN. *(Countering:)* Manhole—you have a hole in *you.*
Where the spear can shove its way up and through
the meat of your body, out your mouth.
A brighter, bloody tongue flickering, catching the light.

>   *(Pause.)*

GIL. Bring me *another* woman!

>   *(Pause.)*

WOMAN. I *am* telling the truth.
You were never a god. Only part of you.
On your mother's side.

GIL. And a muzzle!

>   *(Pause.)*

WOMAN. Do you stand at a window at night, looking out—
and wonder what that sound could be—
like an endless break of waves on a beach?
Gnashing teeth of the men whose lovers you take—
the weeping of mothers—
their beautiful sons come back to them only in dreams,
in a haze of vultures…

(Pause.)

(Challenged, GIL *stares at himself in a mirror.)*

GIL. Look at my reflection:
I am the strongest man, the bravest—

WOMAN. And your people want you to choke on a piece of gristle.

(Pause.)

CHORUS. Let him choke on a piece of gristle.
Let his blow-dryer fall in his bath,
let him wake in the night with a pain in his chest,
and dial 911, and hear the blatt of a busy signal—
let his brakes fail, let him live too long,
let him find a suspicious mole,
let him have children.

(Pause.)

No—

(A more terrible thought occurring:)

Let him see himself.
Let him open his eyes.

(Pause.)

GIL. *(Looking into the mirror:)* No man is my equal.

(He reaches out, to touch his reflection in the mirror. It dawns on him:)

I am completely alone.

(To the WOMAN:*)*

Get out of here. *Go!*

(The WOMAN *moves off.* GIL *shouts.)*

Do I have one waiting who's deaf and *dumb?* Bring her!

(Far off, the roar of a terrible beast. GIL, *out of habit it, ignores it—but finally looks out the window, wondering how distant is the danger.)*

(2)

Two Young Men wander cautiously up a mountainside.

YOUNG MAN 1. My father would fucking kill me.

YOUNG MAN 2. So don't fuckin' tell him. Genius.

YOUNG MAN 1. *(Looking back from where they came:)* If the flock wanders off—

YOUNG MAN 2. "We were chasing away a lion—"

*(*YOUNG MAN 1 *whirls around.)*

YOUNG MAN 1. Where??

*(*YOUNG MAN 2 *gives him a look.)*

Oh: a "lion."
But you did see—something horrible?

(YOUNG MAN 2 *nods.*)

Were you afraid? Because I'm shitless.

(*Pause.*)

YOUNG MAN 2. See—don't tell me that. I kinda hate you,
when you tell me that.

YOUNG MAN 1. It walked like a man—but it wasn't a man?

YOUNG MAN 2. It was eating grass, by the waterhole—you know,
chomp a mouthful, stuff its face...
Then it looked around, and it saw me—
and it stood up—*on its hind legs...*

YOUNG MAN 1. I would've pissed myself.

YOUNG MAN 2. I did.

YOUNG MAN 1. But you said you weren't—[afraid]

YOUNG MAN 2. I was lying!

(*Pause.*)

It was trapped, so it started to charge me—

YOUNG MAN 1. Damn!

YOUNG MAN 2. —and then, right before it slammed into me, it
bounced—

YOUNG MAN 1. It bounced?

YOUNG MAN 2. Like a friggin' gazelle. Up that cliffside. And out of here.

(*Pause.*)

YOUNG MAN 1. (*Trying to get it straight:*) You pissed yourself—

YOUNG MAN 2. Shut up.

YOUNG MAN 1. (*Then why...?*) But you came back.

YOUNG MAN 2. Because—I dunno...
this dream I useta have, about flying—
that's how it ran, up the hillside...

YOUNG MAN 1. Do you think it'll come again?

YOUNG MAN 2. If you shut up. If that would be possible.

(*For a moment they wait in silence, nervously looking in all directions.*)

(*Then* YOUNG MAN 1 *falls into a game they play, speaking softly.*)

YOUNG MAN 1. Keanu!

YOUNG MAN 2. Button it!

YOUNG MAN 1. Play!

(*Pause.*)

YOUNG MAN 1. *Keanu.*

(YOUNG MAN 2 gives in, reluctantly plays the game, to calm his friend.)

YOUNG MAN 2. Gay.

YOUNG MAN 1. Travolta.

YOUNG MAN 2. Gay.

YOUNG MAN 1. Gere.

YOUNG MAN 2. Yawn.

YOUNG MAN 1. Tom Cruise.

YOUNG MAN 2. C'*mon.*

YOUNG MAN 1. Alex Trebeck.

YOUNG MAN 2. He lives with his mother.

YOUNG MAN 1. Mike Piazza.

YOUNG MAN 2. Major homo.

YOUNG MAN 1. Anderson Cooper.

YOUNG MAN 2. He *cries.* He's not even gay. He's a woman.

    (Pause.)

YOUNG MAN 1. You.

YOUNG MAN 2. Busted.

YOUNG MAN 1. Me.

    (YOUNG MAN 2 shrugs.)

I'm not.

YOUNG MAN 2. Fine.

YOUNG MAN 1. I'm *not.*

YOUNG MAN 2. *Fine!*

YOUNG MAN 1. A man can be afraid—

YOUNG MAN 2. Faggots are men. If you want to get technical.

    (Pause.)

YOUNG MAN 1. When you saw the monster—was it dark?

YOUNG MAN 2. No—just before: like this…

things getting lost in the shadows—

    (Just then, NK springs onto the stage, half-naked. He freezes, seeing the men.)
    (They freeze. A stand-off.)
    (They all piss themselves—thunderously, in the case of NK.)

YOUNG MAN 1. Who are you?

What are you?

We are—men. Human—animals.

    (NK sniffs the air.)

Oh. You smell our piss.

We don't want to hurt you—

YOUNG MAN 2. *(Sotto voce:)* And it's going, "Rip, mangle, fuck-suck, shred."

YOUNG MAN 1. You don't know that.

YOUNG MAN 2. Predator. Eyes in the front of its head.

YOUNG MAN 1. So?

    *(*YOUNG MAN 2, *to demonstrate, puts his fists to the side of his head, like eyes.)*

YOUNG MAN 2. Gazelle. The lion is coming right at ya.
But—"What lion?" You're dinner.

    (Challenging, YOUNG MAN 1 *puts his fists next to his eyes.)*

YOUNG MAN 1. Us. *(Using his fist-eyes to "spot" a gazelle:)*
A gazelle! I'm hungry!
Sneak, sneak, sneak—
'Rip—mangle—shred.'
We're the same.

YOUNG MAN 2. Like I said—we're in trouble.

YOUNG MAN 1. *(Asserting a bond:)* Look at him watching us.

YOUNG MAN 2. Not 'him.' 'It.'

YOUNG MAN 1. *(To* NK:*)* Can—you—understand—us?

    (Pause.)

What can he be thinking?

YOUNG MAN 2. *It.*

    (Suddenly NK *bounces at them—they run away, screaming.)*

NK. Why were those animals talking?

    *(*NK *gets on all fours, begins to lap water up from the water-hole.)*
    (Two LIONS *enter, join* NK *to drink. The Peaceable Kingdom.)*

(3)

    GIL *looks out at the night.*
    The CHORUS *mutters softly, in the background.*

CHORUS. Let him have root canal.
Let him be audited.
Let him open his eyes.

GIL. *(Fuming:)* Why are my animals babbling?

    *(*YOUNG MAN 2 *approaches.)*

What now?

YOUNG MAN 2. *(Breathless:)* My lord—I saw it!—a creature—
walks on its *legs!*—teeth like a catamount—
it springs the traps we set, so dinner wanders off, we're starving now,

our women won't go to the watering hole,
we're dying of thirst, my lord—it bounces!
Nothing is good, anymore. We're afraid.
Set *us* free from our fear.

GIL. Has no one tried to kill it?

YOUNG MAN 2. *(Lying:)* We did. But the thing is strong, my lord.
Almost as strong as you are.

> *(GIL is startled.)*

And fast. And very cunning.
And hard to look upon.

GIL. Blood-dripping fangs? One milky eye?

YOUNG MAN 2. Worse, my lord: it's beautiful.
Blinding—like the sun.

> *(GIL is outraged.)*

GIL. Count the number of suns in the sky.

YOUNG MAN 2. *(Puzzled:)* My lord, there is only one.

GIL. There can only be one. Do you understand?

> *(Clearly not understanding, YOUNG MAN 2 nods.)*

Go to the temple—choose among the whores,
and pick the ripest.
The one who seems about to burst her skin.
Take her to the watering hole.

YOUNG MAN 2. And then, my lord?

GIL. Let her burst.
Let her open the creature's eyes.

(4)

> *At the watering hole.*
> NK *is drinking, with Other Animals.*
> *Suddenly, they all look up, alert.*

NK. I smell it too. Blood…

> *(The* WOMAN *appears.* NK *and the Other Animals—moving as one—
> dash away. The* WOMAN *laughs.)*
>
> *(A moment later* NK *returns—cautious but very curious.)*

WOMAN. Did it hurt? When you fell from the sky?

NK. Birds fall from the sky. I'm not a bird.

WOMAN. My mistake.

> *(Pause.)*

NK. You're wounded.

WOMAN. No.

NK. Bleeding.

WOMAN. Yes. That time of the moon.
Do you mind?

NK. I don't know.

> *(Far off, an ominous roar.)*

WOMAN. What was that?

NK. The terrible guardian of the Cedar Forest.

WOMAN. The giant?

NK. *(Nodding:)* Why are you shaking?
He is very far away.

WOMAN. You think that because you're not human.
You don't know that he's always standing here—

CHORUS. Artery clogging, mutating virus,
friendly fire, drunk at the wheel—

WOMAN. —beside us, ready to part us.
Ready to carry us off to the Land of the Dead.

NK. I'm not afraid.

WOMAN. That's why I'm shaking.

> *(She touches his face, tracing the line of his jaw with a finger.)*

You smell like a goat.

NK. Do you lie with goats?
You smell like—

CHORUS 1. —trip on the stairs?
Touch a live wire?
Choke on the cap of a nosespray bottle?

CHORUS 2. Those are human smells. He doesn't recognize them, yet.

NK. You smell like—

WOMAN. …color of dawn, the sun rising over
the gleaming walls of the city—

NK. No…

WOMAN. …dust rising up from the street, where the people are dancing—

NK. *(Not knowing the words:)* 'Walls'? And—'streets'?

WOMAN. —and temples, where the priestesses are
waiting, jeweled, perfumed, wet—

NK. NO! You smell like—

WOMAN. —what you've always wanted.
Tell me what that is.

(They begin to touch each other, explore—finally ending up on the ground, entangled.)

CHORUS. For seven days and nights, he was hard—
she rode him like an animal.
For seven days and nights, he fucked her,
screams, laughter, panting, stench—…
Finally, after seven days and nights,
they came up for air.

WOMAN. Why are you crying?

NK. I'm not.

(Pause.)

I'm stronger than the other animals.
How were you able to pin me?

(The WOMAN lights an after-sex cigarette.)

(The Other Animals have crept back on, to watch.)

WOMAN. Because—the more we fought, the more you needed me.
So I got stronger.
That's why you can't allow my sex to go to war.

NK. Why?

WOMAN. If a woman is killed, the men around her will
stop—to grieve over the body.
They forget where they are—and then
they remember too late.

NK. If you fell, the herd would leave you behind.
I wouldn't even remember your face.
I'm an animal—I'm not a man.

WOMAN. You are now.
Ask the wildebeest.

(In disbelief, NK approaches the animals.)

(They sniff him, in alarm—and then bolt.)

(He chases them, but they vanish.)

(He stands at the edge of the clearing, shouts to the animals:)

NK. Come back!

(He understands, now. To the WOMAN:)

What have you done to me?

(She asks her riddle again.)

WOMAN. Something you dreamed about—
even when you ran on all fours, like an animal—
something you've always wanted…
Tell me what it is.

(NK looks out again, at his vanished animal comrades.)

NK. COME BACK!

(To the WOMAN:)

Why did you do this?

(It sinks in.)

I am completely alone.

WOMAN. You were always alone. But you didn't know.
Now you can be with the rest of us.
Remembering a face you saw, one night,
at a lighted window.
Or the touch of a hand on your back, how good it felt,
that single moment—
and then never to see that face again,
or feel those fingers tracing your spine,
how it all goes away—and you go, too.
Now you can be with the rest of us.
What have you always wanted?

(NK discovers the truth, as he speaks it.)

NK. A friend.

(With new consciousness comes suspicion.)

Why did you come to this place?
Did someone send you?

(Far off, the terrible roar of HUMBABA. Frightened by the monster's cry, the WOMAN tries to move off, but NK grabs her.)

Tell me who sent you!

WOMAN. You can find him in the City.

(5)

In Gil's bedroom.

CHORUS 1. That night the King had a dream…

(GIL finds himself at the edge of the desert, looking out. Behind him, the gentle surf of angry voices.)

CHORUS 1. *(Softly:)* May his ass erupt in boils.
May his children marry badly.
May his prostate grow to the size of a basket—

GIL. SILENCE!

CHORUS. He was standing at the edge of the city,
looking for something he had lost…

(GIL looks around, on edge.)

(Suddenly an enormous boulder falls from the sky, hitting the ground beside him.)

(GIL is astonished but doesn't flinch.)

(He holds his hand to the boulder—but he can't touch it yet.)

He wonders what it is, but there are some things
he can't consider yet:
that it could be a bomb, of course—
or a SCUD, or the random RPG—
or, in happier modern times,
a block of frozen piss and shit from an
airplane lavatory—

CHORUS 1. Why does he not consider these things?

CHORUS 2. Because they are falling long after he is dust.
And his dust is falling…

GIL. It's a rock.
Why is it beautiful?
Why do I want it to spread its legs—like a woman—
and open itself to me?
It doesn't have legs.
Or a mouth I could fill with my tongue.
Or a smell like rain on clay—
It's a rock.
Why do I want to kiss the feet it doesn't have?

>*(Unable to help himself, he tries to pick up the rock.)*
>
>*(It doesn't budge.)*

Wait—…

>*(He tries another tack. No go.)*
>
>*(He squats, tries a dead-man lift—till his eyes bulge and his face is red.)*
>
>*(GIL'S MOTHER approaches.)*

MOTHER. This dream is a good one.

GIL. *(Frustrated:)* Nothing is good.

MOTHER. Your heart is restless—but here is a sign:
this falling star that you love, like a woman—

GIL. Mother, your eyes are clouding.
It's a rock. Too heavy for me to lift.

MOTHER. It's your comrade.
The one you've been waiting for.
Stronger than the animals.
Braver than any man you know.
Only a woman defending her child is braver.

GIL. *I* am braver.

MOTHER. More beautiful than the shadows of clouds
racing across a field.

GIL. My shining *makes* the shadows!
And I've been waiting for *no one!*

MOTHER. You didn't know you were waiting.

> *(In a rage, GIL suddenly lifts the rock he couldn't move before.)*
> *(With a mighty effort, he heaves it offstage.)*
> *(Pause.)*
> *(The rock comes crashing down to earth, from straight above, next to GIL.)*
> *(GIL'S MOTHER smiles.)*

(6)

> NK *at the watering-hole—now wearing clothes.*
> *He gets down on all fours, starts to drink, then catches himself.*
> *He gets back on his feet, cups his hands, dips them into the water.*
> *He tries to drink from his "cup," chokes and sputters.*
> *A* LION *appears, on the other side of the water, staring at him.*
> NK *takes a step, the* LION *moves back.*
> NK *steps back, the* LION *steps forward, stops.*
> *They regard each other—former comrades, strangers now.*

NK. If you come again, I'll kill you.
You mangle other animals we want to eat ourselves.

> *(The* LION *doesn't move.)*
> *(Suddenly* NK *lets out an agonized roar.)*
> *(The* LION *doesn't flinch.)*

That wasn't—how you say 'Go now'?
Am I forgetting the words you taught me?…

> *(He shouts—to the universe, and the king he's never met:)*

Why have you done this to me?

> *(The* LION *starts at the sound of his anguish, then races off.)*
> *(*NK *watches it go.)*

(7)

CHORUS. The Wild Man comes to the City.

> *(*NK *approaches a sorrowful woman.)*

NK. Why are you grieving, woman?

WOMAN. Today is my daughter's wedding day.

> *(Pause.)*

NK. I am new to the ways of the City.

So—your words are strange.

WOMAN. The king is strange.

On the wedding night, he takes the woman first.

His right, he claims.

Only then does he give her, shaken and bleeding, to her husband.

(Two men are passing by, on the street.)

NK. *(Outraged:)* And the people allow this?

(To the men:)

You there!—Are you men, or balls of dung?

MAN 2. *(Whispered, to* MAN 1*:)* Look at his muscles, before you open your mouth.

MAN 1. *(Nodding agreement:)* Balls of dung, my lord.

NK. I'm not your "lord"!

MAN 1. But—aren't you the king?

(Appealing to the others:)

He could be his twin!

As strong, as brave, as beautiful—

MAN 2. A little shorter, maybe.

And doesn't the king have a mole—

NK. I am NOT the King!

I am barely even a man.

MAN 1. *(His point proved:)* Like the king. He's mainly a god.

MAN 2. On his mother's side.

NK. And he's a rapist.

WOMAN. Like the gods.

He wills it and it happens.

Triumph over our enemies.

The mighty walls of our city—look—

like beaten copper burning in the sun—

they will glow forever.

The men of the city, aching to die for their beloved commander.

The women of this city:

happy sacrifice to our good fortune.

MAN. He comes!

(The two men—in their terror of the royal presence—piss themselves.)

(With the WOMAN, *they back off and away.* NK *calls after them:)*

NK. You give him strength, with your weakness!

And your cowardice makes him brave.

And probably he's ugly as the wrinkled ass of a mule—

(GIL sweeps in—astonished to find a man in his way.)

GIL. Behind that door is my bride.

NK. *Your* bride?

GIL. For the night. Get out of my way.

> *(NK doesn't move. They stare-down. GIL realizes:)*

Oh. I had a dream about you.

NK. Did I kill you, in the dream?

> *(Pause.)*
>
> *(Suddenly they fall into a hair-raising bout of wrestling.)*
>
> *(NK finally takes down GIL, who struggles under the former Wild Man.)*

I had a dream about you:
that you sent a temple whore to corrupt me.

GIL. Did she succeed?

NK. She made me human: yes.

> *(GIL flips NK—they both spring to their feet and lock arms—head to head.)*

GIL. You were a star that fell from the sky.
In the dream, I couldn't lift you up—

> *(GIL moves fast, pinning NK in his arms, lifting him off the ground.)*
>
> *(NK struggles in vain.)*

But now I'm awake, and I can break your back
like a hollow reed...

NK. *(Gasping:)* They told me / you were a shepherd to / your people.

GIL. I am!

NK. How can you / tell / when a human is / lying?

GIL. How?

NK. His lips are / moving.

> *(With a roar, NK breaks away from GIL. They circle each other.)*

You lead your men to their doom, in constant war
and dishonor the women. A shepherd??
Why would a shepherd fall upon his own flock?

> *(GIL engages again, in a fury—they wrestle again, break apart.)*

GIL. You were raised by animals?

NK. Yes.

GIL. You speak their tongue?

NK. I did—once.

GIL. They answer me this:
why does a dog lick his balls?

NK. Because he can.

GIL. Are you mocking me?

NK. You would lick your own, if you could.

I would—I've tried.

I can't get my leg that high.

Or my head that low.

Perhaps a "god" would find it easier.

> *(They clash again—a final time.)*
>
> *(Two Soldiers on guard duty wander onto the wall above the fighting. Looking down, they're startled to see the king struggling.)*

SOLDIER 1. Assassin! Help! Murder!

SOLDIER 2. My lord!

GIL. *(As he struggles:)* You come too late. Go back to your watch.

SOLDIER 2. But my lord—

GIL. *Now!*

> *(The Soldiers, disobeying, watch the end of the fight.)*

CHORUS.

As they fight, they cannot help but feel the other's sweat-slick body.

And they have thoughts, without words:

the words come later—thousands of years…

NK. Nice definition, man.

GIL. Thanks.

NK. Biceps?

GIL. Twenty-eight. You?

NK. Twenty-seven.

Forty-eight chest.

GIL. Forty-eight and a half.

NK. Waist?

GIL. Thirty-two.

NK. *("I win":)* Thirty-one.

GIL. *("No":)* Like a girl.

> *(Finally, GIL pins NK to the ground, hard—then suddenly stops, his anger spent.)*
>
> *(Drained, NK doesn't try to move.)*
>
> *(With the show below them over, the Soldiers return to their thoughts.)*

SOLDIER 1. My money was on the Wild Man.

But he's as bad as me. And I'm the world's worst.

SOLDIER 2. No shit.

> *(As the SOLDIERS talk, GIL sits back, studies his fallen opponent's face.)*
>
> *(With his hand, he touches NK's lips—then touches his own, comparing.)*

(He does the same to NK's *eyebrows, nose, forehead.)*

SOLDIER 1. I got my whole squad killed.

SOLDIER 2. It was a training session! Forget it.

SOLDIER 1. But like, when I sent you into that building first?
And rat-a-tat-tat, you're dead.

SOLDIER 2. For awhile.

SOLDIER 1. So then, next time *I'm* going in first,
because I got you killed—even though I'm an officer,
I'm *never* supposed to go in first. And so what do I do?
I take one in the leg. Paint ball. Friggin' sucker
hurts! So I gotta go down, and I'm like
UGH. I can't move because my leg is "shot," so I'm
watching my men just falling, and I look out the window to the
other building and there you are, you're dead and you
just wave at me.

(Pause.)

SOLDIER 2. It was practice.

SOLDIER 1. I know, but—you coulda been dead.

SOLDIER 2. So I got to practice being dead. Shut up.

(Finally GIL *gets up, moves away from* NK, *troubled.)*

*(*NK *gets to his feet.)*

NK. You bested me.

GIL. Not easily.

(Pause.)

NK. There is not another like you in the world.

GIL. Only you.

(They embrace—two lost comrades who have finally found each other.)

The more we fought—the more I needed to fight you.

NK. Because I was stronger than you?

GIL. No.

NK. Braver?

GIL. No.

NK. More beautiful?

(Pause.)

(Suddenly, the two are back to wrestling again—fierce but playful, like lion cubs.)

SOLDIER 2. Maybe that's all life is.

SOLDIER 1. Huh?

SOLDIER 2. Practice.

(Pause.)

SOLDIER 1. For what?

(Far off, the ominous roar of HUMBABA.)

(8)

By the river. NK *and* GIL *look out.*

CHORUS. The king learned much from his friend—
that his power was a gift,
and against the nature of things, to abuse it.
The people were glad.
There was peace, for a time...
But the heart of the king was not easy.

GIL. What do you see out there—that bend in the river...?

NK. Crocodiles? Too dark to tell.
I only see shapes in the water.

GIL. Why would there be so many?

(Pause.)

NK. Feeding time.
You're troubled.

GIL. A toothache. Nothing more.

NK. A gift of the gods.

GIL. What are you talking about?

(NK tries to cheer his friend.)

NK. When the gods created the world,
the lowly worm came to them, with an angry demand:
"What am I to eat?"
They offered him apricots, figs—
he only snickered: "Can I live on *fruit?*
Open this creature 'Man' to me—
and there I will happily dwell—in his mouth!
My wine will be the blood of his gums—
and the roots of his teeth will be dinner!"

GIL. *(Touching his mouth:)* And this pain is a gift of the gods?

NK. Not a gift to *you*—to the worm.

(Put in his place, GIL *laughs.)*

NK. I see you pacing the walls of the city, late and alone,
restless...
I don't think an aching tooth is keeping you up.

(GIL looks back to the river.)

GIL. They aren't crocodiles.

NK. What are they?

GIL. Bodies. Floating down from upriver.
All my life I've seen them go by.
Two or three a week—bloated—
sometimes more, in a single day…

NK. I don't understand—

GIL. We've accepted it.
We don't even see them, anymore.

NK. Where do they come from?

GIL. I've asked them, as they bobble past—
they hold their tongues, but I know—I've always known:
from the heart of the Great Cedar Forest.

NK. *(Uneasily:)* Then it's the work of the gods.
The forest is sacred. No one goes there.

GIL. Have you? When you were wild?

NK. *(Too quickly:)* No.

GIL. How do you know when a mortal is lying?
When you love him.

> *(Pause.)*

Tell me what you saw.

> *(NK is reluctant.)*

I am nothing, if I *do* nothing.
If I accept the world, without changing it.

NK. Is ruling wisely so little?

GIL. There is Evil, in my land—
it has a form, a name—and victims:
bodies floating down river, all my life.
I can put an end to that.

NK. Though even the gods have allowed it?

GIL. *Yes.*
And the cedar trees the giant is guarding?
We can finally take them. Strip the hillside.
Build more temples. Even greater walls around the city.
Monuments: "He freed his people from the dread Humbaba."

NK. I freed the city from *you.* Where is *my* name, in letters
tall as myself, on a great stone tablet?

> *(GIL is relentless.)*

GIL. What did you see, in the Forest?

> *(Pause.)*

NK. I was searching for food, it was late in the winter—
I saw the light of a clearing, through the cedars—
I knew I had come too far.
I turned to go back—but I heard a scream:
not the cry of an animal…
So I made my way to the edge of the clearing.
Then I saw Humbaba.
He held a human child in his arms,
and he was crooning a lullaby:
"Your mother is dead, your father is dead,
your brother is dead, your sister is dead.
The world is dead. The gods are gone.
And you are all alone, alone.
You are all alone."

     (Pause.)

While he was singing, it seemed to be true.
The child stopped struggling.
Humbaba lay the body on the ground.
And then he looked up at me—

GIL. He knew you were there?

NK. He'd always known. He smiled at me.
I ran.

     (Pause.)

I was afraid.

GIL. Don't tell me that.
I hate you, when you tell me that.
Guards!

     (Two SOLDIERS *appear. He points out:)*

There—at the river bend—wade into the water.
Drag a body out.

SOLDIER 2. A body, my lord?

     (To his comrade:)

Do you see any bodies? Maybe logs.

SOLDIER 1. Or crocodiles?

GIL. Then bring me a crocodile.
Whatever you find there, bobbing in the shallows.

     (The Soldiers exit, grumbling. NK *takes up Gil's challenge.)*

NK. I've killed a catamount, on a cold night, to shelter in his carcass.
I've slept in the sticky warm of a life I took.
You don't have to show me the dead.

GIL. And still—you fled like a coward—
that day in the Cedar Forest?

(*NK starts to exit.*)

Where are you going, Coward?

NK. Are you that terrified?

GIL. Of what?

NK. Of being forgotten.

(*GIL is furious at this challenge.*)

I want to see what's washing up on your shore.

(9)

Near the shore.

The two SOLDIERS *enter, grumbling.*

SOLDIER 1. "Bring me a crocodile." Hey, no problem…

SOLDIER 2. "Bring me my head, which I musta lost,
somewhere up my bung-hole."
Like we don't have anything better to do.?
You know why they don't send women on a detail like this?
'Cause they fuckin' *suck.*

SOLDIER 1. Davidson is good. "The Gazelle"?

SOLDIER 2. She's an anomaly.

SOLDIER 1. She's tough and she can keep up.

SOLDIER 2. She's got a moustache.

SOLDIER 1. Nah, she's pretty.

SOLDIER 2. You don't have to carry her fuckin' pack, at least.

SOLDIER 1. And she's cute.

SOLDIER 2. If she took care of that 'stache.

(*SOLDIER 2 suddenly stops.*)

Fuck.

(*SOLDIER 1 looks out.*)

SOLDIER 1. Ok—they aren't crocodiles.

(*NK enters.*)

NK. What have you found?

SOLDIER 1. We can't tell, my lord.

NK. I'm not your lord!

SOLDIER 2. (*Whispering:*) Check for the mole!

(*Ignoring them,* NK *wades into the water, and then offstage.*)

(*GIL enters.*)

GIL. Have you seen my friend?

> *(They point out.* GIL *shouts to* NK:*)*

Get out of the water!

SOLDIER 1. He's safe, my lord.

SOLDIER 2. They aren't crocodiles.

GIL. And why are you not helping him?

(Distracted:) Get out of the water, fool!

The current is strong!

(To himself:) If you were to stumble…

SOLDIER 2. *(Whispered, to his comrade:)* But he's got no problem sending *us* in.

GIL. *(To himself:)* If you were swept away…

> *(He's about to wade in, when* NK *emerges from the water, carrying the body of a* WOMAN.*)*
>
> *(He lays her down on the ground.)*
>
> *(The four men stare at her.)*

SOLDIER 1. *(Whispered:)* I wonder who she was.

SOLDIER 2. *(Whispered:)* Well—whatever she was, before, she's gonna be *that,* for a whole lot longer.

> *(The* DEAD WOMAN *speaks, disturbing the men.)*

DEAD WOMAN. I should never have taken that path.

But my lover was panting for me.

And the sun was still high.

Around a curve in the path, Humbaba was waiting.

He smiled at me.

He knew that I was with child.

And he told me the baby was already dead in me.

> *(Pause.)*
>
> *(*GIL *and* NK *reach a silent understanding.)*

GIL. *(To* NK:*)* I will go before you, down the path.

Leading the way.

You have nothing to fear.

NK. And if you fall—

GIL. Then the world will always remember:

that I was King, and I died in battle,

fighting a terrible monster even the gods refused to humble.

NK. You leave the harder part to me—

bringing the news to your mother.

> *(Pause.)*

GIL. If she gives her blessing, my friend,
will you give over your objections?

(With that question in the air, GIL *and* NK *exit, leaving the* SOLDIERS *with the* DEAD WOMAN.*)*

*(*SOLDIER 1 *points out the abandoned body, calling after them:)*

SOLDIER 1. Did you forget something?

SOLDIER 2. Homos.

SOLDIER 1. The Great Cedar Forest.

SOLDIER 2. Fuck.

(They turn back to the DEAD WOMAN, *afraid.)*

SOLDIER 1. Maybe she was beautiful.

SOLDIER 2. Maybe you wanted to do her.

SOLDIER 1. Maybe she was your mother.

SOLDIER 2. Maybe we're going to die.

SOLDIER 1. Shut up.

DEAD WOMAN. Maybe you ran through the cedars,
and he was behind you, and he was
in front of you, and you kept running,
but he was beside you,
and you fell, and he was on top of you.

SOLDIER 2. Shut *up!*

WOMAN. And he was inside you.

*(*SOLDIER 2 *lashes out, kicking the* WOMAN.*)*

(She lies still.)

SOLDIER 1. *(Shocked:)* What are you doing?

SOLDIER 2. *(Ignoring:)* You wanta get wasted?

(His friend doesn't answer.)

Like *that's* what this country needs: more fuckin' *lumber.*

*(*SOLDIER 2 *storms off.)*

(Alone with the dead, and haunted by it, SOLDIER 1 *does his best to arrange the* WOMAN's *body, with a kind of minimum dignity. Then, heart-sick, he exits.)*

(The WOMAN's *body lies there.)*

CHORUS. That night more bodies came drifting down the river.
Floating past our city, for so many years.
We had accepted them.

(10)

In the Queen's chambers.

GIL *and* NK *are waiting for the* QUEEN *to give her blessing.*

QUEEN. *(Trying out a suggestion* GIL *made:)* Stay behind and wait for you...
I'd rather be flayed alive.
And I would be—by my fear.

> *(Pause.)*

I am nothing, sitting here, doing nothing.

GIL. You gave me life.

QUEEN. Oh. And now I can rest? My work is done?
And if you take my work and you scatter it,
splinter of your bone, gobbet of meat,
on a dark path in a cedar forest?
You aren't a god—

GIL. I know that.

QUEEN. —only part of one—on my family's side.

GIL. *(To* NK:*)* Do you have a mother?

NK. A lioness—but she died.

GIL. Lucky man.

QUEEN. *(To* NK, *bluntly setting things straight:)* Your mother was Aruru, the
goddess of creation.

NK. *(Astonished:)* What?

QUEEN. She made you from a lump of wet clay—
because the people had prayed to her
to deliver them from my son.

GIL. *(Even more astonished:)* What??

QUEEN. My son—who was behaving with the arrogance of a god.

> *(The men are startled—but not completely surprised.)*

GIL. If this is true—

QUEEN. The gods were hoping you would balance each other.
But if *both* of you are fools—

GIL. Why are you angry at me?

QUEEN. *(To* NK:*)* Tell him.

NK. Why do you think I know?

QUEEN. You know.

NK. *(Reluctantly, to* GIL:*)* She's angry, because—
she cannot save you from your fate.

QUEEN. *(To NK:)* And you've forgotten what the animals know:
that no one escapes.
Didn't your mother teach you that?

NK. I learned that from the rabbit—
the one who was dangling, limp, in her mouth.

> *(Pause.)*

QUEEN. *(A final plea to GIL:)* Let Humbaba guard the sacred wood, as he
has forever.

GIL. *(A question:)* Ignore the bodies floating by.

QUEEN. That river flows through all the world, before it makes a loop
into the dark of the sacred trees.

> *(To NK:)*

You've been to the Cedar Forest?

NK. Yes.

QUEEN. And still you want to return?

NK. No.

QUEEN. Why?

NK. Because I'm afraid.

> *(The QUEEN takes this in.)*

QUEEN. My son is not.

NK. He hasn't seen the terrible Guardian of the Wood.
I have.

GIL. *(Sharing his fear:)* Last night I dreamed that I was old—
dozing by the fire. *(To his mother:)* You were dead—

> *(To NK:)*

I don't know where *you* were—
but the room was cold, the wind was howling...
Out a window, I saw the desert moving in, unstoppable—
swirling into the city, swallowing everything in sand...
Long ago, I'd had the chance to *act*—but I had done nothing,
and this was my legacy: a city disappearing.
My name forgotten forever.
How could you believe you were the only one who was afraid?

> *(NK has no answer.)*

I'll lead the way, and keep you safe—

QUEEN. *(Interrupting:)* No—your friend should lead—
he can find the path he took before...

(To NK*:)*

You didn't come out of my body—
but I adopt you, now, as one of my own.
Watch over your brother.

NK. I will.

QUEEN. And bring him safely home, if you can.

(The QUEEN, *unhappy, hurries off, leaving the men alone.)*

NK. Maybe we *are* brothers.
You were raised by a lion as well.

(NK has tried to lighten the moment. GIL *responds with a lion's roar.)*

(NK roars, in reply.)

(They try to best each other with their growls, until they're exhausted.)

(Then, in the quiet, they hear the distant rumble of HUMBABA*.)*

(11)

Two SOLDIERS, *keeping watch on the wall.*

SOLDIER 1 *follows things that float by in the river.*

SOLDIER 1. *(Pointing out:)* Crocodile…crocodile…dead body…croc—

SOLDIER 2. Shut it.

(Pause.)

SOLDIER 1. Will they call us up?

SOLDIER 2. Nah—they'll be going in alone.

SOLDIER 1. Fuck you.

(Pause.)

Dead body…dead body…crocodile…dead body…

(SOLDIER 2 won't rise to the bait.)

I'm hungry.

SOLDIER 2. No you're not. You're afraid.

SOLDIER 1. But it *manifests,* in—I'm hungry.

SOLDIER 2. You got a tapeworm, soldier.

SOLDIER 1. I have a high metabolism.

SOLDIER 2. You know how to deal with a tapeworm?

SOLDIER 1. No. And I'd like to remain in ignorance.

SOLDIER 2. You shove a donut up your ass,
every day for a week. And then,
on the eighth day, you don't.
The tapeworm finally sticks his head out:
"Hey—where's my donut?"
And you hit him with a hammer.

(SOLDIER 1 starts to laugh.)

(Just then, we hear HUMBABA's *roar again, in the distance.)*

SOLDIER 1. What do you think it'll be like?

SOLDIER 2. You know as much as I do.
I mean, there are movies you can watch—
bombs, and people running and screaming and yelling,
but you don't know.
But the bullet gives you instant feedback.
That's when you'll know.

(SOLDIER 1 isn't comforted.)

SOLDIER 1. His breath is like a flame-thrower.
Like somebody pressing your face down
onto a red-hot stove.

SOLDIER 2. You handled worse than that in Basic.

SOLDIER 1. I don't think so.

(SOLDIER 2 takes out a lighter, lights it.)

SOLDIER 2. Hold out your hand.

SOLDIER 1. I don't think so.

(But SOLDIER 2 *waits—and* SOLDIER 1 *reluctantly holds out his hand, above the flame.)*

SOLDIER 2. Closer.

(SOLDIER 1 moves his hand closer to the flame. He's visibly in pain.)

You can cry.
A man can cry.
But just don't break.

(SOLDIER 1, challenged, moves his hand closer. SOLDIER 2 *watches him like a hawk, as he takes the pain.)*

(12)

In the wild.

GIL *and* NK *lead the way, with the two* SOLDIERS *lagging behind.*

CHORUS. The first day they traveled far—
across seven mountains, deep into the wilderness—
and still the Cedar Forest was only a shadow on the horizon...

(NK signals a halt, sits down. GIL settles down beside him.)

NK. That twig you stepped on—did you hear it crack?

GIL. No.

NK. Humbaba did. And he's a thousand miles away.

(The SOLDIERS look around, nervous.)

(GIL and NK *stretch out. In a moment, they're asleep. The* SOLDIERS *move aside, to grumble.)*

SOLDIER 2. We could run for it.

SOLDIER 1. Where? *(Pointing:)* Go that way, we're deserters.

SOLDIER 2. *(Pointing in opposite direction:)* And that way, we get to be dinner.

SOLDIER 1. Take your pick.

SOLDIER 2. Fuck them.

(Pause.)

I don't even think they know we're here, anymore.
We could just take a hike. Like Barton.

SOLDIER 1. *(Trying to remember the name:)* Barton...

SOLDIER 2. Guy flipped out, in training?
Puts trash bags in his clothes and fills em with air and
starts to dog-paddle, across the wide Potomac...

SOLDIER 1. *That* guy. Yeah...

SOLDIER 2. What an idiot.
He coulda just called a fucking cab, or said,
"I don't wanta do this."

(Nearer than before, the offstage cry of HUMBABA.*)*

SOLDIER 1. I don't want to do this.

SOLDIER 2. Walk away.

SOLDIER 1. I would, but—can I live with that?

SOLDIER 2. Key word in that sentence is 'live.'

SOLDIER 1. Huh?

SOLDIER 2. You'd be alive. Could you live with *that?*

(Suddenly GIL *wakes from a dream, with a shout.)*

GIL. *(Anxious, to* NK:*)* Did you call me? Why am I awake?
Something touched me, in the dark—was it you?

NK. You had a dream.

GIL. Did I?

(Remembering:)

We were climbing through a narrow pass, in the mountains...
like we're doing now—
when the sky grew dark, the earth trembled—
and the mountaintops all shattered,
roaring down on us.
We were buried alive.

*(NK *tries to be hopeful.)*

NK. This is a good dream.

GIL. How is it good?

NK. The mountain is Humbaba.
He trembles before you, and you bring him low.

SOLDIER 2. *(Whispering to* SOLDIER 1:*)* —'course, you're also *buried alive!*

NK. *(To* GIL:*)* Go back to sleep.

SOLDIER 2. Fuck.

> *(*GIL *settles back down.* NK *lies beside him, holding his hand.)*
>
> *(In a moment, both are snoring.)*

SOLDIER 1. How do they do that?
Put your head down—boom: you're out.
I toss and turn—

SOLDIER 2. Guilty conscience.

SOLDIER 1. Shut up.

SOLDIER 2. I don't have a conscience.
Helps.

> *(Pause.)*

SOLDIER 1. I'm not guilty—

SOLDIER 2. Fine.

SOLDIER 1. —about anything.

SOLDIER 2. *Fine.*

SOLDIER 1. But…what would that feel like?
Buried alive in a rockslide?

SOLDIER 2. Want me to show you?

> *(The two* SOLDIERS *move away from the sleeping heroes.)*

OK. A rock would hit you—

> *(He hits his comrade, hard.* SOLDIER 1 *stands his ground.)*

Then another—

> *(Hits him.)*

—another…

> *(*SOLDIER 2 *starts to pummel* SOLDIER 1, *who staggers under the blows.)*

Trick would be not to fall.

> *(Hitting harder than ever:)*

If you go down, you're dead.

SOLDIER 1. *(Getting punch-drunk:)* The sky—

SOLDIER 2. What about it?

SOLDIER 1. Growing dark.

SOLDIER 2. It's night.

SOLDIER 1. The earth is trembling—…

SOLDIER 2. That's you.

> *(Keeps hitting:)*

You OK?

> *(Keeps hitting:)*

You're doin' good.

> *(He keeps battering his friend.)*

Don't break. I'm gonna make a man out of you—

SOLDIER 1. It's a dirty job—

SOLDIER 2. —if it kills me.

(13)

CHORUS. Finally they came to the Gate that leads to the Cedar Forest.

> *(The four men stare up at the awesome gate.)*

SOLDIER 1. That's a *gate?*

SOLDIER 2. It's a mountain.

SOLDIER 1. It's a gate the size of a mountain.

GIL. Like the mountain that fell on me, in my dream.
Seventy cubits high, at least—twenty-four in width…

SOLDIER 1. How can it swing open?

SOLDIER 2. How can a mountain move?

NK. *(Deeply uneasy:)* Something about this gate is—wrong.

SOLDIER 2. *(To* SOLDIER 1*:)* Where does a giant shit?

> *(*SOLDIER 1 *says nothing.)*

Wherever it wants.

> *(Thinking* SOLDIER 1 *doesn't understand:)*

Because it's a giant…

> *(Silence.)*

You son-of-a-bitch. You're running away.
In your head.
You're fucking *leavin'* me

> *(He hits* SOLDIER 1 *hard.)*

Don't leave me!

> *(He hits* SOLDIER 1 *again. Near the breaking point,* SOLDIER 1 *hits back.)*
>
> *(For a moment, both are in shock.)*
>
> *(They fall on each other like animals, fighting to the death.)*
>
> *(Startled,* GIL *and* NK *wade in and pull the men apart.)*

GIL. What are you doing??

SOLDIER 1. Nothing.

NK. They're afraid.

SOLDIER 2. No sir!

NK. Two trembling girls.

GIL. *I* was shivering, in fear—last night, in my dream.

> *(To the* SOLDIERS*:)*

Do you want to go home?

SOLDIER 2.	**SOLDIER 1**
Yes sir!	No sir!

GIL. Sit by a fire, dozing with the women, the rest of your days…

SOLDIER 1. *Yes!*

SOLDIER 2. *(Less certain:)* No…

GIL. Then— *(To* SOLDIER 2*:)* —you go.

> *(To* SOLDIER 1*:)*

And you can stay.

SOLDIER 2. Inflate my trash-bag water-wings—
across the wide Euphrates—
dog-paddle the fuck away…

> *(To the heroes, of his friend:)*

I can't leave this pussy behind.

NK. Because you love him?

> *(The* SOLDIER *can't answer.)*

You don't.
When the danger is past, and you're far from here,
you'll never see him again.

> *(Closer than ever comes the roar of* HUMBABA.*)*

You won't remember why he even mattered.

SOLDIER 1. With all respect—fuck you, sir.
I'd die for him.

NK. In the heat of battle.
That isn't love. It's clinging to your mother's teat.

GIL. *(To* NK*:)* Why do you shame this man?

> *(To the* SOLDIERS*:)*

I was wrong to bring you.
Go back to your wives and children.

> *(The* SOLDIERS *hesitate—unable to meet each other's eye.)*
>
> *(The roar of* HUMBABA, *closer.)*

Go.

(A moment—then both of the SOLDIERS *run.)*

*(*GIL *and* NK *watch them go.)*

You were cruel.

NK. I wanted to spare their lives.

GIL. My dream foretold a victory, you said.

NK. For *you*—alone…

GIL. But I'm not alone. You're a part of me.

*(*NK *turns away.)*

You know you are:
blood, bone, sweat, smile,
muscle, cock, shining eye…

NK. An arm can be lopped off—
an eye can stare at nothing, forever…

(Pause.)

Something about the Gate is—wrong.

GIL. *(Looking up at it:)* It's too big.

NK. I knew it had to be big.
I've seen Humbaba, remember.

GIL. Take an axe and break it down.

NK. Why do I want it to open itself to me?
Because it's beautiful. Gleaming hinges—
polished wood…

GIL. Beautiful things are easily broken—

(More firmly:)

Shatter it with your axe.

NK. *No.*
I don't think it's locked.
Maybe that's what's wrong with the Gate.

(Warily, he approaches the towering Gate—gives it a push.)

(The Gate swings open, with a groan of mighty hinges.)

*(*NK *stares at his hand that touched the Gate.)*

Don't come any closer.

GIL. Why?

(Pause.)

NK. When I touched the Gate—and it started to move—
the strength drained out of my hand…
through the opening, I thought I saw—you…
standing at the edge of the forest,

hovering over—something…
the body of an animal, or—…

GIL. It was a waking dream. I haven't moved:
I'm right behind you.

NK. You looked up at me—through the open gate:
like you'd always known I was coming.
You smiled at me. There was blood…—
I wanted to run.

> *(Pause.)*

I'm afraid.

GIL. Don't tell me that.
I hate you, when you tell me that.

> *(Pause.)*

This Evil in my land is real—
it has a form, and a name—

NK. *What* name?
You've never seen the Guardian of the Wood.

GIL. My mother said:
our life is a breath: in—out—gone.

> *(Pause.)*
>
> *(*GIL *goes up to the partly-open gate.)*
>
> *(He pushes it open more, with a groan of hinges.)*
>
> *(He walks through the opening.)*

I'm through. And nothing happened.

> *(Pause.)*

Now I *am* looking up, and smiling at you.
Forget death.

NK. Tell me how.

GIL. Love something more.

NK. I do.

> *(He follows* GIL *through the Gate, to the edge of the Forest. Suddenly, he stops.)*

That twig I stepped on—did you hear it crack?

GIL. Yes.

> *(Holding their breath, they wait—but the giant doesn't appear.)*

NK. Humbaba must be sleeping.

GIL. Then we should wake him up.

> *(Pointing skyward:)*

Which is the tallest cedar?

NK. That one, rising up into the clouds…

GIL. Let it be the first.

> *(He raises an axe, ready to chop down the tree.)*

(14)

> *In the wild.*
>
> *The two* SOLDIERS *run on, exhausted—and stop to catch their breath.*
>
> *They can't look at each other.*
>
> *From off, there's a very loud chock, of an axe digging into wood.*

SOLDIER 1. What the hell was that?

SOLDIER 2. They're chopping down the cedars.

> *(Pause.)*

What our country needs right now:

more fucking lumber.

That we stole from the *gods*.

Like—they're not gonna miss it—right?

Fuckin' HOMOS!

> *(The sound of chopping echoes.)*

SOLDIER 1. Are we lost?

SOLDIER 2. No.

SOLDIER 1. Then where is the path?

SOLDIER 2. Shut up.

> *(More chopping.)*

Shut up!

> *(Pause.)*

SOLDIER 1. What do you think that feels like—

being chopped down?

SOLDIER 2. You want me to show you?

SOLDIER 1. *No.*

> *(He starts to exit.)*

SOLDIER 2. Or do you wanta keep running?

> *(*SOLDIER 2 *picks up a dead tree limb, hefting it like an axe.* SOLDIER
> 1 *stares at him, mesmerized.)*

(15)

Humbaba's lair.

HUMBABA *is asleep.*

CHORUS. Deep in the forest, Humbaba is dreaming:
no one hears him cry out.

> *(Very loud, the thock of an axe.* HUMBABA *sits up, wide awake.)*

HUMBABA. Something touched me in the dark—
who's there?

> *(He hears the drawn-out crash of a tree as it falls—and can't believe what he's hearing.)*

> *(*HUMBABA 2 *joins him, to make a larger creature.)*

HUMBABAS 1 and 2. No—I must be dreaming...

> *(Another thunderous crash.)*

> *(Then another. A third* HUMBABA *makes the creature complete.)*

3 HUMBABAS. Would any man defy the gods like this?

> *(CRASH.)*

> *(Pause.)*

> *(CRASH.)*

But I hear it. I can *hear* it...
Trees falling / and I stand here, not believing...
The gods said, Guard the wood.
But I was sleeping.
What have I done?

> *(He croons to himself, in his misery, as he moves off to slay the barbarians.)*

"Your mother is dead, your father is dead,
the trees are dead, the world is dead—"

(16)

Near the Gate.

GIL, *exhausted, drops his axe.* NK *watches him, on edge.*

GIL. Why doesn't he come?

> *(Shouts:)*

WHERE ARE YOU?

NK. Maybe there is no Humbaba. [giant]
Maybe you made him up.

> *(Quoting* GIL:*)*

"Best to honor the sacrifice of our fallen troops—"

> *(Pause.)*

> *(*GIL *lashes out, hitting* NK *so hard that he falls to the ground.)*

(NK doesn't get up.)

Your name in letters as tall as a man:
"He killed the giant…delivered his people…
brought the wealth of the sacred Forest
into the City…"

GIL. Get up.

(NK doesn't move.)

Get *up!*

(Pause.)

NK. I think I hear him coming.

(Both men are silent, listening:)

3 HUMBABAS. *(Off:)* "…and you are all alone, alone.
You are all alone."

(Shaking, NK gets to his feet, as the 3 HUMBABAS enter.)

(The giant contemplates the two frightened men.)

My turds are bigger than you are!

GIL. I had a dream that a mountain was falling on top of us.
Was that you?

3 HUMBABAS. Why have you desecrated this place?

GIL. *(Unnerved:)* There are bodies—in the water…

3 HUMBABAS. They were there, before the river ever made its way
into my forest.

NK. *(Whispered, to GIL:)* The earth is quaking beneath us—can you feel it?
He's afraid. Of us!

(Overhearing, HUMBABA whirls around, confronting NK.)

3 HUMBABAS. Have we met?

(NK fights back a sickening urge to run.)

At the edge of a clearing.
I looked up, and you were standing there—
shaking—like you are now—and staring at me
—do you remember?
I spared your life—

NK. *(To GIL:)* Don't listen to him!

3 HUMBABAS. —and now you want to take mine?

(Trembling, GIL steps forward.)

GIL. I was the one who led this journey—
I cut down the trees of the gods—

3 HUMBABAS. And you are the one who will suffer—yes.
After death has taken your friend—

GIL. Where?

NK. Nowhere! Don't you see?
It's a trick! Words are his only weapon—

3 HUMBABAS. NO!

NK. Then why are we still alive?
Why haven't you already torn us apart?

3 HUMBABAS. A man without mercy is already dead.

> *(To GIL.:)*

And you know that.
That's why your hand is on the axe, but you hesitate—

NK. Kill him *now!*
Or were they lies you were telling me—
about evil, in this land?

3 HUMBABAS. I'm guarding the forest, as I was ordered by the gods.
"Evil" is only a word you like to use—to justify evil.

NK. But it's not just a word! It has a form and a name—
and turds as big as a man!

> *(To GIL.:)*

You said, "Forget death." Did you mean that?
You told *me* we had to die:
a breath—in, out, gone…
Kill him. Before the gods look down,
and see what we're doing.

> *(GIL swings his axe and connects with the giant's body.)*
> *(HUMBABA 3 separates from 1 and 2.)*

3 HUMBABAS. *(To GIL.:)* Your friend will sicken and die, now.
When he's gone, your life will be over.
But you'll live on—waiting for your own death,
which is far away.
You'll hold his body in your arms for a week,
til the flesh is rotting, and a worm
falls out of his nose—

NK. Nothing's falling out of my nose but snot!
Don't let him get away!

GIL. But he's dead!

NK. No—he's moving! Swing AGAIN!

> *(When GIL hesitates, NK swings his axe, breaking off HUMBABA 2 from 1.)*
> *(HUMBABAS 2 and 1 meet up with 3 as separate parts, surrounding NK.)*

HUMBABA 3. *(To* NK:*)* When you enter the House of Dust,
your eyes will make out shapes in the dark—

HUMBABA 1. Dust is the air you breathe forever.

HUMBABA 2. Clay is your food.

HUMBABA 3. Nothing changes.

NK. *(To* GIL:*)* Why won't he die?

GIL. *(Surprised:)* He's dead!
He lies in pieces on the ground.
The stink of his blood is on me—

3 HUMBABAS. Nothing changes.
You wait for light—it never comes.

NK. *(Close to delirium:)* But I hear him—I can hear him…

GIL. What is he saying?

> *(Pause. All is quiet.)*

It's only the cry of birds. Wind in the cedars.
The beat of your heart.

> *(Pause.)*

We need to tell the people the monster is dead.

> *(He gestures to* NK *to follow him out.)*

Come.

> *(*GIL *moves off, assuming* NK *is behind him.)*
> *(*NK *starts to follow—when the* 3 HUMBABAS *grab him. They drape him
> in a tattered cloak of feathers.)*

3 HUMBABAS. You lie in dust.
Your food is clay.
Feathers cover your body—
But you can never fly out of the darkness…

> *(Pause.)*

Why did you kill the Guardian of the Wood?
WHY DID YOU DO IT?
Why did you swing the axe and sever his head?
WHAT HAD HE DONE?
Why did you swing the axe again, and mutilate the body?
HAD HE HURT YOU? HAD HE HURT ANYONE?

NK. There were bodies in the river…

> *(Pause.)*

3 HUMBABAS. Say, "I didn't do it.
It was my friend, who grabbed the axe.
My friend who plotted to kill you—to glorify his name."

> *(*NK *says nothing. The* 3 HUMBABAS *push him away.)*

Fly home.

(*NK looks at his moth-eaten feathered cloak. Watching the giant warily, NK flaps his "wings."*)

(*It's not an impressive display.*)

FLY HOME!!!!!

(*In a total panic, NK staggers off. HUMBABA watches him go.*)

You are home.

(17)

In the wild.

The two SOLDIERS *stumble on*—SOLDIER 1 *is bloody,* SOLDIER 2 *still carries the "club" he was using to beat his friend.*

SOLDIER 1. Are we lost?

SOLDIER 2. No.

SOLDIER 1. Then where is the path?

SOLDIER 2. You fuck up everything.

(*Off but near, a lion roars. The Soldiers barely react.*)

SOLDIER 1. Here, kitty, kitty…

(*SOLDIER 2 stares at him, dumbfounded. Then he starts to laugh.*)

(*SOLDIER 1 grins at him.*)

Here kitty, kitty, kitty, kitty, kitty…

(*Now* SOLDIER 1 *starts laughing, too. The men are close to hysteria. Off-stage, the lion roars again. Slowly, the Soldiers quiet down.*)

SOLDIER 2. Everything. You fuck it up.

SOLDIER 1. I know.

SOLDIER 2. I mean, fuckin' *everything*. You're an officer. You *never* go in first—

SOLDIER 1. We were training! You *said!*

SOLDIER 2. (*Ignoring:*) —but right, you gotta redeem yourself. So there you fuckin' are, leading the charge— and in the first five *seconds,* you take one in the leg, you haveta go down— all your men are falling now, because you led them into a trap— you look out the window, there *I* am, I'm dead—

SOLDIER 1. —and then you waved at me.

(*At that moment,* GIL *staggers in, carrying* NK *in his arms.*)

(*The* SOLDIERS *are stunned.*)

SOLDIER 2. Sir—

GIL. I need water.

> *(SOLDIER 1 produces a wineskin.)*

SOLDIER 1. What happened to him?

GIL. I don't know.

> *(GIL gently puts the barely conscious NK down on the ground.)*
>
> *(Offstage but close, a lion roars.)*

SOLDIER 2. *(Looking around, anxious:)* Is the giant—

GIL. We killed him.

> *(GIL puts a little water to NK's lips—it dribbles out.)*

SOLDIER 1. Where is he wounded?

> *(GIL doesn't answer.)*

Sir?

GIL. I don't know.
The battle was over. We were heading home.
And then he collapsed.

> *(Offstage, the lion roars again.)*

That lion is hungry.

SOLDIER 2. Yes sir.

GIL. Since daybreak—she's been tracking us.
Why?

> *(He runs his hand over NK's face.)*

There isn't any blood.

SOLDIER 2. They understand weakness. Sir.

GIL. You men will need to keep watch tonight,
over my friend.
I have to sleep.

SOLDIER 1. Sir.

> *(GIL lies down beside NK, takes his fevered hand, and falls asleep in a moment.)*

SOLDIER 2. *(Relentless, to his comrade:)* You look out the window, there *I* am,
I'm dead—

SOLDIER 1. And then you waved at me.

> *(Pause.)*

I thought, because—

SOLDIER 2. —I forgave you?

> *(Pause.)*

If we get back, I never wanta see your fuckin' face again.

(18)

CHORUS. They returned to the city—
to a mournful celebration:
the monster Humbaba was dead—
the king's beloved was dying.

(GIL *sits beside NK's sick bed.*)

GIL. *(To* NK:*)* I had a dream about you:
that you fell to the earth, like a star.
You were blazing…
I couldn't pick you up.

NK. You told me that dream—it was long ago.

GIL. Don't leave me.
Please—don't leave me.

(Pause.)

NK. There was something wrong, with the Gate.
I thought it was only wood—but it wasn't.
It was flesh. It was an opening into the body.
I shouldn't have touched it.
If I had slashed it open with my axe…

(Pause.)

I should never have touched that temple-whore—
the one you sent, to infect me.

I had never wanted a friend.
And now I did. I had to find *you.*
I had to fight you, and share in your glory,
and love you like a brother. Like a woman
Like my life.

(Pause.)

Happiness means nothing to an animal.
I had to learn it. And how it passes:
here, now, gone…

(Pause.)

I curse that Gate.
I curse that whore who left her human stink on me…

(Calling out his curse:)

Shamat! May the men who lie with you
be fat, and reek, and come too soon.
May they turn you out on the street,
where only drunks and lepers will have you,
may the mangy street-dog get a whiff of you,
and lift his leg, in salute,

may you lie in your filth at the end of the day…
…at the end of the day…

> *(GIL, shaken, thinks he's done—but NK goes on, cursing Shamat.)*

May a toothache keep you up all night—
and while you toss and turn,
may you remember a face you saw—
or the touch of hand—

> *(He stops, exhausted.)*

GIL. If the priestess hadn't come to you…
you would never have met me.

> *(Pause.)*

NK. Then I withdraw the curse.

GIL. Do you? Tell me the truth:
do you?

> *(NK won't oblige him with answer.)*

NK. Where am I going now?

GIL. I don't know.

NK. WHERE AM I GOING?

> *(Silence.)*

A place without light, the monster said.
Dust—clay…
I'll sit in darkness—with kings of the earth,
their crowns lying forgotten, in a heap,
on the floor.

> *(Pause.)*

I have one hope for you:
that you die in battle, like a man.
I die here, in the luxury of my bed, in the palace,
in shame.

GIL. But my friend—…

NK. Remember what the animals know…

GIL. What? *Tell* me…

CHORUS. But no words would come.
The heart of his friend was still.

GIL. Open your eyes.
Open them.
Please.
Open your eyes…

> *(NK is still.)*

(19)

Some time later.

GIL *pulls the cloak of feathers from the body of his friend.*

He touches NK's *cooling naked flesh, puzzled.*

GIL. If you mother was a lion…
wouldn't you be a dead lion?

(*Pause.*)

If your father was a gazelle—
wouldn't you be a fallen gazelle?

(*Pause.*)

Your mother was the Earth.
Now you're dust. Beautiful dust.
And the places where you ran and fought
and played and killed and loved—
they all wait for you to come drifting down,
in the afternoon light…

(*He gathers* NK's *body in his arms.*)

I thought I'd never be alone again.
Now I am.

(*Pause.*)

I was never afraid of dying.
Now I am.
What have you done to me?

CHORUS. In that chamber, time had stopped.
But in the world, a week was passing…

(*GIL'S MOTHER enters.*)

MOTHER. You have to give the body up, to be buried.

(*GIL doesn't move.*)

Will he hear you crying for him—
and wake up?
That cannot happen.

(*Pause.*)

That maggot on your arm—

(*GIL looks, horrified.*)

—fell from his nose. Give up the body.

(*Pause.*)

GIL. You told him—to watch over me.

MOTHER. And he did.

GIL. And he did. I survived.

(Pause.)

Why did I survive?

MOTHER. I don't know.

GIL. Is it a punishment?

(Pause.)

There is a man called "Faraway."

He was spared, when the gods destroyed the world,

in a Flood.

Man, woman and child—they were swept away.

Only he survived.

(Pause.)

Why was he spared? So many years ago…

why was I?

QUEEN. He lost an entire world. You lost a friend—

GIL. He *was* an entire world.

I lived in him.

Where am I living now?

(Pause.)

QUEEN. You'd have to cross the Ocean of Death.

Where the way is guarded by Scorpions.

They'll see you're alive.

They'll never let you pass.

GIL. Now that my friend is lost,

I'm the strongest man alive, again,

the bravest and the most beautiful…

(GIL "disguises" himself, by donning NK's tattered cloak of feathers.)

And I'm smarter than a scorpion.

(20)

CHORUS. This time he went alone—

walking a thousand miles in a day,

sleeping just a few hours at night.

One afternoon he came upon two lions

at play in the sun.

(TWO LIONS enter.)

(They fight, as Gil and NK had fought, the day they met.)

(And they roar—like the two human friends, when they had a "roaring contest.")

He saw the animals glorying in life.

(GIL approaches the LIONS silently.)

(In a blur of motion he grabs one, breaking its neck.)

*(The other tries to run—*GIL *chases it, grabs it, dragging it back onstage, where he breaks its neck.)*

*(*GIL *looks at the two dead animals. Something in him is satisfied, for a moment.)*

(Then he moves on.)

(21)

On the shores of the Ocean of Death.

The two SOLDIERS—*now* SCORPIONS—*are on guard-duty.*

But they aren't watching, as GIL *approaches.*

SCORPION 2 *has a cattle-prod. He wants to use it on* SCORPION 1.

SCORPION 1. I don't know if I can take another twenty-five…

SCORPION 2. That's right—you don't know.
So let's find out.

SCORPION 1. Please…

SCORPION 2. Please—*what?*
How many times did you get me killed, in Basic?

SCORPION 1. Not on purpose.

SCORPION 2. When you ran away, in the Forest—

SCORPION 1. You ran, too!

SCORPION 2. I was trying to catch you!

SCORPION 1. I was afraid…

SCORPION 2. So you're gonna run away, for the rest of your life?

(Reluctantly, SCORPION 1 *'takes the position'—getting down on his knees, putting his hands behind his back.)*

SCORPION 1. Do it.

(Pause.)

DO IT.

(Before SCORPION 2 *can do anything,* GIL *approaches.)*

SCORPION 2. You shouldn't be here, dead man.

GIL. I know.
I have to get to the other side of the Ocean of Death.

SCORPION 2. Start swimming.

SCORPION 1. There's something wrong with this—dead man.

SCORPION 2. What?

SCORPION 1. Well—I don't think he's dead…

SCORPION 2. Say what?

SCORPION 1. And I don't think he's a man…

> *(They regard* GIL *with unease.)*

GIL. I *am* a god—but only on my mother's side.
I'm mortal.

SCORPION 1. Then it isn't your time to cross over.

SCORPION 2. So get the fuck out of here.

GIL. I need a boat.

SCORPION 1. The sea is too rough.

> *(*SCORPION 2 *approaches* GIL, *leading with his cattle-prod.)*

SCORPION 2. I'm amping this up to "high"…

SCORPION 1. *(To* GIL:*)* Who have you lost?

GIL. My only friend.

SCORPION 1. There's a skiff, on the other side of the cove.
But no one has taken it out on the open water…

> *(*GIL *starts to move off,* SCORPION 2 *steps in front of him.)*

SCORPION 2. *(To* GIL:*)* I could stop your heart.

GIL. You're too late.

> *(Finally,* SCORPION 2 *gives up the staring contest, steps aside.* GIL *exits.)*
> *(Humiliated,* SCORPION 2 *approaches* SCORPION 1 *again. He kicks* SCORPION 1, *who falls on his side.)*

SCORPION 2. Get up.

> *(*SCORPION 1 *struggles back into position, on his knees, hands behind his back.)*

You ready?

> *(*SCORPION 1 *doesn't answer.)*

I'm ready.

> *(Pause.)*

OK: this is the story:
You've been captured. You're knee-deep in shit.
They wanta ask you things—but they don't care what the answers are.

> *(Slipping into the role of Interrogator:)*

Are you afraid of me?

SCORPION 1. No.

> *(For that response,* SCORPION 2 *zaps* SCORPION 1, *who stifles a scream.)*

SCORPION 2. Why are you afraid of me?

> *(*SCORPION 1 *doesn't answer.* SCORPION 2 *shocks him again—* SCORPION 1 *sobs and falls on his side. Slowly he struggles back into position.)*

Are you in love with me?

SCORPION 1. No.

> (SCORPION 2 *shocks him again.* SCORPION 1 *cries and falls over. He lies there, trembling.*)

SCORPION 2. Why are you in love with me?

> (*No answer.* SCORPION 2 *puts down the prod, sits beside* SCORPION 1 *and holds him in his arms.*)

You did good. You took it all.
You don't have to pretend you're a man, anymore—
or *act* like a man.
You *are* a man.

> (*Hearing these words of blessing,* SCORPION 2 *starts to sob.*)

All my life—I wanted to be alone.
Then I enlisted.
I had to depend on people again—for awhile:
I fuckin' *hated* that.
Because—most people are worthless.

> (*Stroking* SCORPION 1's *face:*)

Like you—you fuck up everything...
I was *dead*...

SCORPION 1. But you weren't. You waved at me.
I thought, because—you forgave me.

> (SCORPION 2 *holds his weeping buddy close.*)

(22)

CHORUS. He found the skiff, and started to row—
but the sea ate away at the oars...
so he held up an animal skin, for a sail—
the wind died down.
Between two shores, adrift,
he was tormented by his thoughts...

GIL. (*To the absent* NK:) Where are you?
Are you suffering?

> (*Pause.*)

Are you dead because of me?

CHORUS. No answer—only the gentle slap of waves against the boat...
in all the vast of the dark, only that plash...plash...

GIL. Sometimes—I can't remember, what you—...[look like]
let me see your face...

CHORUS. Plash...

GIL. Sometimes I can't remember if I killed you.
Did I kill you?
CHORUS. Plash…
Finally a wind came up, driving the little skiff before it,
to the most distant shore.

(23)

CHORUS. Faraway had seen the boat approaching.
He went down to the beach.
FARAWAY. *(To* GIL:*)* Who are you?
GIL. Does it matter?
I was the strongest man alive—
the bravest, and the most beautiful…
But my friend has died.
And I realized I was nothing.
　　　(Pause.)
Less.
FARAWAY. You dress like one of the dead,
but you're alive.
Why have you come here?
Across the desert, through the mountains,
over the Ocean of Death, to this shore?
　　　(Pause.)
GIL. Why were you spared—
when the gods destroyed the world?
　　　(Pause.)
I have to know.
　　　(Pause.)
FARAWAY. I wasn't a better man than my neighbors—
braver, or more beautiful.
But I was warned, in a dream, to build a boat.
So I did. And it started to rain…
　　　(Pause.)
I watched the world disappearing
under the waves. Everything I had loved…
It doesn't rain—here—for which I am grateful.
I don't like the sound.
GIL. You didn't answer my question:
you survived—
FARAWAY. I don't know why.

(Pause.)

All the good people I knew in my life were taken.
Why was I saved?

(Pause.)

Do you think—if you had been a better man—
your friend would have lived?

(GIL is silent—but the answer is clearly 'yes.')

Would he have lived forever?

GIL. No.

FARAWAY. That's why you feel like less than nothing.
That's why you can't fall asleep,
and food is like dirt in your mouth—
you aren't safe.
You never were.
He was always going to leave you.
Before you ever saw him, he was already disappearing.

(GIL suddenly looks around.)

GIL. Wait—are you alone?
Has he come to this place?

FARAWAY. Do you see him?

GIL. I thought I could hear him laughing—
running along a path, up into the hills—
I thought I could smell the sun on his skin,
his hair soaked with sweat—
is he here?

FARAWAY. How did he die? In battle?

GIL. No.
I led him into the Cedar Forest—

FARAWAY. Why?

GIL. I wanted to kill the giant—

FARAWAY. Why?

(Pause.)

GIL. The gods—gave me a restless heart—
I DON'T KNOW WHY!

(Pause.)

FARAWAY. Because you were afraid of being forgotten.
Disappearing.
Like your friend.

GIL. *No.*

FARAWAY. *(A challenge:)* "The smell of his hair."
Soaked in sweat, shining in the sun—
So—tell me the smell of his hair.

> *(GIL is silent.)*

His laughter—echoing in the hills, as he ran—
what is that sound?

> *(Pause.)*

Even now you can barely remember.
You try—but it's like waking up from a dream
that's already fading away.

GIL. Why are you lying to me?
I *know* he's here—on the other side of a—door,
a—gate…

FARAWAY. If he were, you still couldn't bring him back.

GIL. Why not?

FARAWAY. Because you aren't man enough.

> *(Pause.)*

GIL. Tell Death—if he's willing to fight me—

FARAWAY. He would laugh till his bones were clattering.
Even his brother Sleep could take you, with one drowsy arm
behind his back.

GIL. *Another* lie.
Sleep is afraid to come near me…

FARAWAY. Prove it.
Stay awake for seven days.
And if your love for your friend is stronger than sleep,
it may be stronger than death.
Then, perhaps the gods will let you plead your case.

> *(Pause.)*

What *is* your case?

> *(Pause.)*

GIL. I want my friend beside me,
at the end of an endless day.

FARAWAY. Is that all?

GIL. I want him there forever.

FARAWAY. Is that all?

> *(GIL can say nothing.)*

Sleep is at the door. I'll let him in.

> *(FARAWAY exits. A moment later NK enters, a cattle-prod in his hands.)*
> *(GIL, with his back to the door, doesn't see him—but can sense him.)*

CHORUS. Had he lived forever, he might have met *this* man, one night—
in the dark of the meat-packing district, at the end
of a rotting pier…

NK. Who gave you my name?

(GIL *doesn't answer.*)

A newbie, huh?

GIL. *(Deflecting:)* How long were you in the Marines?

NK. Long enough.
I taught the men how to survive,
if they were captured by the enemy.
And then—since I liked my work, you might say—
I started to teach you civilians.

GIL. And the ones who come to you—

NK. *(Not sure of Gil's commitment:)* These are men with a *serious* prison fetish—

GIL. —when you—teach them, they remember things?

NK. Sometimes. Why are you asking?

GIL. That's what I heard.

NK. Is that what you want?

(GIL *hesitates, still not sure he can trust this guy.*)

I had a client once—lost 12 days of his life—
completely gone. He'd served in Vietnam.
Did not even know his brain had been wiped.

GIL. Then why did he come to you?

NK. Since he got out, he'd been looking all over,
for a challenge.
He hadn't found one. Nothing real, anyway.
Then he heard about me.
He wrote me a letter describing a scene that spoke to my
fondest desires. I tell you, it made my heart sing.
No one had broken him.

(*Pause.*)

I broke him in all of 35 seconds.
Using 3 rubber bands.

(*Pause.*)

GIL. How?

NK. I just came at him from a direction he had not anticipated.

(*Pause.*)

He kept coming back, and then, one day, when I was
testing his mettle—
he had—not even a memory, just an image—a flash, gone:

a terrified woman, pregnant, being gutted with a K-bar…
that was it for awhile, and then there was more:
smell of burning flesh… children running screaming into
a clearing, being shot…
took a while, but over time, he got back all of those
lost 12 days.

    (Pause.)

And then he was able to sleep again.
What have *you* forgotten?

    (Pause.)

GIL. My buddy and me—we were following a trail, into this forest…
I remember a lot of blood—
I think I led him into a trap…

NK. What else?

GIL. *(Fighting to remember:)* What else…
He asked me a riddle:
why does a dog lick his balls?
Because…

    (He can't recall.)

NK. Because he can.

    (Pause.)

GIL. Anything we can imagine:
if we can do it, then we do it…
defy the gods, kill a giant, chop down every tree in sight…

NK. Make the world a wasteland.

    (GIL is fading, NK helps him out of the feathered cloak.)
    (GIL stretches out on the floor, fighting sleep.)

What else have you forgotten?

    (NK stretches out beside him, curling around him.)

This…

GIL. How could I forget—this…
I was running, and you were behind me, and you were
in front of me, and I kept running,
but you were beside me—
I fell, and you were on top of me.

    (Pause.)

And you were inside me…
And you said—the last thing you said:
"Remember what the animals know…"
But I've forgotten…

NK. No one escapes.

GIL. No one…

(In a moment he's sleeping in NK's arms.)

(When he's certain GIL won't wake, NK rises. With a final look at his friend, he exits.)

(GIL sleeps on. FARAWAY enters, a sack in his hand.)

FARAWAY. Wake up.

(GIL wakes, with a start.)

GIL. Where did he go?

FARAWAY. Who?

GIL. *(Quickly covering:)* No one.

FARAWAY. You were dreaming.

GIL. No!

I wasn't asleep, I was just—drifting off…

FARAWAY. You've been asleep for a week.

GIL. *(Less certain:)* No…

(FARAWAY takes a loaf of bread from his sack.)

FARAWAY. I knew you would lie. It's what men do.

So I baked a loaf of bread, the first day of your nap…

(He tosses the loaf at GIL—it hits the floor like a brick.)

And then another.

(He pulls out another loaf, tosses it at GIL.)

One loaf a day, every day…

(He empties the sack on the floor—four more loaves fall out.)

Soggy, moldy, mildewed, stale…

And today—the seventh day of your sleep—

the bread is baking now.

(GIL knows what this means—he's lost everything.)

(Long pause.)

GIL. I'm hungry.

FARAWAY. Eat.

(GIL picks up the stale loaf, rips off a chunk—starts to eat, steadily but not ravenous.)

(FARAWAY watches him.)

(GIL starts to cry.)

GIL. My friend is dead.

I sleep and eat.

Like nothing happened.

(Pause.)

Scratch myself,
eat again, take a shit—
sleep…

> *(In his agony, he tears apart the loaf of bread.)*

FARAWAY. Go back to the people who wait for you.

> *(GIL looks around, as if slowly waking up from a dream.)*

Go back to the City.

GIL. My city was beautiful—
beside a river—walls inlaid with copper…

FARAWAY. It hasn't vanished yet.

GIL. It will.

FARAWAY. Then love your people *now*.
Rule them wisely. While you can.

> *(Pause.)*

A wind is rising.
It will bring you home.
Get down to the boat.

> *(Pause.)*

> *(GIL starts to move off.)*

Take off the dead man's cloak.

> *(GIL stops—but he's reluctant.)*

GIL. Something of his…[to remember him by].

FARAWAY. Not this.
Remember him running beside you,
up into the hills above your City…

> *(GIL relents, lets FARAWAY help him out of the cloak of feathers.)*

> *(GIL stares at it in FARAWAY's hands.)*

GIL. Will I ever see him again?

FARAWAY. I don't know.

GIL. Will I recognize him?

> *(Pause.)*

FARAWAY. When the rain had finally stopped—
and the water slowly receded—
I looked around, and I was afraid.
Mountain, river, forest—
they were all there.
Like nothing had happened.
All of it—like it was before.
And I didn't recognize anything.
I cried, "What is this terrible place?"

(Pause.)
GIL. I think I know:
The rest of my life.

> *(As* FARAWAY *watches,* GIL *moves off, down the path that leads to the shore.)*
> *(The lights fade.)*

End of Play